Microsoft®
SQL Server 2005
Reporting Services

FOR

DUMMIES®

Microsoft® SQL Server 2005 Reporting Services

FOR DUMMIES®

by Mark Robinson

WILEY

Wiley Publishing, Inc.

Microsoft® SQL Server 2005 Reporting Services For Dummies®

Published by
Wiley Publishing, Inc.
111 River Street
Hoboken, NJ 07030-5774
www.wiley.com

WILEY

About the Author

Mark Robinson has been active in the field of business intelligence since the early 1980s. He is current directing the business intelligence (BI) practice at Greenbrier & Russel, a business and technology consulting services company and a gold BI partner with Microsoft. For the last two years, he has participated quarterly in the Microsoft BI Partner Advisory Council meetings in Seattle where he has mingled with developers, partners, trainers and marketing professionals and has provided input into the direction of SQL Server 2005. He has been involved in selling and delivering BI solutions involving the Microsoft SQL Server platform as long as SQL Server has been a product.

As a consultant, Mark has worked side by side with some of the pioneers in the field of decision support and business intelligence. He has been communicating the value of business intelligence in executing on the business strategy to his customers over the past twenty years. He has been involved in over fifty implementations covering a wide range of reporting and analysis tools. He has written many articles on a variety of topics including what business management should know about data warehousing as well as what the future holds for business intelligence.

Mark is a veteran of reporting and analysis solutions that deliver significant business value to his customers. During his experience in business and technology fields, he has performed various leadership roles performing traditional leadership roles in IT management, product management and practice management. Mark has led practices for a variety of consulting services companies in Emerging Technologies, eCommerce Solutions and Business Intelligence. He has led companies in strategic transformation efforts via investments in business intelligence. He has worked for and consulted to financial services institutions (insurance and banking), retailers, manufacturers, healthcare providers, software and technology services companies, and professional services firms with an emphasis on technology solution strategy, architecture, and delivery. He currently serves in a strategist role in the architecture, design and delivery of business intelligence solutions for his clients.

After receiving a B.A. in physics from the University of Chicago, he enrolled in the business school and received his MBA from the University of Chicago in the following year. Thinking he was well trained in operations research and finance, he began his business experience in new business development at Corning in 1979. When IBM came out with the first personal computer in 1982, he switched his focus and joined up with Andersen Consulting (now known as Accenture). He has been on the business and technology track ever since. His work experience has spanned software vendor companies (Softbridge and Hyperion), a business technology group at Baxter Healthcare as well as other consulting firms (Computer Power Group, Parian, Cysive and marchFIRST).

If you have any questions for him about this book or to find out what he can do for your organization, he can be emailed at mrobinson@gr.com. He lives in the Chicago area with his wife and two daughters.

Author's Acknowledgments

A veritable army of people contributed their time and energy toward the publication of this book. I may have achieved some sort of record in terms of the number of people involved in this project at Wiley. During this quest, I have worked with a pair of each of the key coordinating roles — acquisitions editors, project editors, copy editors and technical editors. My initial contact at Wiley, acquisitions editor Terri Varveris, was extremely helpful in coordinating the right resources and getting me started down the right path. As part of this process, I have developed working relationships with many new people and feel that everyone involved has helped to improve the content of this book.

I also need to acknowledge the loving support of my wife Cathleen and daughters Ellen and Rose. I appreciate their understanding of my time away from the family over the many evenings and weekends required to finish this book. They provide the inspiration and support necessary for beginning, enduring and completing any journey of this magnitude.

Publisher's Acknowledgments

We're proud of this book; please send us your comments through our online registration form located at www.dummies.com/register/.

Some of the people who helped bring this book to market include the following:

Acquisitions, Editorial, and Media Development

Project Editor: Christine Berman

Acquisitions Editors: Terri Varveris, Tiffany Franklin

Copy Editor: Christine Berman

Technical Editor: Dan Meyers

Editorial Manager: Jodi Jensen

Media Development Supervisor: Richard Graves

Editorial Assistant: Amanda Foxworth

Cartoons: Rich Tennant (www.the5thwave.com)

Composition Services

Project Coordinator: Jennifer Theriot

Layout and Graphics: Andrea Dahl, Joyce Haughey, Barbara Moore, Barry Offringa, Heather Ryan

Proofreaders: Leeann Harney, Jessica Kramer, TECHBOOKS Production Services

Indexer: TECHBOOKS Production Services

Publishing and Editorial for Technology Dummies

Richard Swadley, Vice President and Executive Group Publisher

Andy Cummings, Vice President and Publisher

Mary Bednarek, Executive Acquisitions Director

Mary C. Corder, Editorial Director

Publishing for Consumer Dummies

Diane Graves Steele, Vice President and Publisher

Joyce Pepple, Acquisitions Director

Composition Services

Gerry Fahey, Vice President of Production Services

Debbie Stailey, Director of Composition Services

Contents at a Glance

Table of Contents

Introduction

Twenty-five years ago, people developed reports using an advanced programming language that usually ran on the mainframe. With the advent of the personal computer in 1982, it was possible to use a programming language called Basic to write some basic reports with formatting. In the mid-1980s, Microsoft Excel came along and many people began to use the formatting capabilities and developing reports directly in Excel. Since then, Excel has continued to be the preferred tool for reporting and analysis for financial analysts and accountants due to its ease of programming formulas and formatting capabilities.

Beginning in the 1990s, Microsoft began the development of a database management system called SQL Server. The early versions of SQL Server were clunky and the solution was not as popular as other database management solutions on the market. The first serious scalable version of SQL Server was SQL Server 7. In 2000, the SQL Server 2000 database was launched and until recently has been a scalable database system for developing enterprise solutions, especially for departments of large companies or midmarket companies. The price of the software running on Windows was a compelling feature of this database product.

In the last few years, Microsoft began to expand its reach into reporting tools. Microsoft began developing Reporting Services. It was originally conceived to run as a Web service on top of a database in SQL Server 2000 and leverage the Web services – based architecture of the .NET framework. The design goals for the product were to include tight integration with Visual Studio .NET, leverage the overall extensibility of the framework, and offer a short learning curve to developing reports. In January 2004, Microsoft launched Reporting Services 2000 and offered it as a free download from their Web site. When it was launched, a Webcast was done to communicate the features of Reporting Services. This Webcast was the second most popular Microsoft Webcast ever, with 5,000-plus people viewing! Also, in just a short time, the number of downloads for Reporting Services outnumbered the number of known licenses of Crystal. This was a sweet spot in the marketplace. There was demand for an intuitive reporting tool that was an extension of a powerful database management system.

Then in April 2004, Microsoft acquired a company called ActiveViews. ActiveViews provides an ad hoc reporting system that takes advantage of the .NET framework and SQL Server Reporting Services to allow users to do ad hoc reporting within Reporting Services. Since then, Microsoft has been integrating the technology into Reporting Services to integrate and enhance the ad hoc reporting capabilities within Reporting Services. This new component has been added to the Reporting Services 2005 product in the form of a tool called the Report Builder. It is now available in Reporting Services 2005.

Microsoft SQL Server 2005 Reporting Services For Dummies helps you explore all the capabilities of this exciting new reporting tool. This book gives you the basics for all components of Reporting Services 2005. Although this book doesn't make you an expert at using all the features, it shows you how to use the key capabilities to produce some outstanding reporting solutions. It provides a great roadmap for exploring the key capabilities and gets you started on the path to mastering advanced features.

This book is for you if you're interested in developing reports from any database management system that runs in Windows (SQL Server, DB2, and Oracle), because there are tools in SQL Server that can integrate information from any of these other database management systems.

Because Reporting Services 2005 comes as part of SQL Server 2005 (no extra cost!), if your organization is using SQL Server as a Department of Enterprise Database solution, you should explore the capabilities of this exciting new tool as soon as you can. This book is your quick-start guide to beginning to create powerful new reports that can help you easily unlock and explore data stored in myriad systems.

How This Book Is Organized

To help you find what you need quickly, this book is divided into seven parts. Each part covers a certain topic about using Microsoft Reporting Services 2005. Whenever you need help, just flip through this book, find the part that covers the topic you're looking for, and then toss this book aside and get back to work.

Part 1: Just the Basics

Microsoft Reporting Services 2005 is a powerful reporting platform that requires an introduction to the basics of Web-based reporting. The key considerations of reporting are described as an introduction.

I provide a quick summary of some database concepts to give you a refresher on database access. Because you'll be querying database tables for information to report, you need to be aware of how to access tables and what SQL queries are all about. With this knowledge, you're ready to begin to build reports.

Part II: Building Reports — Your Creativity Options

Microsoft provides a simple interface for constructing reports quickly with a Report wizard. A first pass through this wizard provides a glimpse of the steps required to assemble a report from scratch.

As all carpenters have tool belts to provide quick access to tools for construction, Microsoft Reporting Services provides a toolbox that provides quick access to tools helpful in designing and building reports. SQL has many tools, and I help you get to know the advantages and disadvantage of each in special reporting situations.

Basic actions such as sorting, grouping, and filtering information presented in a report add to your intended users' understanding of the information to be delivered in your reports. Basic capabilities for producing ad hoc reports (reports you can create quickly on the fly through drag and drop operations) are covered through a description of how the Report Builder tool works.

Part III: Publishing, Accessing, and Subscribing to Reports

Professors in college know the phrase "publish or perish" — they need to publish articles and books to continue their tenure at the college or university. Well, for other reasons, you also need to know how to publish a report so that others can benefit from your information. You can publish reports so that users can access them whenever they need to. You can also publish reports so that they appear in e-mail messages to business users on a regular basis.

Reports can be pushed to users through e-mail or sent directly to Web sites. Reports can also be pulled by business users who can find the report and desire to see the content on demand. Microsoft Reporting Services 2005 supports both the push and the pull models for report access.

Part IV: Maintaining Your Reports

A Web interface that comes with Reporting Services 2005 manages your reports in folders to make access quick and easy. This interface is the Report Manager. In general, you can publish reports to the Report Manager and manage these reports and who can access them through some security and site settings.

Security is an important topic when sensitive business or personal information is available on the Web. In this part, I fully explore security options for reports and for the overall Web site. Database security can also provide ways to lock down secure information so that information is provided according to any standards and guidelines that corporations today enforce for business information distribution.

Optimizing the performance of reports can be a consideration if you have many users accessing vast amounts of data at the same time during peak times. If you're responsible for the overall end-user satisfaction with your reporting facility, you will probably need to remember a few principles for maximizing the execution performance for your reports.

Part V: Developing Advanced Reports

Interactive reports are valuable to users who need to see many facets of the data they're looking at. Reporting Services lets you drill down from summary information to see greater detail and then shift your view across many parts of the organization with an array of reports that are linked together. Microsoft Reporting Services 2005 enables you to create some interesting linked reports which together provide an intuitive navigation interface to begin exploring information in more detail.

Drilling down to see more detail, showing navigation links on reports which bridge you to other views of the information, and transparently passing parameters from one view to another are all possible with Reporting Services 2005. You have all the features to provide a report that can be easily understood by an executive and allow for further exploration of the detail.

Part VI: Migrating from Other Reporting Tools

Undoubtedly, before obtaining Microsoft Reporting Services 2005, you have used other tools to provide needed reporting. I have noted some comparisons of Microsoft Reporting Services 2005 with other popular reporting tools. And if you're used to developing reports in Microsoft Access, you will be interested in learning how to convert Access reports into Reporting Services reports.

Part VII: The Part of Tens

For those people who just want to find shortcuts and tips for working more efficiently with Microsoft Reporting Services 2005 (so they can take the rest of the day off), this part of the book provides some cool tricks, resources you can spot on the Web for more information, more interesting information about the rest of the Microsoft BI platform, and finally a list of third-party tools that further enhance your productivity or extend the capabilities of Reporting Services 2005.

This part is intended as a reference for tips and resources that make Reporting Services 2005 seem a lot easier than the incomprehensible manuals. Just remember that if anything in Reporting Services 2005 confuses you or doesn't make sense, it's not your fault — it's Microsoft's fault, so feel free to blame these developers for failing to anticipate your needs appropriately and selling you a not-always-intuitive product.

How to Use This Book

You can use this book as a reference or as a coffee table decoration (especially if your color scheme includes a cheery yellow!). Unlike novels, this book is not designed for people to read from cover to cover, although you can if you want to. Instead, just browse through the parts that interest you and ignore the rest.

If you plan to take full advantage of Microsoft Reporting Services 2005, read Part I first so that you can acquaint yourself with the more common Reporting Services features.

The other parts of this book are here for your reference and amusement. Though you may not care about ad hoc reporting with the Report Builder at first, some day you may want to play around with it just to see what it can do. To your surprise, some features you thought you would never use may turn out to be more useful than you ever imagined. Then again, the features may really turn out to be useless after all, but you'll never find out until you try them.

Foolish Assumptions I Make about You

First of all, you should already have Microsoft Reporting Services 2005 installed on your server at work or on your desktop. Note that you can install the full SQL Server 2005 including Reporting Services 2005 on the Windows XP and Windows 2000 Professional operating systems.

Icons Used in This Book

 This icon points out things that make using Reporting Services for tasks quicker and easier.

 This icon denotes information to keep in mind as you're using Reporting Services.

 This icon explains important stuff you need to know to prevent really awful things from happening.

 You can skip these paragraphs unless you really want to get into complicated subjects.

Getting Started

By now, you're probably anxious to start trying out Microsoft Reporting Services 2005. Turn on your computer and get ready to jump miles ahead of the competition by having the foresight to use the world's most powerful reporting infrastructure in Reporting Services 2005.

Part I
Just the Basics

The 5th Wave   By Rich Tennant

DATA MINING

Hold on Brad—I forgot the canary.

DOWN

In this part . . .

To make life easier, Microsoft has built in some powerful features to create reports useful for transforming data into information. I provide an overview of the reporting principles and challenges and then introduce you to the key features of *Microsoft Reporting Services 2005*. I also show you some basic features of the SQL Server 2005 database that will help you access databases for the reports you want to build. I demonstrate how to get a basic report up and running with data just waiting to be tapped for a database.

Microsoft Reporting Services 2005 may seem confusing at first with functionality that is unlike other reporting tools. But after you build your first report, you'll have a clearer understanding of the features and functions available to produce very robust reports.

Chapter 1

Getting Familiar with Reporting Services

Corporate data is growing at an extremely fast clip, meaning that more data is collected about business events and business transactions than ever before. It has been noted that data storage capacity of every company of every type doubles every 12 months. This data is stored in a great variety of formats — databases, spreadsheets, files, and documents. And as a direct consequence of this infinite variety, there's never very much uniformity to the data, so it often just sits in locations, never to be examined with any real efficiency.

The challenge in business today is to tap into this data that's just sitting around idle in an organization and then transform it into information and eventually into the kind of knowledge that can result in a competitive advantage. This transformation needs to evolve in baby steps. The first step is to identify what kind of data exists and where it resides. The next step is to create reports from this information.

A *report* is basically a simple document that can present numbers, text, and/or graphical information. Reports are necessary to combine information from various data sources and present that information in a coherent manner to business people. This information enables us to understand what is happening in some aspect of the business and can even (hopefully) enable us to make decisions based on this information.

In this chapter, I provide an overview of reporting in the business world so that you have some perspective. I then show how Microsoft Reporting Services meets the challenges and provides a great way of doing reports. You'll be surprised what capabilities Microsoft has packed into this extension of SQL Server 2005.

Dealing with Reporting Challenges

A good reporting tool must address many challenges, based on the need for versatility, accessibility, and automation. Versatility is important because of the great diversity of applications in business today that require reports in many forms. Accessibility is important because information is more frequently utilized in a business process if you can get to it easily. Finally, automation is important because access to key reports on demand at a moment's notice can greatly speed business processes that are dependent on the information.

The first challenge is versatility. For a reporting tool to do just the basics for you, it needs to wear a lot of different hats. The reporting tool must be able to handle both standard reports (regular weekly reports that are core to your business) as well as ad hoc (where you construct a report on the fly to answer a new question) reporting and analysis. The reporting tool also needs to span a multitude of data sources and data formats in a variety of database management systems (DBMSes for short). Today, companies focus on driving the business as it is today, as opposed to investigating historical information, so being able to put key performance indicators on a dashboard that allows for drilling down into more detail enables this forward-looking ability. Finally, the ability to be able to develop a generalized report with dynamic filtering can serve multiple purposes and thereby reduce the total number of reports required to support the enterprise reporting needs.

The next challenge for reporting tools is accessibility. Today, information technology (IT) departments respond to requests from various business groups. IT typically experiences large backlogs and might have some dissatisfied users as a result. Also, some reporting tools are used to distribute information predominantly on paper. Providing self-service and Web-based reporting capabilities, in which business users can go to a Web site to get the information they need, does two things:

 ✔ **Information is delivered when it is needed (if the data is available).**

 ✔ **IT is freed to do more value-added activities.** Report information can also be provided on an extranet site to service partners and suppliers.

Having access to historical information via the Web provides perspective to the information so that trends can be identified. Even beyond this, you can mine the historical information for predictive modeling purposes to help see into the future, based upon assumptions related to the key factors or drivers of the business.

The next challenge for reporting tools is automation. Reporting capabilities have traditionally been defined by the IT department. IT is constantly challenged with having to retrieve information from multiple data sources and delivering reports with a variety of tools. Being able to automate the integration of data sources and the production of reports so that information is pushed to business people in the form of reports and alerts enables knowledge workers to be more proactive. Alerting reports can also be produced when key operational metrics look to be out of whack, indicating that a situation needs attention — again, a proactive, enabling capability.

You'll get a chance to see how Microsoft SQL Server 2005 Reporting Services rises to these challenges and provides some excellent reporting capabilities. The great feature about Reporting Services is that it is an extension of the SQL Server database management system. As such, if you have an SQL Server license, you have Reporting Services.

Mastering Reporting Principles

Have you ever wondered why some reports are immediately understood while others lead to blank looks and questions about your competency? Reports that resonate with others generally satisfy the key principles of reporting. In this section, you get the chance to explore the key principles to follow to create good reports.

Presenting the right information

The first "good reporting" principle is presenting the "right" information. The right information can be current or historical, subtotal amounts by category, running totals by reporting group, trend lines sales over time, or just vertical bars showing how your product sales ended last quarter. The right information depends on the nature of the business question that you're trying to answer.

In order to be right, the information should be timely for the question being asked, as accurate as the business process allows, as relevant to the business question as possible, and also consistent with information from multiple functional areas (such as finance, sales, and operations) in the company. The report should also provide some additional insight into the situation.

Another benefit of reporting the right information is that the report should be *actionable*. That is, the best reports show the type of information that you (or anybody else equally intelligent) would use to make an immediate decision. This could take the form of an exception report that shows business events that require immediate attention. Or it could be a chart illustrating that the inventory levels of a certain raw material — compared with component sales — indicate that a reorder needs to take place immediately. Whether a decision can be made based on the information presented in a report is an important criteria in the value of that report. It also is a guiding principle when determining what information belongs on a report.

Microsoft Reporting Services allows you to report information from nearly every type of data source you can find — from a legacy system to a spreadsheet to relational databases and even OLAP (online analytical processing) databases. Within a report, Reporting Services allows you to report from multiple data sources in order to provide the right information in the report. It provides access to the data sources essential to presenting the right information.

Using the right medium

"The medium is the message," advertisers tell me. The messages or information that you deliver in a report should be versatile enough to allow viewing from virtually any media. The choice of media appropriate to the report depends mostly on the type of action that the report should evoke. For example, if the report needs to be easily accessible and represents a key variable of the business, the report needs to be shared in many contexts. This type of report should be available on the Web and available to all relevant business users for collaboration. If the report is part of a regular briefing, is reviewed with many other such reports, and might need to be referenced intermittently, it might be best to print the report to include in a book of reports for review. If the report needs to be sent to a person in the field for immediate action, it should be available on a PDA in electronic form. If the report will be subject to further analysis by a financial person, creating the report in an Excel spreadsheet might be best.

Guess what? Reporting Services provides you with the capability to produce reports on the Web and to export them into a number of formats such as PDF and Excel. Reporting Services also allows you to print the report as well as to distribute reports via e-mail or even integrate your reports within your company intranet. You can also embed Web-based reports within business applications or information portals, such as a corporate intranet. You should know the context for a given report and make it accessible in the best manner to enhance the productivity of the business consumer of that report.

Presenting to the right audience

If you're like me, you need to create reports and share them with other people in the company so that they understand something about the data — and then hopefully have them interpret or explain the business context to everyone else. Depending on the functional role of the person with whom you'll be sharing the results, the style of the report is sure to be different. Some people react better to a pure numbers presentation. Others respond better to a graphical view of the information, perhaps showing a trend over time or a comparative chart of performance compared with other like aspects.

Reporting Services allows you to customize your information to suit the preferences of a wide variety of consumers of information. Reporting Services allows you to create traditional reports as well as free-form reports. It also allows you to create interactive reports that can drill into more detail by linking directly to another report. If you're making a presentation to the board of directors or perhaps creating a list of To Do's for yourself, knowing your audience helps you define the best style and format for your report.

Offering the right content and design

When somebody walks up to me at the copy machine and asks me, "What is this report that Accounting sent me last week supposed to be telling me?", I usually wonder about two things. First, is this guy testing me with something that I'm supposed to be able to pick up quickly? Then, after rapidly scanning the information and concluding that it is not a test, I'm usually shocked by how poorly organized the information in the report actually is. Finally, I have to shrug my shoulders and confess that I am just as confused as he is.

The moral of this story is that many bad reports are out there! Reporting can be improved by taking advantage of features that present the right information clearly so that you have no question about the right interpretation. A report with the right content and design is easy to understand by ordinary people like you and me.

Designing a report so that the content is easy to figure out can be a challenge. For example, it's difficult right off the bat to interview a business professional and puzzle out from the interview all of his or her reporting needs. Even if the interview session goes well, determining what reports are best for his or her purposes and perspectives is difficult. To do a great job at this, you need to have an understanding of all the information coming from the key data sources within the organization. Therefore, good information content in a report requires that you have a holistic understanding of a great many aspects about the business and its operational data assets.

By using Reporting Services, you have many content design approaches that you can put to use because of the many elements in the report toolbox that you can use in any report. In addition, you might want to provide for ad hoc query and analysis. The ad hoc nature of asking questions, getting answers, and integrating these answers together to gain an understanding of what's really going on is what most business analysts and their managers need to do. They need the capability to ask a variety of questions and filter the report dynamically or drill down to see more detail within the underlying data. Perhaps they want to be able to jump from one view to another, with a parameter passed to the second report that shows a different view for that aspect of the initial report. Reporting Services was designed to provide these kinds of capabilities.

The design surface or user interface used to create reports for Reporting Services includes a wide variety of tools that can provide just the right content to clarify the information so it's clear to your audience. For example, tabular or list reporting might be appropriate for financial analysis, but subreports could provide other views that clarify the meaning of the information reported. Charts provide for graphical views that allow the user to easily visualize trends and anomalies. Free-form reporting tools such as lists and rectangles (containers used for placing other controls that allow more free-form reporting) allow much more flexibility than ordinary banded-style (columnar reporting with little flexibility to change column spacing and subtotaling formats) reporting tools most of us have had to settle with.

Providing the right security

Information provided to the wrong people can lead to some huge problems. For example, if personal information from Human Resources (like your employees' Social Security numbers) was available to everyone in your company as well as to your customers and prospects, this could lead to an identity theft situation and some disgruntled employees. If you provide access to information that is not appropriate for some class of business users, you could open up your company to unwanted lawsuits and other nuisance issues that could result in your own trip to your HR department.

Reporting Services allows you to properly secure the information by requiring users to submit both a user ID and a password if they want to access key information sources. Proper credentials must be provided to the server for any user to gain access to any major feature of the product. Reporting Services can also limit the access and distribution based on the access group defined in Windows-based security by your network administrators. Reports with sensitive information won't appear to users who don't have proper permission.

Investigating Business Data

Many company managers and analysts today are preoccupied with investigating business data. For companies that still have legacy systems — systems installed in the 1980s or 90s that were developed on mainframe platforms or other platforms that new systems no longer use — accessing the data for reporting and analysis can prove a challenge. Many business people have turned to spreadsheets for rekeying legacy data and creating some analysis based on the data. Databases such as Microsoft SQL Server and Oracle are becoming the information storage system of choice. Databases allow for easyaccess to information in tables that can be queried with reporting tools. Applying good reporting principles to the information in these databases can provide valuable insight into business operations.

Being able to drill down into information for more detail or charting information to see trends in the information is *business intelligence.* Business intelligence (BI) solutions integrate information from multiple data sources and realign the data into structures that are ideal for reporting, drilling down, and trending. These hybrid data models provide greater value for users, including more insightful information content in reports. Smart users who know the tools can then explore information effectively to gain insight into the underlying information.

In a well-executed BI solution, users have self-service access to reporting tools like Reporting Services. Self-service reporting for everyone is a nirvana state of business intelligence. Business people need to be able to freely explore appropriate information with interactive reports or view relevant performance data through dashboards. Dashboards are a common user interface for executives who typically have little training or knowledge in computers and therefore require very intuitive controls for interacting with the information. These varied reports become a truly analytical support system that can provide the perspectives necessary to increase the agility of your organization. Reporting Services is one tool that can be leveraged to provide this type of analytical framework.

Uncovering the Major Features of Reporting Services

Earlier sections in this chapter spell out in general the many principles related to creating, distributing, and managing those reports supported by Reporting Services. Now it's time to do a bit of our own "drilling down" by examining in greater detail the basic capabilities of Reporting Services proper. Hopefully, a few simple illustrations of Reporting Services features and capabilities will provide you with a perspective on how to work with the tool. Don't worry if you don't catch on during the first reading of this section. I'll backtrack and cover all these areas in greater detail in subsequent chapters of the book. This tour will enable you to appreciate the power at your fingertips with this new reporting service.

It's a Web service

Reporting Services gets its name from the fact that the report server is a Web service. A *Web service* is a software component that runs independently on a server and can be accessed by other applications running on the World Wide Web. The Web service runs on the report server. The Web-based reporting functionality of the reporting service provides a single platform for producing Web-based reports for all types of data. The reporting service enables you to embed reports within any Web application and make them available to users with any Web interface. It also allows you to save or view report information in a number of different formats, ranging from images to Excel workbooks.

Any application that can make use of Web services can present information through Reporting Services. One particularly useful set of applications enables you to manage many aspects of report processing as part of the report service — retrieving data, transforming the report layout into a device-specific format *(rendering),* delivering reports to specific formats, and securing the access to reports, to name just a few.

Working with the design surface

The design surface is the user interface used to create reports for Reporting Services. The primary design interface provided by Microsoft for creating reports is Visual Studio. Visual Studio hosts *Report Designer,* which is the application that allows the user to select a data source, build a query, lay out the report elements, preview it with sample data, and finally publish the report to the report server. Report Designer is a powerful tool for developing flexible and complex reports. It offers maximum programmability of the report to provide reports that are structured or free-form, static or interactive, parameter-based or hyperlinked, graphical, tabular, or matrix. It saves developers from the hassle of having to know the gory details of Structured Query Language (SQL) or eXtensible Markup Language (XML) — or Multidimensional eXpressions (MDX) if you're accessing *data cubes,* the OLAP data stores that allow fast reporting of summary information. When you use Visual Studio to develop your reports, they are actually built within a *Report Project.* Project *properties* let you control where the reports are saved and where they are viewable when the report is published.

Third-party tools from Microsoft partners are also available for creating reports using Reporting Services. See Chapter 23 for a list of supported third-party products.

Continuing the tour of Reporting Services features and/or terminology brings us to the *Report Manager,* an ASP.NET application built into the Web service to enable you to manage the reports that you create. This tool organizes reports into easily maintained folders of reports, data sources, and report resources. It allows an administrator to control access, security, and extended usage and also provides an interface for end users to access and view reports easily. Report Manager has features that allow you to create Report History snapshots for point-in-time information. You can also define subscriptions that allow reports to be delivered to users via e-mail or through Web sites. Report Manager also controls server functionality, such as the report cache, and other features that influence overall report distribution performance. I'll be saying lots more about the Report Manager in later sections, where I concentrate on managing, securing, and distributing reports.

Another tool available from the Report Manager is *Report Builder,* which is a report authoring tool that complements Report Designer. It is a "click once" Windows application and is run from a full Windows application running on the report server. Whereas Report Designer can create very flexible and complex reports, Report Builder is designed for the business end user who needs to create an ad hoc report. Business users can drag and drop key information elements without having to know anything about the databases they come from. As such, Report Builder supports a more intuitive style of building reports.

When I talk about Report Builder, I'm talking about a *thin* application — meaning that it is a small separate application that starts up quickly and runs within Reporting Services — that is downloaded to your machine when you access it. It provides a rich development environment displaying more information about all the relationships and hierarchies (such as models) in the data sources that you use to create the report. A Model Builder utility for maintaining these relationships and hierarchies is accessible through Visual Studio.

Connecting to a data source

In order to create reports, you must first connect to a source of data. Reporting Services allows access to any data source with an ODBC (Open Database Connectivity) driver. It also supports OLE DB (Object Linking and Embedding database) connectivity to a wide variety of data sources, including some legacy data sources and most other relational databases such as Oracle, DB2, and Informix. You can also access flat-file data sources (text files) and hierarchical data sources if an ODBC driver supports it. This provides flexibility in sourcing the information for further data processing and any resulting analyses. Applications can be written to connect to SQL and even OLAP data sources as well as OLE DB-compliant data sources.

One key feature of Reporting Services is that it allows multiple data sources to be used within a single report, a unique capability that allows for truly robust reports.

Creating the layout

Regardless of the design surface (Visual Studio or Report Builder) that you use, you have many report items in the toolbox of report controls available to you for building reports. Some of these items are independent items — meaning that they're not associated with a particular data source. Examples of these report controls include the Textbox, Line, Rectangle, and Image report items. Rectangles can be used to group other report items or to add page breaks.

Other report controls organize data for presentation and are known as *data regions.* Examples of these report controls include the List, Table, Matrix, Chart, and Subreport controls. Tables are used for tabular displays; matrix report items are excellent at creating cross tab reports; subreports act as containers for other reports; and charts create graphical content. You can also add headers and footers at the report, page table, or group level within a report. The heart of creating reports is knowing the ins and outs of working with the various report items as objects in your reports. I talk about these capabilities more in several chapters of this book, beginning in Chapter 3.

Using expressions and formulas

Inserting expressions into reports can sometimes be tricky, so it's good to know that Reporting Services has a robust Expression Editor to help in this task. You can create custom fields from columns you return from your data source and then create expressions in a textbox for descriptive text based on elements from your data sources for the report. When it comes to formulas, you can make use of aggregating functions such as SUM and AVG or COUNT and even set up conditional formatting so that various intersections of your report stand out because of distinctive back color, fonts, or other properties. Finally, you can create your own functions and utilize them with a report.

Filtering, sorting, and grouping

Think of *filtering* your report data as a way of providing an appropriate amount of data to meet what is known in the business as your "information delivery requirements." Not everybody needs every bit of information, so go ahead and set up parameters in your query to reduce the amount of data returned. (See more on parameters in the next section.) Alternatively, you can add fields to a report item with a basic drag-and-drop maneuver. Then, groupings of report items can be created with an Insert Group command on a table report item. Expressions can be used for the Group On value and Sort value. A report table can be sorted on any field in the table. This allows for robust control over your reports so that a single report with parameters the user can specify could replace a whole book of reports, which are hard-coded or preprogrammed for only certain combinations of parameters.

You can create reports with interactive sorting capabilities, which enables the user to sort the data within the report. Reporting Services supports group sorts and various techniques to control the scope of the sort. The Interactive Sort control appears in the Report view as a control that shows the direction of the current sort and highlights which columns can be sorted interactively. The advantage of using this technique is that it interacts with the data that has already been retrieved from the server into the report. All the sorting is performed on the client application without having to query the server again. This provides another option for controlling the overall reporting solution performance.

Defining parameters

Parameters are variables that determine the filtering for the data presented in reports. You can use parameters in queries to specify report content. All you do is specify your parameter values in a report prompt within the report; they are then passed through to your query to generate the specified report. Parameter values can also be provided by another report so that reports can be linked to create a guided analysis across multiple reports. Report parameters are passed into the report, either through a parameter prompt or directly from another report. Query parameters are specified in the query of the data source that generates corresponding report parameters. You can select one or multiple values in the parameter value list to determine what parameter values are reported for a parameter-based report.

Navigating and fact-seeking

Being able to find something quickly in a long report can be a real plus, as anyone who's scrolled through pages of reports looking for an elusive fact can testify. You can use Reporting Services to control whether your report displays with a *Document Map;* it also lets you control what aspect of the report a Document Map is based on. Document Map allows the user to click a control in the report to jump to the bookmark represented by that value of the report variable. If you set up your Document Map wisely, you can then use the feature to quickly find the info you want.

Document Map is a great idea for documents that work like catalogs. You can also specify whether clicking a cell will jump to another report or to a URL location on the Internet. Using this capability can produce some interesting drill-down analysis capabilities or hyperlinking to get more information from another Web service or Web page about a particular subject.

You can also control the *visibility* of each component of the report so that it can be initially visible (or not) but turn invisible (or visible) based on another report item, an action, or a conditional function. This feature allows for interesting drill-down effects within a single report, where you can initially hide a detail section and toggle between showing or hiding that section with a control that appears on the report.

Formatting the content

Reporting Services provides you with a variety of devices to control simple text formatting. They include toolbar controls for font and style of your text, menu controls which allow you to change foreground or background color, and text properties that allow you to adjust the format of numbers or general text for display.

Text and numbers are sure to make up the greater part of your reports, but you're sure to face situations in which you'll want to add images to your reports. Maybe you want to provide some concrete visual information, or you just want to spice things up a bit. With Reporting Services, you can add images to your report as part of the header, display a picture of a catalog item, or even add a background image to every page of your report. And when it comes to how images get attached to your report, you have the option of embedding images directly in the report, referencing an image on the Web via its Web address (or URL), or storing the image as a field in a database. (Talk about flexibility!)

You can set project properties to control the location of the report server as well as the name of the folder that the report will be created in when saved and deployed. Report properties can reference *custom assemblies* or code that can be run to handle special display formats for numbers in a field. You can also control XML data output options. Many charting types are supported (22 to be exact) with smoothing and 3-D effects that can be added.

You can also make use of templates and styles to create interesting reports. This works similar to how you use templates in Excel or Word, where many aspects of the formats are available as predefined settings to save you time in getting to your final destination layout format.

Saving a report

In Reporting Services, you save any report you create by using Report Definition Language (RDL). RDL, an XML-based schema for report content that allows report definitions to be exchanged between different systems or different reporting tools, is an open specification that Microsoft has published. Some leading reporting tool vendors have announced that they will support this standard. This is a great development because it ensures that in the near future, you'll be able to move reports between different reporting tools without losing formatting or data.

The properties of the project dictate where you save the report when the project is actually built and deployed. For example, you can build the report and deploy it to a folder in the Report Server. This enhances your ability to navigate to the report you need when you need it.

Displaying a report

You can preview your report layout in the Preview window of whichever design tool — Report Builder, Report Designer, or some third-party (non-Microsoft) tool — you choose to work with. After you're happy with the layout, you can print from the Design tool. This is one way to see the results of your work. After you save your report to the server, you can use the Report Manager to access and view the report.

Another way to access your report is to use a technique called *URL access,* which allows you to type in a URL directly in a standard Web browser to render the report in your browser. With this method, you have the option of displaying the report without the headers and other toolbar and control features that the Report Manager provides. I discuss this further in Chapter 9.

After you actually produce a report, you can render it in a variety of formats, including TIFF, JPEG, PDF, HTML, XML, Excel, and Word. You cal also use Open API (application program interface) formats, which can be utilized to render in many more output formats. Third-party vendors have also developed rendering extensions for Word, Excel, and even bar codes. With these rendering approaches, Reporting Services can serve information to a variety of devices such as PDAs, Web sites, wireless desktops, and any computer on a corporate intranet.

Managing reports

Remember that managed reports are reports stored on the report server, where they can be stored in folders within the Report Manager. You can add reports to folders, move reports between folders, create new folders, rename old ones, and create folders within other folders, much the same way you'd work with folders for your computer's file system in something like Windows Explorer.

You publish your data sources to the report server when you deploy your report project; these data sources can be shared among many reports. You control access to such data by using data source connection properties to set the access permissions of a data source. Within Report Manager, you can move shared data sources into their own folder if you so desire. You can also save images used in your reports as resources in your folders, thus providing for easy access and maintenance. Report Manager also allows the administrator to control which users have access to which specific folders.

Report Manager also provides access to various *report properties* that govern how reports will execute (such as scheduled runs or execution frequency), how reports should use the memory cache (cache temporary copy when run, when to expire the cache), how parameters are used (default parameter values, parameter interactivity), report-delivery techniques, and how users will be able to interact with the report content. You can use Report Manager to create snapshots of the report, and you can save report histories so that you can review how the data has changed over a period of time. All these properties provide great control over your managed reporting environment. I describe the capabilities in more detail in Chapter 9.

Securing a report

Reporting Services has a robust security model. It makes use of a role-based, user-based, and task-based security model to ensure proper permissions are established for access to critical business information. The security model can also be extended, and Microsoft will provide the bits for security model extensions to support proprietary authentication schemes. A role is a way to categorize users into groups based on the way they need to interact with the system and its resources. Users can belong to many roles like content manager, publisher, or browser (of information). User-based security is specific to a specific user in unique aspects of how they interact with the system. Tasks are different functions that a given user can perform.

Distributing a report

The most popular way to distribute a report is to print it. The printed report is then copied for all report consumers and distributed at an appointed time. Footers usually record the time the report was run as well as the time the data source was last refreshed.

Many years ago, environmentalists took the bull by the horns and recommended to corporate America that Business (with a capital B) should consider how many trees were being chopped down in the name of printed report distribution. Deforestation worries intensified the environmentalists' resolve. Even recycling experts could not make a decisive argument against the environmentalists, so corporate America began to embrace the online report distribution best practice. The ubiquitous Internet came along and further popularized this trend, which means that reporting in the modern age is becoming increasingly paperless.

To accomplish paperless reporting, Web services like Reporting Services are required. Using Reporting Services, you can author a report and then publish it to a folder to be accessed by Report Manager. *On-demand* reports are reports that do not cache temporary copies of reports when they are run. *Subscriptions* can be defined to "push" reports to users: Subscriptions can be scheduled to execute regularly to deliver rendered reports to end users.

One delivery option for subscriptions is to have the subscription send an e-mail containing a hyperlink, a notification, or a rendered report attachment. Another delivery option is to have the subscription execute a file delivery to send the report to a file location that an intranet can access easily.

Accessing and Looking at Reports

Now you can catch your breath after that rapid tour of Reporting Service capabilities. The following chapters of this book dive much more deeply into each of these subject areas.

One of the very first things that you might want to do with this new tool is to see how you can get to a report and view it. Consider this dipping your toes into the vast ocean of Reporting Services. You can follow this road with me if you have access to the sample reports provided in the Reporting Service installation software. (You'll find the sample reports in the file system folders that you name during the installation process.)

Printed reports versus online reports

Reading a printed report doesn't require any technical sophistication. And with a printed report, you get a paper copy of key information that you can refer to. Paper reports, however, do not offer any interactivity where you might click on some hyperlink to further explore the underlying details of some information on the report. It is helpful to display the date and time when the report was run, as well as the time when the data was last refreshed. This allows you to budget the currency and relevance of the information displayed in the report. But there are a few limitations in having access *only* to a printed report:

- ✔ **The report is not connected to a live data source.** With a live connection to the data source, you can get information since the latest refresh of the database. For daily cumulative reporting, it is best to work with live data source connections if you really want to understand the current dynamics of the business.

- ✔ **Graphical information has a single "shade of gray" display.** This can present some difficulties when you review a bar chart with a multitude of different categories, but your printer produces only black and white. Using colors — yes, that includes shades of gray — improves the visibility of the dynamics of your business as viewed through the reports.

- ✔ **You have no drill-down capability.** With a live database connection on a report with drill-down capabilities, you can easily navigate to see a more detailed perspective of the information presented from a summary report. You also have a choice on what areas you want to drill down into detail. This need might change from period to period, so a live report with dynamic drill-down capability in several report variables clearly provides a much better analysis.

- ✔ **You cannot take hyperlinks that jump from one view to another view.** With hyperlinks, you can set up jumping within the report to link to a section grouping of the report, or you can set jumping outside the report to go to another report entirely or to a hyperlink on the Internet. Without the ability to hyperlink, you might have to flip through lots of reports trying to locate the data that you're trying to analyze.

Viewing a report

Viewing a report with Reporting Services requires that your computer at least have a connection to the server that's running the report server. If you've installed the sample reports from the Reporting Services installation CD, you should be able to view a sample report by following these steps:

1. **Connect to the Report Manager by pointing your favorite Web browser to** `http://localhost/reports.`

   The Report Manager home page appears, as shown in Figure 1-1. You'll see a folder for Sample Reports as well as any other folders defined on your report server. You'll also see the menu options related to site settings and subscriptions. The view in the figure shows how it looks after you click the Show Details button, which then toggles to a Hide Details button (shown in the upper-right of Figure 1-1). You can see who created the folders and when they were last modified.

2. **Select the folder that you want to view and click it.**

   Report Manager displays the contents of the Sample Reports folder, as shown in Figure 1-2. The folder consists of reports, resources, and (possibly) other folders defined on the report server. Each report in the Sample Reports folder can have a description (if provided) as well as a listing of the last date modified and who modified it. It might also show the last date run if configured in this way. You can click the column headings to sort all contents in that column in either an ascending or descending order. You can edit report properties by clicking the Edit symbol — the tiny-hand-over-the-report-page icon. You can also move or delete reports by marking the check box in the far-left column and clicking the Delete or Move button.

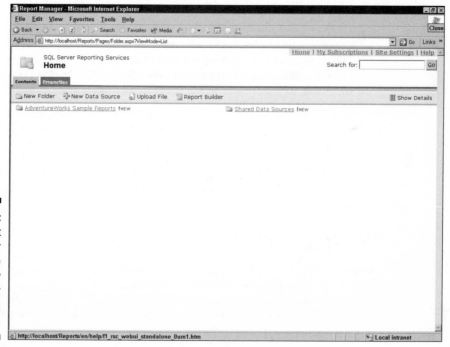

Figure 1-1:
The Report Manager home page is the entry point for viewing reports.

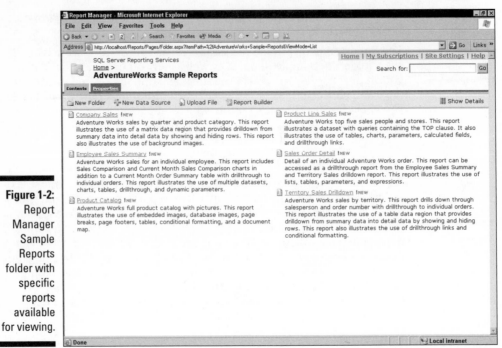

Figure 1-2:
Report
Manager
Sample
Reports
folder with
specific
reports
available
for viewing.

3. Select the report that you want to view and click it.

Report Manager displays the report, as shown in Figure 1-3. Notice that the report shows all the information based on any parameter value sentered as well as on the security enforced on the report server. If this is an interactive report, you might see rows highlighted, indicating that a hyperlink exists to another report or a bookmark within the same report. Reporting Services reports can be developed to include graphics like bar and pie charts that are linked to the data shown in the same report. You can also design parameters in the report so that the user can change the parameter value and rerun the same report and see an entirely different slice of the data in the report. For example, you can select different product categories or different time ranges to see a different slice of the information. Note that there is an option on the toolbar to export to a different format. This is a way to change the reported information into a spreadsheet or a PDF for sharing and collaborating with others.

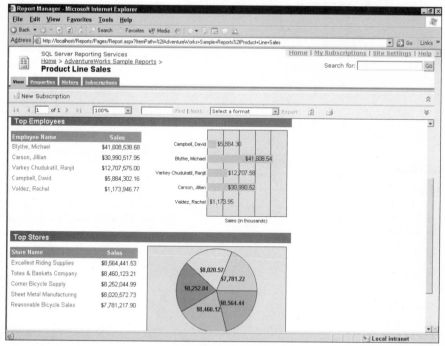

Figure 1-3:
Report
Manager
with the
Product Line
Sales report
displayed.

4. Click the Back button when you finish viewing the report.

Alternatively, you can link back to the original report folder by clicking the link on the breadcrumb trail in the top-left of the Report Manager window.

Chapter 2

Retrieving Data from a Database

. . . .

. . . .

*I*n Chapter 1, I start you off with tons of great info about how a cool new reporting tool — Microsoft SQL Server 2005 Reporting Services — can help you write better reports. (I know, because I put the info there.) What Chapter 1 doesn't cover are the basic, everyday database concepts — concepts that might prove useful to anyone who, say, actually wants to work with a database.

And this is why Chapter 1 inevitably leads to Chapter 2. Rest assured that after reading this chapter, you'll have enough background and knowledge to be able to handle most of what you'll ever encounter when accessing data from relational databases. Okay, you might come across some higher-end issues that a real database administrator (DBA) should deal with, but even there, I show you how to phrase a request so that your organization's DBA will be impressed by your sharp business sense and acumen.

Discovering What Makes a Database

A *database* is nothing more than a collection of data stored in some organized fashion. Databases use the concept of *tables* as the organizing scheme. Just like working with a filing system to organize your papers, tables are used to store structured data of a specific type. And as long as I'm defining stuff, another name for a table is an *entity* — a thing that can be distinctly identified. For example, orders and customers are examples of entities. They are things that are distinct from each other but relevant to your business. In a relational database named SALES, you'd expect to find two distinct entities named ORDER and CUSTOMER.

Tables are the backbone for any database. Each table comprises columns and rows designating attributes of the data you want to store. The best way to envision a table consisting of columns and rows is to think of a table as a grid in which the columns and rows of the grid correspond to the various attributes for that table. For example, the ORDER table might contain rows for each order and columns for the date the order was entered, who entered the order, the customer for which the order was placed, the promised ship date of the order, and so on. The specific products contained in a customer order might be in another related table called ORDER DETAILS.

Each column has a *data type* associated with it that describes what type of information is stored in the column. If the column is to contain a number, the data type is a numeric data type. Data types can be numeric, text, decimal, currency, notes, and so on.

Keying In on Your Data

For any given table in the database, you have at least one attribute that uniquely identifies it. (There might be an order number column for this purpose, for example, conveniently called OrderID.) In the world of database management, you call such a column (or set of columns) whose value uniquely identifies every row in a table a *primary key*. An example of a primary key for a PERSON table is an American's Social Security number because this number is unique for every person in the United States. Having a primary key is great because when you later have to manipulate all the data you've stored, you can access each record uniquely by referring to the value of its primary key.

Any primary key you choose to set up for a table has to meet the following common-sense requirements:

- ✔ **No two rows can have the same primary key value.**
- ✔ **Every row must have a primary key value assigned to it.**
- ✔ **The column containing the primary key value cannot be modified or updated.**
- ✔ **Primary key values can never be reused.**

In your database travels, you are likely to encounter the concept of a *foreign key*. Don't despair or think that you suddenly have to learn some foreign language in order to crack a secret code. A foreign key is simply a primary key for one table that is kept in another table to make it easier to join the two tables to query information from two related tables.

Striking up a Relationship with Your Data

A *relationship* is a connection between tables in the database. As you might expect, many types of relationships can exist in a database. The *one-to-one* relationship, for example, means that for each row in one table, there is at most one associated row in another table. If you want to get concrete, I can tell you that for each husband, there is at most one (legal) wife, and a wife has at most one (legal) husband — at least in this country.

You can also have *many-to-one* relationships, indicating that for a given row in a table, there can be multiple related rows in another table. A woman, for example, can have zero or more children. And then there are *many-to-many* relationships, in which there are no restrictions on the number of rows related to the row of a specific table.

As I discuss in the preceding section, a *foreign key* in a database table is a key from another table that is contained within the table in question. The foreign key in a specific table is most often the primary key of the related table. Foreign keys complete an association or *relationship* between two tables by identifying the parent entity. Foreign keys provide a method for navigating between different instances of an entity (sometimes referred to as *referential integrity*). Every relationship in a database must be supported by a foreign key.

The rule for referential integrity is that if a relational table has a foreign key, every value of the foreign key must either be null or match the values in the relational table in which that foreign key is a primary key.

As you might expect, a *relational* database is in fact a set of tables with *relationships*. The job of a DBA is to select the appropriate relationships for the database being modeled. When the DBA completes a model for a database, he or she publishes it in the form of an *entity-relationship* (ER) model. An *ER diagram* is the document that communicates how all the tables in a database are related. It is also the roadmap for how to query a database for reporting purposes.

You can see an example of an entity-relationship diagram in Figure 2-1. (The sample AdventureWorks database depicted here comes with SQL Server, so it's going to serve as my handy sample database of choice in this and many other chapters of this book.) The relationships between sales order, sales detail, territory, salesperson, and customer are clearly shown in this ER diagram, so it's easy to see how tables link up. Note that the scope of this diagram is not the entire database but merely the Sales Order table relationships in the database. This diagram was created as a database diagram with the SQL Server 2005 Management Studio, which I talk more about in Chapter 12.

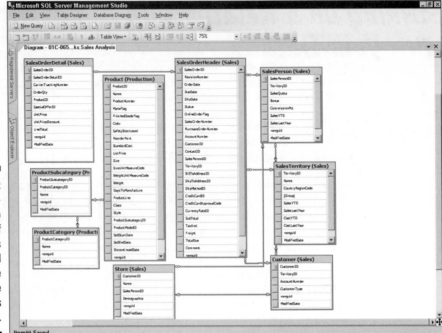

Figure 2-1:
Entity-relationship diagram of the Sales Order model from the Adventure Works database.

SQL Server 2005 does not have a diagramming tool, but Microsoft Visio 2000 has a technique known as *reverse engineering* a database to create a diagram of the related groups of tables in a database. This is the technique that I use to create the ER diagram shown in Figure 2-1.

It pays to have a closer look at Figure 2-1, so here goes. The most detailed table in the diagram is SalesOrderDetail. A foreign key — FK1 — in this table relates to the Product table. The Product table, in turn, is related to the product subcategory (ProductSubCategory) and the product category (ProductCategory) tables. The information from these product-related tables can be combined to define a product *hierarchy.*

A *hierarchy* describes how particular business terms are grouped into categories, which in turn are grouped into higher level categories. For example, the *product* hierarchy represents how products roll up (indicating the hierarchy of products) to subcategories and then to categories. A *territory* hierarchy, on the other hand, represents how salespersons roll up to territories. Each grouping within a hierarchy is a *level* of the hierarchy. The product hierarchy has three levels (products, subgroups, and groups), and the territory hierarchy has two levels (salesperson and sales territory).

Another look at the ER diagram in Figure 2-1 shows you that a salesperson is *related* to a customer — which is another way of saying that a salesperson has responsibility for a customer. You'll also find tables (SalesOrderHeader and SalesOrderDetail, for example) that contain attributes that relate to money transactions between customers and the company.

Building a SQL Query

Having all your stuff nicely stored in a database (relational or otherwise) is a nice start, but if you can't access your information quickly and efficiently, you'll find yourself up a certain creek rather quickly without a certain paddle. This is where *querying* a database comes in. As you might expect with anything involving computers, a specific language is needed to enable us humans to communicate with that laptop or desktop machine and actually do something with the information stored in that database on the hard drive. This language is Structured Query Language (SQL). SQL was specifically designed to work with databases and can be used to access data (to be displayed in a report), update data within a table, or insert new values into the table. For the purposes of working with Reporting Services, you need to focus only on using SQL to display information.

Being SELECTive

You build SQL statements or queries by stringing together terms — including one or more *keywords* — that look pretty much like plain old English. The SELECT keyword, for example, indicates that you want to retrieve information from one or more tables in the database to which you are connected. When you use the SELECT statement, you also have to indicate what you want to select as well as from which table in the database. The keyword FROM is used to precede the names of the tables in which the selected columns are located. For example, the following syntax retrieves the customer ID, order date, and subtotal from the SalesOrderHeader table:

```
SELECT customerID, OrderDate, SubTotal
FROM SalesOrderHeader
```

Refer to your handy entity-relationship (ER) diagram (see Figure 2-1) for the column names and then use those names as the columns to select in the SQL statement. If you do not correctly spell what you want to select, or you don't use the proper syntax, you'll receive an error. The error message can look like Incorrect syntax near... or Invalid object name....

Follow along with SQL Server Query Analyzer

Getting a handle on SQL statements takes some doing, so it wouldn't hurt to get some practice. Here's what I suggest: If you have SQL Server (or its utilities) loaded on your computer — either at home or at the office — you should be able to run the program Query Analyzer. (Query Analyzer for SQL Server works like most database SQL command processor utilities in that it allows you to connect to databases and write SQL queries to return result sets.) Follow these steps to start Query Analyzer and connect with the AdventureWorks sample database:

1. **Start the SQL Server Management Studio by choosing Start⇨All Programs⇨Microsoft SQL Server 2005⇨SQL Server Management Studio.**

   The SQL Server Management Studio main window appears along with the Connect to Server dialog box.

2. **Connect to the server.**

   The Connect to Server dialog box is shown in Figure 2-2. It prompts you for the server type, server name, and authentication. You have several options for server type: Database Engine, Analysis Services, Reporting Services, and others. In order to write queries for this example, select Database Engine as the server type. Also specify the server name to which you are connecting and select Windows Authentication in the third combo box. If you specify Windows Authentication, you do not need to provide any more information. For SQL Server authentication, you need to provide user ID and password information for a valid SQL Server access. Then click the Connect button to connect to SQL Server.

Figure 2-2:
The Connect
to Server
dialog box.

3. **Select the database you want to query.**

In the Management Studio, you should be viewing the Object Explorer window on the left side. If it is not displayed, you can open it by choosing View⟹Object Explorer. Object Explorer uses a tree structure to group information into folders. Expand the folder named Databases to show all the databases available to you. For this example, click the AdventureWorks database.

4. Open the Query Editor and begin constructing your SQL query.

Right-click the database named AdventureWorks and you will see a pop-up menu of options. Select the New Query menu item and you will see the Query window open to the right of your Object Explorer. Note also that a new toolbar displays after this action. The second toolbar is the SQL Editor toolbar to help in executing SQL queries.

An alternative way of opening the Query Editor is to click the New Query button on the standard toolbar to do this. However, if you use this method, you will be prompted to connect to the server with another Connect to Server dialog box like the one shown in Figure 2-2. In this case, you need to select Database Engine as the server type and make sure it is connecting to the same server with the same authentication as you entered in Step 2 above. Then click the Connect button to open the Query Editor window.

You see a dialog box similar to the one in Figure 2-3. You can now enter SQL statements to execute on the server that's running SQL Server 2005.

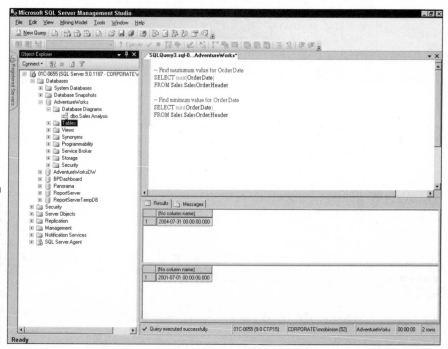

Figure 2-3:
Query Analyzer with a connection to the Adventure Works database.

The examples shown are run with the database AdventureWorks, which is installed as part of the Documentation and Samples option in the SQL Server 2005 installation.

Suppose you were interested in querying the Sales.SalesOrderHeader table in the AdventureWorks database. You might start with the following query:

```
SELECT count(*) FROM Sales.SalesOrderHeader
```

The count function used here tells SQL Server that it is interested in returning the number of rows in the database table. The count function is not case-sensitive and it requires column reference(s) in parentheses after the function name to indicate which columns it is counting. The use of the asterisk is a short-hand way of indicating all columns referenced in the FROM clause. The answer SQL Server returns is that 31,465 orders are in the Sales.SalesOrderHeader table.

That's a lot of orders! Before you start plowing through that data, how about finding out the date of the last order as well as when the first order occurred? (Basically, I'm talking about the *date range* of the table here.)You can do that in the Sales.SalesOrderHeader table by using the following two SQL statements or queries:

```
-- Find maximum value for OrderDate
SELECT max(OrderDate)
FROM Sales.SalesOrderHeader

-- Find minimum value for OrderDate
SELECT min(OrderDate)
FROM Sales.SalesOrderHeader
```

Figure 2-3 shows the result set for these two queries. Note that the results window is split to show the results of all queries in the query window. Also note that I can use dashes (--) to indicate that what follows on that line is a comment and is not to be evaluated as part of the SQL statement. You can use this technique to *comment* your statements. You can use comments to explain in English what is being queried or to explain what to do with the results of the query in the flow of processing that follows.

By looking at the result sets in Figure 2-3, you can conclude that the Sales. SalesOrderHeader table contains orders dating from July 1, 2001, through July 31, 2004.

If you would like to see all the columns of a table, you don't have to spell out all those column names in your SELECT clause. Rather, you can use the following convention:

```
SELECT * FROM Sales.SalesOrderHeader
```

If you need some more support on writing SQL queries from within Query Analyzer, click the Help menu and select the Transact-SQL Help topic from the menu. Search for SELECT, which is a good place to start with more detail on syntax. Transact-SQL is the SQL syntax that SQL Server 2005 understands. Other variations of SQL have been developed for other database engines.

WHERE you join the party

If you would like to retrieve information from columns of multiple tables, you first need to join the two tables. You do this by referring to both tables in the FROM clause of your query and then adding a WHERE clause to stipulate what criteria SQL should use to find which columns to search. And what might that criteria be? Easy. By setting the primary key of the first table to the foreign key of the corresponding related table, you tell SQL that the two tables are linked and are therefore fair game for whatever search you undertake. (For more on primary and foreign keys, see the earlier section, "Striking up a Relationship with Your Data.")

You can use this approach only when the two tables have a *common key* on which to join information. For example, if you refer to the ER diagram in Figure 2-1, you can see that a CustomerID key is common to both the SalesOrderHeader and Customer tables.

Check out how this works on real tables. Say you want to query the account number, order date, and subtotal amount for SalesOrderHeaders (info that is stored in two separate tables — the Customer table and the SalesOrderHeader table). To do that, you use the following syntax:

```
SELECT s.AccountNumber, OrderDate, SubTotal
FROM Sales.SalesOrderHeader s, Sales.Customer c
WHERE s.customerID = c.customerID
```

I referred to columns located in two tables — SalesOrderHeader and Customer — so that SQL Server needs to *join* the tables on a common key. The FROM clause contains the tables that contain the columns I want to seeas results. The WHERE clause indicates how the tables should be joined by their respective keys. This works here because customerID is the primary key for the Customer table, and it is also a foreign key for the SalesOrderHeader table.

You'll notice that this query has what might be considered an interesting additional quirk. (That's how some refer to it, but others might use a different language.) First and foremost, the name customerID is clearly a column name that exists in both the SalesOrderHeader and Customer tables. (I say "clearly" because this whole process works only if tables share a common key — and how could a key be common if it did not share the same name?) That sounds logical — and is logical — but having a single name for what seem to be two separate items in two distinct tables is going to confuse SQL's computer brain further down the road if you don't intervene now.

To that end, do exactly what I did in the preceding query and provide an *alias* in the FROM clause for each of the tables that you want to work with. (I usually use the first initial, or at most a two-letter alias, for my tables.) As long as you define the alias for each table in the FROM clause and use the alias in the rest of the SQL query to uniquely show where columns are sourced from, SQL Server will know how to process your query. The alias saves you from having to enter fully qualified names for the columns in your query. In this way, you can simply refer to the non-unique column customerID but prefix it with the alias of the table in which to find this column. The alias and column name combination must be a unique reference in order that the SQL can be understood and executed by the database. (Of course, when you get to the WHERE clause in your query, you'll have to use the same aliases referenced in the FROM clause; only then can the WHERE clause look in the right place for what you want.) If you want to use an alias that has spaces in it, you must use double quotation marks around the alias name. It is best to use text letter(s) for the aliases because most symbols produce SQL error messages.

You should also use the alias concept when you want to see a non-unique column (such as customerID) in the result set. For example, to retrieve customerID in the result set, if you don't preface the column name with an alias, you receive the system-generated error message:

```
Ambiguous column name 'CustomerID'
```

To resolve this issue, use the alias with the non-unique column name in the SELECT statement.

It does not make a difference which table alias you use in the following example:

```
SELECT c.customerID, s.AccountNumber, OrderDate, SubTotal
FROM Sales.SalesOrderHeader s, Sales.Customer c
WHERE s.customerID = c.customerID
```

The WHERE clause also enables you to filter your query. For example, if you are interested in orders in 2004 listed in the sample AdventureWorks database, you could issue the following query:

```
SELECT s.AccountNumber, OrderDate, SubTotal
FROM Sales.SalesOrderHeader s, Sales.Customer c
WHERE s.customerID = c.customerID
and OrderDate >= '1/1/2004'
```

Note that I started a new line in the WHERE clause for each condition to enhance the full statement's readability. Also, I need to enter single quotes around that date field value so that the data field OrderDate can be evaluated with a literal value of the date. SQL Server only recognizes date and time values enclosed in single quotes. This query returns 13,951 rows indicating the number of orders taken with order dates on or after January 1, 2004.

ORDER in the court

Seeing all orders for a year in a particular order might prove useful to you (or to some higher-up in your company). One common way to look at sales — especially when it comes to handing out bonuses — is to look from highest to lowest. This sort order is a *descending sort order*. The way to specify the sort variable and direction on your SQL command is to use the ORDER BY clause. To see the results from highest to lowest subtotal in the sample AdventureWorks database, use the following syntax:

```
SELECT s.AccountNumber, SubTotal
FROM Sales.SalesOrderHeader s, Sales.Customer c
WHERE s.customerID = c.customerID
and OrderDate >= '1/1/2004'
ORDER BY SubTotal desc
```

The result set will be ordered from highest to lowest value of column SubTotal for all account numbers in the SalesOrderHeader table. Note that the desc keyword is an abbreviation for *descending*. If you want an ascending sort, use the keyword asc. As always, the FROM and WHERE clauses make liberal use of aliases, as spelled out in the "WHERE you join the party" section, earlier in this chapter.

GROUP BY for subtotals

Variety is the spice of life, so go ahead and group your orders by the AccountNumber field. The GROUP BY expression specifies the groups into which output rows are to be placed. The SQL expression you'll write looks like this:

```
SELECT s.AccountNumber, SUM(SubTotal)
FROM Sales.SalesOrderHeader s, Sales.Customer c
WHERE s.customerID = c.customerID
and OrderDate >= '1/1/2004'
GROUP BY s.AccountNumber
ORDER BY SUM(SubTotal) desc
```

Notice that for this example, you use an aggregate function (SUM) in the SELECT expression. You use the SUM function to indicate that you're interested in getting the sum of the sales SubTotal based on the selection criteria of the query (which in this case, was a restriction only on the OrderDate). When you use an aggregate function like SUM, you also need to have a GROUP BY expression to indicate that you still want to group by the other SELECT variables that don't use an aggregate function. You could specify multiple GROUP BY variables in the query, which would indicate where subtotals would occur in the result set.

The SQL query here returns a result set that groups a sum of the sales SubTotal amount by account number and then orders these groupings from highest to lowest so you can determine which accounts represent the most revenue to the company. Note that the GROUP BY expression precedes the ORDER BY expression. If you forget the order of these expressions, your SQL analyzer tool reports a syntax error and lists the keyword where the error occurs. In this case, the error is at the GROUP BY keyword — SQL's little signal to you to get the expressions in the right order!

HAVING for filtering

Want to try for more? How about an example that tells you how many orders there were for the account that ended up being the total sales winner in the query. You need to use the COUNT function, which returns the number of rows satisfying each grouping of the result set. To make it even more interesting, go ahead and add just a little new wrinkle and specify the column names to be shown on the results set listing. This can be done by using the AS keyword after the variable in the SELECT expression, followed by the title to be displayed in quotes. Finally, for the pièce de résistance, set it up so that SQL looks at orders only where the sales SubTotal is greater than $200,000. When you have all your SQL ducks in a row, the resulting query should look like this:

```
SELECT s.AccountNumber as 'Account',
count(*) as '# Orders',
SUM(SubTotal) as 'Total Order'
FROM Sales.SalesOrderHeader s, Sales.Customer c
WHERE s.customerID = c.customerID
and OrderDate >= '1/1/2004'
GROUP BY s.AccountNumber
HAVING SUM(SubTotal) >200000
ORDER BY SUM(SubTotal) desc
```

Now I'll use another language to describe the effect of this query — *voilà!* (That's French, Morticia!)

Note: Sharper eyes will have noticed a new keyword — the HAVING keyword — used here with the aggregate sum(SubTotal). Why does one have to have HAVING? Well, the only way to filter an aggregate function (a function like SUM, MAX, or MIN) is to use it in a HAVING expression. You cannot use an aggregate function within a WHERE expression. As a final note, the HAVING expression comes *after* the GROUP BY expression and *before* any ORDER BY expression.

One final example, and you'll have completed a great SQL workout! Just imagine that you want to specify the year for which you want to analyze sales. Instead of specifying in your WHERE clause a start date (>= January 1 of the year) *and* an end date (<= December 31 of the year) in the query, you can use a *date function* on the OrderDate field. Date functions, to no one's surprise, are used to display information about dates. Specifically, you can use the YEAR function to return an integer that represents the year part of a specified date. The function YEAR(OrderDate) = '2004' in the WHERE clause specifies that you want orders where the order data was sometime in 2004. The resulting query is

```
SELECT s.AccountNumber as 'Account',
count(*) as '# Orders',
SUM(SubTotal) as 'Total Order'
FROM Sales.SalesOrderHeader s, Sales.Customer c
WHERE s.customerID = c.customerID
and Year(OrderDate) = '2004'
GROUP BY s.AccountNumber
HAVING sum(SubTotal) >200000
ORDER BY sum(SubTotal) desc
```

Creating views in the database

Bear in mind that it might be easier to request that a database administrator create a view to query from. A *view* is a virtual table that represents the data in one or more tables in an alternative way. A view can simplify the tables and bring them together to make writing SQL much easier than working with the original underlying tables. This approach is a design consideration that can greatly simplify the work of getting information out of the database. A view can reference a maximum of 1,024 columns and can filter unwanted data or embed some business rules in how tables should be combined for reporting. You can also UNION together tables that can be created for a specific year so you can query data for several years in a single view. (The UNION command is a way of combining the results of two similar queries in the same result set.) The columns need to match in terms of number and data type between the two SQL statements being combined. The UNION command should be considered a way to make querying information easier within a complex or confusing database model.

When used with the AdventureWorks sample database, this query returns seven rows indicating that for the year 2004, seven customers had more than $200,000 in sales.

As a final illustration, Figure 2-4 shows a slightly revised SQL statement to retrieve the `Store Name` and include it in the result set called up by our SQL query. Notice that I had to include a join from the Customer table to the Store table in order to return the `Store Name` info instead of the `AccountNumber` in the `SalesOrderHeader`. This was accomplished by adding a condition to the WHERE clause that `s.CustomerID = c.CustomerID`. All this works because `CustomerID` is a key in the Customer table and a foreign key in the Store table.

Respecting the stored procedures

All you power users out there are going to love this one. It's time to talk about the last concept in my introductory tour: the stored procedure. The *stored procedure* is a query that is compiled as code on the server. Nice, but nothing to write home about, you say? How about if I told you that the execution plan for the query within the stored procedure is also fixed when the procedure is stored? The execution plan refers to the method that the SQL Query Optimizer will use to retrieve the data. For stored procedures, the query execution plan is stored and executes quickly. Queries that are not in stored procedures are evaluated at run-time to generate a query execution plan and are then executed, introducing delays in the processing.

The stored procedure can be used in a report and executes faster than normal SQL because it was already compiled when it was created. The database engine does not have to evaluate it as closely as SQL code that has not been stored as a procedure. *Note:* I refer to SQL Server syntax in this section. Other database management systems have their own quirks in terms of syntax and conventions, so if you go the non-SQL Server route, you're on your own.

Another nice thing about stored procedures is that you can pass *parameters* — the specific values of variables defined in the stored procedure — into them. (Parameters are the variables whose values can be changed upon each execution of the SQL expressions within the stored procedure.) For example, you might want to write a procedure that has a `Year` parameter and a `Minimum Threshold` parameter as part of your investigation of account sales. To do this, you would need to declare variables `@year` and `@amount` and reference these variables in the stored procedure. (The `@` symbol is what you use to identify a variable in a stored procedure.)

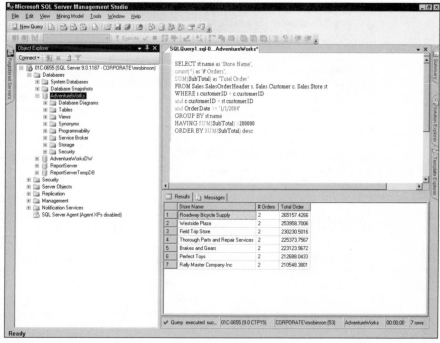

Figure 2-4:
SQL state-
ment and
the result set
displayed
in Query
Analyzer.

Using the last SQL query in the earlier section, "GROUP BY for subtotals,"
you can create a stored procedure that meets all necessary requirements
doing the following:

1. **With Management Studio open, find your database in the Object
   Explorer window and click on the folder named Programmability
   to expand within your database folder.**

   All the subfolders underneath Programmability are displayed.

2. **Right-click the Stored Procedure subfolder in the tree.**

3. **Choose New Stored Procedure from the pop-up menu that appears.**

   A template for creating a stored procedure in the Query Editor window
   appears. Delete all the text before the PROCEDURE statement and enter
   the procedure name as **TestProcedure**.

4. **Define the parameters for the stored procedure.**

   For this example, you want to define two variables: Year and Threshold
   value for sales. Enter the parameter name as **@year**. Because year is a
   four-digit character, define the data type to be char(4). Threshold is

going to be a dollar amount, so define the @threshold parameter data type as money. Your stored procedure code should then look like this:

```
CREATE PROCEDURE TestProcedure
Add the parameters for the function here
@year char(4) ,
@threshold money
AS
BEGIN
```

5. **Enter the SQL query for the procedure.**

The SQL statement substitutes @year for the year 2004 and @threshold for the SubTotal amount in the WHERE clause of the last query in the earlier "GROUP BY for subtotals" section. The statement should be as follows:

```
SELECT s.AccountNumber as 'Account',
count(*) as '# Orders',
SUM(SubTotal) as 'Total Order'
FROM Sales.SalesOrderHeader s, Sales.Customer c
WHERE s.customerID = c.customerID
and Year(OrderDate) = @Year
GROUP BY s.AccountNumber
HAVING SUM(SubTotal) > @Threshold
ORDER BY SUM(SubTotal) desc
```

6. **Check your stored procedure by using the Checkmark button on the SQL Editor toolbar.**

You'll receive error messages if there are any issues with the statement you entered — which should not happen if you follow these instructions.

7. **Save the stored procedure by right-clicking anywhere in the editor window where you have built the SQL statement and choosing Execute Item from the pop-up menu that appears.**

You have now created a new stored procedure. The final procedure code should look like this:

```
CREATE PROCEDURE TestProcedure
        -- Add the parameters for the function here
        @year char(4) ,
        @threshold money
AS
BEGIN
SELECT s.AccountNumber as 'Account',
        count(*) as '# Orders',
        SUM(SubTotal) as 'Total Order'
        FROM Sales.SalesOrderHeader s, Sales.Customer c
        WHERE s.customerID = c.customerID
        and Year(OrderDate) = @Year
        GROUP BY s.AccountNumber
        HAVING SUM(SubTotal) > @Threshold
        ORDER BY SUM(SubTotal) desc
END
GO
```

You can then run this stored procedure in your SQL Analyzer with the
expression

```
EXEC QUERYSALES '2004',200000
```

This statement passes the values of the two parameters into the stored procedure. It tells SQL Server to run the QUERYSALES stored procedure with
@year = '2004' and @threshold= $200,000.

Impressed yet? By now, the power of the SQL Server database management
system — a system that puts the power of the relational database at your fingertips — should be pretty obvious. Even better news is the fact that you can
harness this database access power and use it to retrieve information from
a database for the kinds of reports you would want to build with Microsoft
Reporting Services.

In this chapter, you began your journey to construct reports. Knowing the
basics of SQL and stored procedures serves as a good foundation for creating
powerful reports using Microsoft Reporting Services.

Chapter 3

Building and Running a Simple Report

*R*eporting Services is all about letting you create reports — a no-brainer if there ever was one. The somewhat trickier part involves getting all the groundwork done so that Reporting Services can do its job — preparing the soil, as it were, so that your little report can flower. *Groundwork* in this context means

✔ **Defining your data sources:** Where is the hiding place of the data you want to work with?

✔ **Defining your query:** What exactly is it that you're looking for?

✔ **Formatting your results set for your intended user:** What's the best way to present this information, given your intended audience?

Then all you have to do is run the darn thing and print it out.

This process may sound like a lot to take care of, but don't worry too much. In this chapter, I walk you through all these steps, using as my data source the handy AdventureWorks database, which is included as part of SQL Server 2005. Before I can do that, however, I have to take you on a tour of the Reporting Services workspace, known affectionately as the BI Development Studio. (BI is short for *B*usiness *I*ntelligence; now, does anybody remember the old joke about Military Intelligence?)

Facing Down the BI Development Studio

You work with Report Service's Report Designer tool whenever you want to build a report, so it won't be too long before you become intimately familiar with it. (Report Designer is just one of the authoring tools within Reporting Services, but it is definitely the most powerful and flexible for creating the widest range of report styles.)

Report Designer runs within the Business Intelligence Development Studio, so if you ever actually want to use Report Designer (and I'm guessing that you will), you have to launch Report Designer — and set up a new project for it — from within the BI Development Studio. Here's how that's done:

1. **From the Windows taskbar, choose Start⇨All Programs⇨Microsoft SQL Server 2005⇨Business Intelligence Development Studio.**

   The Business Intelligence Development Studio displays onscreen, providing the environment where you'll design your reports. Frankly, it's not much to look at. All you'll see for now is a blank Explorer pane (known as the Solution Explorer pane) on the right, a blank Output pane at the bottom, and a big gray expanse in the middle.

   If the Solution Explorer pane is not visible, choose View⇨Solution Explorer from the main menu to see it.

2. **Get the process for a new project started by choosing File⇨New⇨ Project from the main menu.**

   The New Project dialog box appears onscreen, as shown in Figure 3-1.

3. **In the New Project dialog box, verify that the Business Intelligence Projects folder is selected in the Project Types pane.**

   Reporting Services adds the Business Intelligence Projects category at installation. This project type contains all the report tools that you need to design and build reports using Reporting Services.

4. **In the Templates pane, select the Report Server Project Wizard.**

   The BI Development Studio allows you to create a report from scratch or to use one of the Visual Studio installed templates.

5. **Enter the name for your report in the Name field of the New Project dialog box.**

   If you refer to Figure 3-1, you can see that I chose the evocative name *Example Project* for my new project.

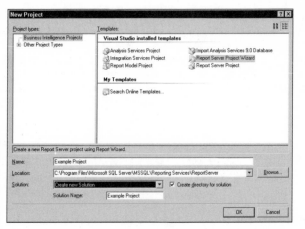

Figure 3-1:
Specify
project
types here.

6. **In the Location field, enter the directory path under which you want to save your report project. You can alternatively click the Browse button and then navigate to the folder you want.**

7. **Click OK to close the dialog box.**

An icon representing your new project appears in the Solution Explorer pane.

Working with Your Reporting Project

After you set up a new project in the BI Development Studio (see the preceding section), it's time to get down to the nitty-gritty of report building. Note that the Solution Explorer pane of the BI Development Studio initially shows an icon bearing the name of your report project as well as two folders associated with that project. You can use the Solution Explorer pane to view the contents of these folders, set the properties of such contents, and — most importantly — add your data sources. To see how this works, go ahead and right-click the Shared Data Sources folder. Doing so displays the Shared Data Source dialog box, as shown in Figure 3-2.

If you don't see the Solution Explorer pane at first, choose View➪Solution Explorer from the main menu.

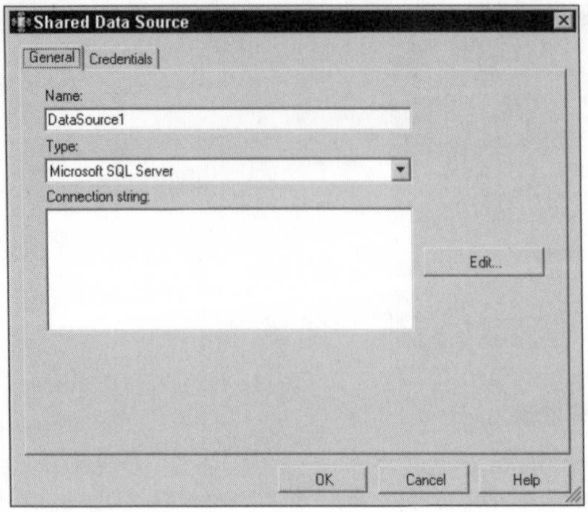

Figure 3-2:
Specify
your data
source here.

Establishing a shared data source

Your report will get its facts and figures from some kind of source — more likely than not, a database-oriented one. The Connection Properties dialog box (refer to Figure 3-3) lets you define that data source — and for good measure, lets you refer to that source as your Shared Data Source, where *shared* means that it can be referenced by many reports within the same report project. Here's how you specify a data source:

1. **In the Solution Explorer pane of the BI Development Studio, right-click the Shared Data Sources folder of your new project.**

   The Shared Data Source dialog box appears. (*Note:* For more on setting up a new project, see the "Facing Down the BI Development Studio" section, earlier in this chapter.)

2. **On the General tab of the Shared Data Source dialog box, select the data source type that you want.**

   Your choices here could include OLE DB providers (for Oracle, SQL Server, Outlook, and Directory Services); ODBC drivers (for a wide variety of relational databases); SQL Server Analysis Services, SAP; and others. Your choice here sets the context for the next action.

3. **If you specify a data provider for a relational database, click the Edit button and the Connection Properties dialog box will appear (see Figure 3-3).**

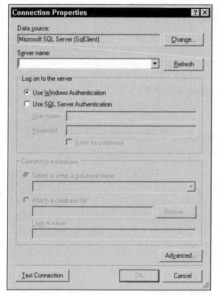

Figure 3-3:
Specify your
connection
properties
here.

Supply the information needed to log on to the server. This consists of the server name and the database name running on that server. You can supply user ID, password, and workstation ids specific to an individual user if necessary by clicking the Advanced button and specifying these property values.

4. **Click the Test Connection button located at the bottom left of the Connection Properties dialog box to confirm that you entered the correct information for the database connection.**

   If the test is successful, Reporting Services will notify you that the test connection succeeded. When you have successfully created a connection, click OK to proceed.

   If you need to enter more advanced information about the connection (like a timeout setting), you can use the Advanced button of the Connection Properties dialog box.

If you crossed your i's and dotted your t's and faithfully followed my instructions, you should now have a solid connection to your data source. Need reassurance? Then check whether a new icon bearing the name of the database you just connected to appears in the Shared Data Sources folder in the Solution Explorer pane. If the icon pops up there, you are now ready to define the query you want to use as the basis of your report.

Welcome to the Report Designer

Nestled within any new project listed in the Solution Explorer, you will find two folders: a Shared Data Sources folder and a Reports folder. (You can read about the Shared Data Sources folder in the preceding section.) Now is the time to move on to the next stage of creating a report: the *Add a Report Object to Your Report Project* part. Here's how:

1. **Make sure that the Solution Explorer pane is displayed on the right side of the BI Development Studio.**

   If it's not visible, choose View⇨Solution Explorer from the main menu.

2. **Right-click the Reports folder.**

   A handy pop-up menu appears indicating your choices for how to add a report.

3. **Choose Add⇨New item from the pop-up menu, taking your cue from Figure 3-4.**

   The Add New Item dialog box appears, as shown in Figure 3-4. Here you'll find templates for use in creating a report. Right off the bat, your choices are slim pickin's — Report Wizard, Data Source, and Report, to be precise — but that will change as you add new templates.

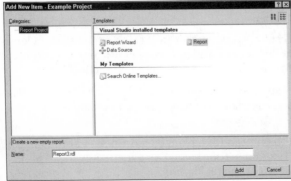

Figure 3-4:
Settling on
the right
template.

4. **In the Add New Item dialog box, click the Report template icon and then enter a name for your report in Name field.**

   Something like CustomerSales would do nicely. Note that Reporting Services wants you to end your filename with the `.rdl` file extension. (RDL stands for Report Definition Language, which is what Reporting Services creates for you while you build your reports.)

5. **Click the Add button.**

The previously useless gray area of the BI Development Studio is now populated with the kinds of tabs and windows that you expect in a development environment — which means that you are ready to rock.

Working with your data

When you have the wonders of the Report Designer tool spread before you in all their glory, you'll notice the Solution Explorer pane on the right, displaying a shared data source in its Shared Data Sources folder and a report in its Reports folder. You can "pin" the Solution Explorer pane open so that it shows all the time, or you can "unpin" it so that it shows only when you move your mouse over the far right margin of Report Designer. (This pinning and unpinning business is what the push-pin icon is for.) On the left, you'll see either a Fields pane or a Toolbox pane. These panes become important after you define the query from your data source — so more on them later.

To get Report Designer to work for you, you do have to bring some stuff to the table. More specifically, you need to know which tables in your database contain the information you seek, as well as which columns you need in order for the report to patch together a SQL query. If this doesn't sound familiar, visit Chapter 2, where I cover basic SQL and database matters.

To define a query that returns the data you want, you need to set up a *dataset* because that's where you store your query information for a report. First make sure that the Data view is front-and-center in Report Designer — which should look like Figure 3-6. After ascertaining that fact, do the following:

1. **Choose New Dataset from the Dataset drop-down menu.**

   The Dataset dialog box makes an appearance, as shown in Figure 3-5.

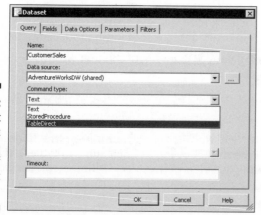

Figure 3-5: The Dataset dialog box from the Data tab of the Report Designer.

2. **On the Query tab of the Dataset dialog box, enter a name for your query in the Name field.**

   Again, CustomerSales has a nice ring to it.

3. **Choose your data source (usually a database name) from the Data Source drop-down menu.**

   Selecting AdventureWorksDW (shared) would be a good choice here. Use the button with the ellipsis (...) to modify any aspect of the data source. Clicking this button brings up the Shared Data Source dialog box shown earlier in Figure 3-2.

4. **From the Command Type drop-down menu, choose Text.**

   Other choices here include StoredProcedure and TableDirect. Don't worry about them for now; just concentrate on the basics.

5. **In the text window beneath the Command Type drop-down menu, enter the following SQL query:**

   ```
   SELECT Name AS 'Store Name',
   COUNT(*) AS 'Num Orders',
   SUM(OrderHeader.SubTotal) AS 'Total Sales'
   FROM       Sales.SalesOrderHeader AS OrderHeader,
   Sales.Customer AS Customer,
   Sales.Store AS Store
   WHERE      OrderHeader.CustomerID =
              Customer.CustomerID
   AND    Customer.CustomerID = Store.CustomerID
   AND    (YEAR(OrderHeader.OrderDate) = '2004')
   GROUP BY   Store.Name
   HAVING     (SUM(OrderHeader.SubTotal) > 200000)
   ORDER BY   SUM(OrderHeader.SubTotal) DESC
   ```

   Note: This query is based on tables found in the AdventureWorks sample database shipped with SQL and is asking to return the store name, the number of orders, and total sales amount in 2004 for orders greater than $200,000. This requires looking at three tables in the database: OrderHeader, Customer, and Store. The query further requires that the results be returned in order of highest to lowest total sales amount.

6. **When done entering your SQL query in the text window, click OK in the Dataset dialog box.**

   Your SQL query returns your result set: 2004 Store Sales from highest to lowest.

Note that if you click the Generic Query Designer button (the button in the Data view toolbar with the icon showing a pencil and two tables), the SQL changes into a lovely graphical view of the query environment, which includes these panes:

✔ **Diagram pane:** Shows the tables in the query

✔ **Grid pane:** Shows the columns selected from the tables and various properties defined by the query itself

✔ **SQL pane:** Shows the SQL query you entered previously or generated from selecting tables and columns

✔ **Results pane:** Shows the rows returned from the tables after running the query

You can show or hide these panes based on your preference by clicking the tools in the toolbar sprawling across the top of the Data view window.

You can see the whole shebang in Figure 3-6. You can also run — *execute,* if you prefer — this query and test to make sure that the SQL query brings back a results set. You can execute the query you have designed by clicking the ! button in the Data view toolbar. The query results are shown in the grid at the bottom of the Data view window shown in Figure 3-6.

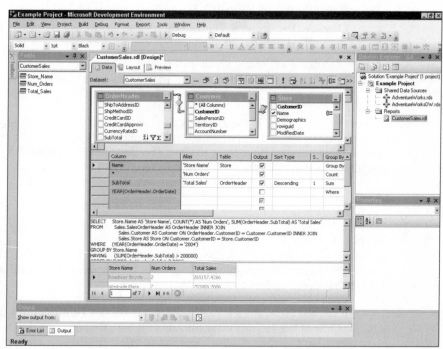

Figure 3-6:
The Data view within the Report Designer showing your result set.

Sketching out your design layout

After you have your query defined as a dataset in the Data view of Report Designer so that it returns a result set you like, you can move further along the Report Road by clicking the Layout view. The Layout view provides you access to the fields of your dataset defined in the Data view as well as access to a toolbox of report items that you can use to place the info from your datasets where you want it. Before I let you go down that road, however, I want you to get acquainted with all the windows and panes in the Layout view of the Report Designer — the basic building blocks for all the spiffy reports you're about to create.

The first pane is the Toolbox pane, as shown in Figure 3-7. Two types of report items are available to you in the Toolbox:

✔ *Data regions* are areas on a report that contain data from a data source that is repeated. Examples of data regions–type tools are the `List`, `Matrix`, `Table`, and `Chart` controls — which, as you might suspect, are used to set up and format lists, matrices, tables, and charts, respectively.

In the upcoming steps, I show you how to use a `Table` control to create a nice little mini-spreadsheet within your report.

✔ *Independent items* are areas on a report that are not associated with a dataset. A text box, for example, represents a text constant for titles or comments in a report. I discuss report items in depth in Chapter 5.

The next handy pane is the *Datasets* pane, shown on the left in Figure 3-8. When a dataset is created, the Report Designer retrieves a list of fields from the data source and populates the list. This list of fields is available for dragging into the Layout view to populate those controls that you have previously had the presence of thought to drag from the Toolbox window onto your report template. Very handy.

You can select from the report items in the Toolbox to create a simple report from your dataset. The placement of report items in a report is completely free-form. You can place them anywhere in the body of the report. To see how you can put such freedom into action, try the following. Build your first report by following these steps:

1. **In Layout view, drag a `Table` control from the Toolbox onto the layout region of the Layout view and drop it into the area. (If the Toolbox pane isn't visible, on the View menu click Toolbox or click the folder named Toolbox on the far left side.)**

   A `Table` control appears in the report, as shown in Figure 3-8.

2. **To switch from the Toolbox pane to the Datasets pane, you can click the View menu and select Datasets or click the Datasets tab on the far left.**

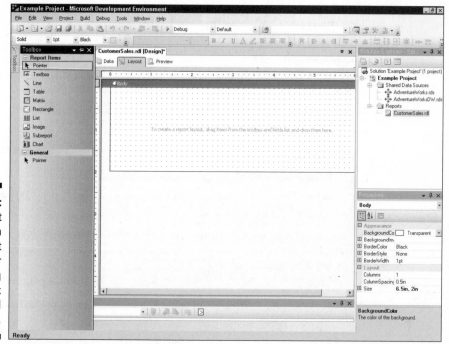

Figure 3-7:
The Layout
tab within
the Report
Designer
showing
a toolbox
with all
report items.

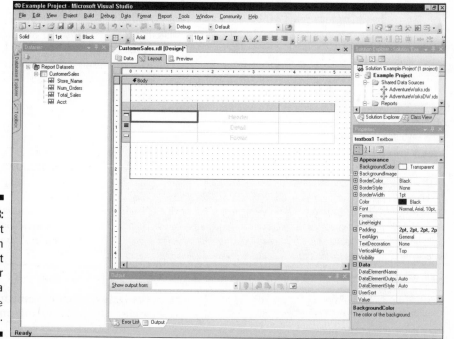

Figure 3-8:
The Layout
tab within
the Report
Designer
showing a
`Table`
control.

3. In the Datasets pane, click the columns of information that you want on the report and drag them onto the Detail section (center row) of a column in the `Table` control.

This automatically defines a cell in the Detail section of the column and creates a header with the field name as the header text. You can edit the default headers to whatever you care to see in the columns.

In Figure 3-9, you can see that I dragged the store name into the Detail section of the first column, the number of orders into the Detail section of the second column, and the sales total into the Detail section of the third column.

4. Click the Preview tab in the Report Designer.

Reporting Services executes your query and formats it as you defined it on the Layout tab.

The report preview for your report appears, as shown in Figure 3-10. You can click the Save toolbar button to save your work-in-progress report if you want to at this point.

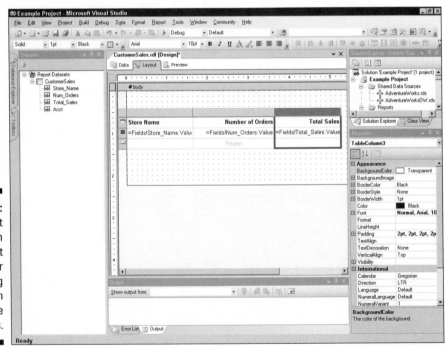

Figure 3-9:
The Layout tab within the Report Designer showing fields within the table columns.

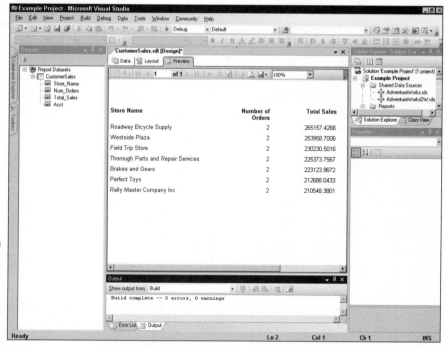

Figure 3-10:
The Preview
tab shows a
preview of
the report.

Modifying Your Report

A loosely formatted report of customer sales — like the one I built in the preceding section — is the design equivalent of a sticky note on your computer monitor. It has its uses, but it's probably not the report you'd use to distribute to others! With Reporting Services, you have at your fingertips a variety of other tools and techniques that allow you to enhance that report's readability. This section shows you a few basic options you can use to improve readability and appearance.

Formatting in Layout view

Want to improve the readability of your report in one fell swoop? Add a title. You can do this by clicking and dragging a Text control from the Toolbox onto the report template just above your Table control. When you have the Text control in place, just type the name of the report.

Another way to get the titling job done is to add a page header. If you use a report header, the report title is repeated automatically on every page of the report. Furthermore, you can control whether it prints on the first page or the last page of your report by setting properties for the page header. Here's how:

1. **Right-click the area of the Layout view just to the left of the left margin of the layout page and select Add a Report Header from the pop-up menu that appears.**

   The header section is magically added to the report.

   You can also add a report header by clicking anywhere on the report and choosing Report⇨Page Header from the main menu.

2. **Click and drag the `Textbox` control from the Toolbox pane onto the header section.**

   A text box appears in the header section.

3. **Click anywhere within that text box and start entering your report title.**

   `Customer Sales for 2004,` anyone?

   You can make this title bold (for readability) by highlighting the text and clicking the B (bold) button on the Report Formatting toolbar.

Anything else strike your fancy? How about making column headings bold so they stand out a bit better? To do this, click in the table header section of the table control, highlight the text, and then click the B (bold) button on the Report Formatting toolbar.

To adjust the format of the displayed numbers in the report, right-click the table column detail cell that contains one of your fields and select the format you want from the Textbox Properties dialog box that appears. (Format choices here include Number, Date, Time, Percentage, and Currency.) You might want to change the Account column format to Number and the Sales column format to Currency, for example.

To add a footer to the report, right-click in the area just left of the margin of the layout and select Page Footer from the pop-up menu that appears. (Alternatively, choose Report⇨Page Footer from the main menu.) You can create expressions for fields in the footer that appears on each page. First, go to the Toolbox pane and add a `Text` control to the footer for each element you would like to include in the footer. You can then enter expressions in each text box that define what the text box displays when the report is previewed.

For example, you could enter the following expression to make the footer display the current page of the total page count:

```
="Page " & Globals!PageNumber & " of " &
          Globals!TotalPages
```

You could also add the following expression, which makes the footer display the time of execution:

```
= Globals!ExecutionTime
```

Put all these tweaks together, and you've got a revised format which could be presentable to your reporting audience. This layout is shown in Figure 3-11. (I cover expressions in great detail in Chapter 5 and more advanced topics in Chapter 7.)

Click the Preview tab in the Report Designer to see how the report appears to the user. This more polished report is highlighted in Figure 3-12.

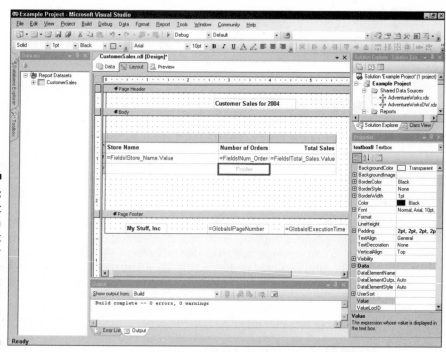

Figure 3-11: The Layout tab within the Report Designer showing a header, footer, and formatted columns.

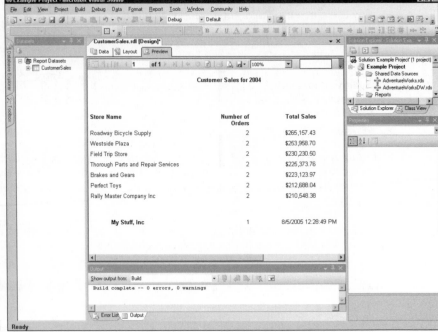

Figure 3-12:
The Preview
tab within
the Report
Designer
showing
a more
polished
report
format.

Saving your report

You can save the entire report at this point by choosing File⇨Save All from the main menu. Doing so saves the entire report project, including all reports within the report project for the dataset(s) defined. The report is saved in the Business Intelligence Project for which it was created. The project maintains many logically related reports that use the same shared datasets.

Saving the report created in the Report Designer creates an RDL file. *Report Definition Language* (RDL) is Microsoft open standard for the report specification. You can view the RDL code for this report by right-clicking the report in your Solution Explorer and selecting View Code from the pop-up menu that appears. This RDL file is a standard XML file with markup tags that define all the properties of the report.

Printing the report

Printing a report in the Report Designer is very simple. In the Preview tab of the Report Designer, click the printer icon in the toolbar or choose File⇨Print⇨Printer from the main menu. Then print the report the same way you would print any document in Windows.

Part II

Building Reports — Your Creativity Options

The 5th Wave   By Rich Tennant

"WELL, SHOOT! THIS EGGPLANT CHART IS JUST AS CONFUSING AS THE BUTTERNUT SQUASH CHART AND THE GOURD CHART. CAN'T YOU JUST MAKE A PIE CHART LIKE EVERYONE ELSE?"

In this part . . .

After you know how to create reports based on data in a database, you're ready to move to the next level. *Microsoft Reporting Services 2005* provides a wizard to kick start the report development process. When you see what the Report wizard can do, you'll know just how fast you can create dynamic reports. This part also introduces you to the process of developing reports through the Report Designer interface in the BI Development Studio.

You can use the styling features provided in the toolbox of report controls to create interesting new reports. You can sort and filter information at will. You can have the user select what type of filter to use for a view of the report through the use of a parameter. These fundamentals provide the foundation for creating powerful reports.

You may also need to provide the user with a way to create a custom report. This capability is provided within the Report Builder tool. This aspect of *Microsoft Reporting Services 2005* provides the platform for how Microsoft will extend future generations of this product.

Chapter 4

We're Off to See the Wizard

In This Chapter

▶ Getting help from Report Wizard

▶ Accessing Report Wizard

▶ Stepping through the wizard

▶ Previewing results

*I*n this chapter, I cover another technique for authoring reports quickly — namely, the Report Wizard. This chapter gives you a kick-start in developing reports with more formatting and linking features, which are topics I talk about in more detail in later chapters. The Report Wizard can help you get information into a starting format. You can then modify an initial report to meet your accessorizing needs.

The Report Wizard provides a simple step-by-step interface that walks you through the process of assembling a report. It provides two output format templates to choose from, requires you to select data elements from a dataset that will become its report columns, and asks you for a sort order and a grouping level for the report. In a few simple and direct steps, you can quickly form a report that can serve as a starting point for further formatting and enhancement. It is the best way to learn how Reporting Services assembles the right components together to create reports.

Accessing the Wizard

From the Business Intelligence Development Studio, you can start the Report Wizard in one of three ways:

✔ In the Solution Explorer for a Report Server Project already open, right-click the Reports folder and select Add New Report from the menu that appears.

✔ Choose Project⇨Add New Item. The Add New Item dialog box appears. Select the Report Server Project Wizard in the Templates pane, fill in the name of your report, and click Add.

✔ From the file menu, choose File⇨New⇨Project. In the resulting New Project dialog box that appears, you can select the Report Server Project Wizard.

Congratulations! You have started the Report Wizard, as shown in Figure 4-1.

Figure 4-1:
The Report
Wizard
startup
screen.

Establishing the Data Source

After you start the Report Wizard, you need to choose which data source to work with. You have two databases from the SQL Server 2005 installation samples — AdventureWorks and AdventureWorksDW. In this example, I'll use the AdventureWorks database.

In the previous chapter, I describe how to define a shared data source in the report project. If this is not set up already, use the following steps to do so. Figure 4-2 shows the options you have on the screen. This is the second step of the Report Wizard.

1. **In the Select the Data Source dialog box, click the New Data Source radio button; make sure that Microsoft SQL Server is selected in the Type drop-down list, and then click the Edit button.**

The Connection Properties tab appears.

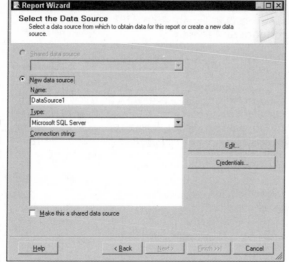

Figure 4-2:
The Select
the Data
Source
page is the
first step in
the Report
Wizard.

2. In the Connection Properties dialog box, type your server name.

3. Use Windows NT Integrated security to connect to the server.

4. Select AdventureWorks from the database list and then click OK.

5. Verify that your server and the AdventureWorks database are both listed in the connection string.

6. Test this connection by clicking the Test Connection button.

7. Click OK.

Querying the Data

Suppose you want to specify a query that will bring in the product hierarchy with the sales information from 2004. Here is the SQL statement you can use:

```
SELECT     Production.Product.Name as Product,
           Production.ProductSubCategory.Name AS
           SubCategory,
           Production.ProductCategory.Name AS Category,
           Production.ProductModel.Name AS Model,
           Sales.SalesOrderDetail.OrderQty,
           Sales.SalesOrderDetail.UnitPrice,
           Sales.SalesOrderDetail.UnitPriceDiscount,
           Sales.SalesOrderHeader.OrderDate
```

```
FROM        Sales.SalesOrderDetail,
            Sales.SalesOrderHeader,
            Production.Product,
            Production.ProductModel,
            Production.ProductSubCategory,
            Production.ProductCategory
WHERE       Sales.SalesOrderDetail.ProductID =
            Production.Product.ProductID
AND         Production.Product.ProductModelID =
            Production.ProductModel.ProductModelID
AND         Production.Product.ProductSubCategoryID =
            Production.ProductSubCategory.ProductSubCategor
            yID
AND         Production.ProductSubCategory.ProductCategoryID
            = Production.ProductCategory.ProductCategoryID
AND         Sales.SalesOrderDetail.SalesOrderID =
            Sales.SalesOrderHeader.SalesOrderID
AND         YEAR(Sales.SalesOrderHeader.OrderDate) = 2004
```

Copy the preceding statement to the clipboard. Then, on the Design the Query page, paste this SQL statement into the Query String text box by clicking the Query String box and pressing Ctrl+V. You now have a source of data to report. When you click the Query Builder button, you will see the Query Builder window, as shown in Figure 4-3.

After you decide on the data source to report from, you need to define the type of report you want to produce.

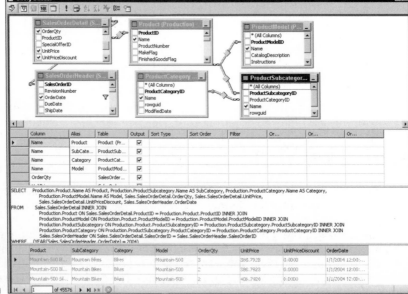

Figure 4-3:
Query
Builder
window
showing the
graphical
data source.

Designing the Table and Styles

You need to make some choices about report style and layout. Initially, you need to choose between a *table* and a *matrix* style report in the Select the Report Type window of the Report Wizard, as shown in Figure 4-4.

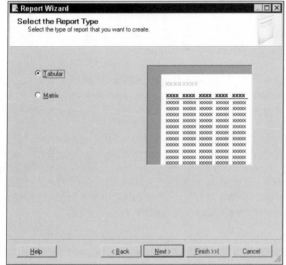

Figure 4-4:
Select the
Report Type
of the Report
Wizard.

The matrix style of report is more like a cross-tab report where rows and columns correspond to two different reporting variables (like product and time). The tabular report is a more common report style required for reporting and is like a listing with multiple columns. I discuss these styles in more detail in Chapter 5.

Laying Out the Report — Layout and Style

The choices presented by the Report Wizard become a little more complex and perhaps a bit intimidating

One choice is the table layout. You can select the stepped layout, include subtotals, and enable drill-down analysis in the report. Then, you should decide what table style you want to use for the report. Your choices include bold, casual, compact, corporate, and plain. The Report Wizard will create controls with fonts and colors using the theme that you select. These properties can be modified in Report Designer when the Report Wizard has completed its process. Think of these as templates for the report you're building. In this example, I use the Corporate style.

If you used the Report Project Server Wizard project template, the wizard will then prompt you for the Report Server name and the deployment folder. Just take the defaults here, so that the deployment folder name is the same as the name of the project you are creating.

Finally, name the report and review a summary of the choices made during the previous steps using the Report Wizard.

The Report Wizard will build the controls for the report you have created and return you to the Report Designer in the Layout view as shown in Figure 4-5. You can review the layout and make any modifications you need at this point.

This gives you a report with a page break for each *Product* and *Model.* In addition, *Product Category* and *Product Subcategory* will appear as groupings for the report. These groupings will initially appear collapsed with an expand icon, allowing for interactive expanding and collapsing. The remaining columns will show the detail at the lowest detail level of the report. You can see this in the Preview mode by clicking the Preview tab.

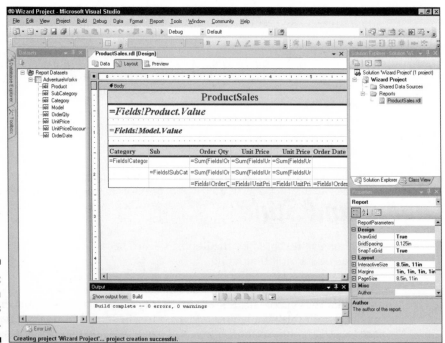

Figure 4-5:
Layout tab in the Datasets view pane.

Chapter 5

Styling with Report Types

*J*ust as you and your hairstylist can choose from among a variety of vogue hairstyles, Reporting Services gives you a multitude of choices in styling reports. The key prerequisite for styling report layouts is that you've started a report document and completed the Data tab where you connected to a data source, and you've created a specific dataset for data access.

A *dataset* is the result set of a query defined in the Data tab of Report Designer. In this chapter, I explore all the different report items and data regions you can choose from to build impressive reports using Reporting Services.

Report Design Surface

The design surface is a design environment that gives you flexibility in designing and building reports. It consists of a set of windows, views, data fields, and tools. In the following section, I talk about the two most important aspects of report styling: the toolbox and fields list.

Using your toolbox in the workshop

You need to become acquainted with the View and Window main menu options of the Report Designer before you get started. All report items and data regions are located in the Toolbox. They are your tools for building reports. If the Toolbox doesn't display by default, you can see it by choosing View⇨Toolbox in the Business Intelligence Development Studio.

To work with any report item or data region, you must select the item from the Toolbox. (The toolbox is usually hidden in the left margin and you need to move the mouse over the region to open the toolbox.) The toolbox is shown in Figure 5-1. You can find this window on the left side of the Report Designer.

Figure 5-1:
The
Toolbox and
Datasets
windows
in Report
Designer.

The secret to working with the Toolbox is keeping it visible when you want it. Here are some of the ways you can maneuver the toolbox:

✔ Open the toolbox by choosing View⇨Toolbox.

✔ To make the toolbox close automatically, click the toolbox to open and then, on the Window menu, select Auto Hide.

✔ To keep the toolbox open, click on the toolbox and then, on the Window menu, clear Auto Hide.

✔ To move the toolbox to a different location, click on the toolbox and then, on the Window menu, clear Auto Hide, and then select Floating. Drag the toolbox to the desired location.

✔ Hide the toolbox by selecting Hide on the Window menu. (To reopen the toolbox, click Toolbox on the View menu.)

✔ Reset default settings by clicking the Window menu and selecting Reset Window Layout.

Notice that each window has a stick pin icon that is equivalent to an Auto Hide toggle option. Click the icon, and it turns on Auto Hide. Click it again, and it turns off Auto Hide. You can use this same technique for the Fields, Solution Explorer, and Properties windows. You can also use the Window menu to select Auto Hide All, which hides all windows in the Report Designer.

Interacting with datasets

After you specify your query that defines a dataset within the Data tab of the Report Designer, you will see the query result set columns in the Datasets window within the Layout tab. If you want to add data to your report, you start with the fields appearing in the Datasets window. A sample Datasets window appears beneath the Toolbox in Figure 5-1. Note that all datasets appear in the window for the report being edited. You can expand each dataset to see the selected columns from the query corresponding to that dataset.

You can also create calculated fields that are derived from the dataset fields available in the Datasets window. All fields have names and, unless an alias field name was supplied in the Data tab where the query was defined, the field has the same name as the column in the select statement.

To add a field to the fields list, follow these steps:

1. **In Layout view, expand any dataset appearing in the Datasets window.**

2. **To add a field, right-click anywhere in the list of fields, and then click Add. (To edit a field, right-click an existing field, and then click Edit.)**

   The Add New Field dialog box appears.

3. **Type a name for the field.**

   Names must be unique within the dataset.

4. **Click the Database Field or Calculated Field radio button, and then type a value.**

   For a database field, this must be the name of a field returned by the query in the dataset. For a calculated field, this must be an expression (which is like a formula). Click the expression *(fx)* button to build an expression.

You can drag a field from the fields list onto the report. When you do, Report Designer creates a textbox with a field expression in it. If you drag a field onto a structured area such as a table or a matrix cell, or onto an existing textbox, an expression referencing the field (or field expression) is placed in the cell or textbox. I talk more about expressions in the next section and at great depth in Chapter 6.

Working with Data Regions and Other Report Items

Report items are the controls that appear in the Toolbox, shown in Figure 5-1. Report items can be containers to data from datasets defined in the Data tab of the Report Designer. Some report items, however, only help you in creating format styles in the report itself. These report items are independent of datasets and don't have changeable values. Examples of these report items are graphical items such as rectangles and lines. Other independent items can link to specific fields in a dataset; images and textboxes are good examples. Finally, there are special report items that are independent but can be containers for other data regions. A subreport is an example of this special type of report item.

Report items are actually controls that run on your report server that extend report processing.

In the following sections, I describe data regions and report items in some detail. I tell you about your options for accessing and customizing them and I give you some examples of how to use them.

Setting report item properties

All report items have basic attributes or properties that you can set in the Properties window, in code or in expressions. Every report item has many types of properties. One group of properties is the *appearance* properties. Except for the line report item (which only has color, style, and line width appearance properties), there are common appearance properties for all report items. These common appearance properties include the following:

- **BackgroundColor:** As its name suggests, this option sets the color for the background of a report item.
- **BackgroundImage:** You can have images appear as the background for controls or for the entire report document. Sometimes graphic designers refer to these kinds of images as *watermarks*.

- **BorderColor:** This property sets the color of the border around the report item.

- **BorderStyle:** This option sets the style of the border. Choices include solid, dotted, dashed, and double-lined, among others.

- **BorderWidth:** The width of the border is controlled with this setting, which can be expressed in points or inches.

- **Padding:** You can set the size of padding between border and text. You can set the property for left, right, top, and bottom padding.

For example, when you use the Report Wizard and choose the corporate style (as described in Chapter 4), the title textbox and header appear as follows: BackgroundColor is LightGrey and Top and Bottom Border colors are DarkBlue; Bottom BorderStyle is Solid; Bottom BorderWidth is 3 points; and all padding settings (top, bottom, left, and right) are 2 points.

In addition, all report items and data regions located in the toolbox have design properties, layout properties (to specify location, size, and/or page break usage), and miscellaneous properties (such as label, tooltip, and bookmark). All report items except image, line, and rectangle have international properties (such as language, calendar, and direction) to specify how text will be displayed.

You can set properties in the Properties window or through other menu options and other dialog boxes. The next few sections describe each report item or data region in more detail.

Using textboxes for labels and captions

The *textbox* is an independent report item but can link to fields in a dataset if required. The textbox is probably the most commonly used independent report item. You can use it as a label with a constant (like "My Report") or an expression as the value. The textbox is the default report item for a cell in the table, where you can place labels or numbers from dataset fields. You can also have the textbox display the value displayed in another textbox in a report.

To add a textbox to a report, follow these steps:

1. **In Layout view, click the Textbox control in the Toolbox, then drag and drop it onto the document.**

2. **On the document, expand the textbox to the size you want it to be.**

3. **Enter the desired text directly into the textbox control in your document.**

Textboxes display content for titles as well as captions in report headers and footers. To have the textbox display a value, set the value property of the textbox. An easy way to do this is by clicking the textbox and typing the text you want it to display.

Typing text is great for static values. But what if you want to set more properties, set the values to the contents of a dataset field, or reference a global variable? In those cases, use the Textbox Properties dialog box. Changing settings in the Textbox Properties dialog box is faster than setting individual properties in the Properties window for the textbox. To access this dialog box, right-click on the textbox and select Properties from the menu that appears. The Textbox Properties dialog box opens, as shown in Figure 5-2.

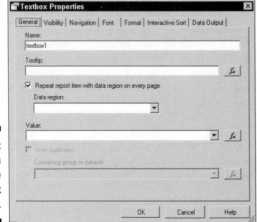

Figure 5-2:
You can
change
key textbox
properties.

The Textbox Properties dialog box allows you to fully specify the properties of the textbox. You can

✔ Define the name of the textbox control.

✔ Enter text in the Value field to define what shows up in the textbox when you run the report.

✔ Set the value to any dataset field available in your report by choosing from the drop-down fields list shown in Figure 5-2.

You must use the expression:

```
=Fields!Store_Name.Value
```

to display the values of fields from the report dataset in any data region, including textboxes.

You can specify that the height of the textbox remain fixed or change with the contents. You can also define the format for the data displayed in the textbox from standard choices or custom choices. Note that you can select the format display by highlighting the standard format of your choice and then selecting the display format that you need. You can click a button for advanced formatting, but I talk more about that later.

If you need to reference global constants and create expressions for what is displayed in the textbox, click the expression (*fx*) button to the right of Value. The Edit Expression dialog box appears, as shown in Figure 5-3.

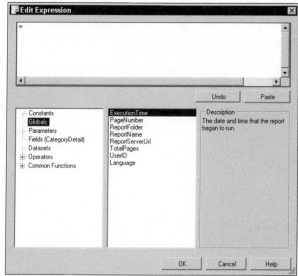

Figure 5-3:
The Edit Expression dialog box gives you options for creating expressions for a report item.

The Edit Expression dialog box enables you to create an expression referring to the global variables, fields, or other dataset references on the left side of the dialog box. For example, if you want a footer that shows the current page number and the total number of pages, you can construct the following expression for the value property of a textbox within the Edit Expression dialog box:

```
="Page "& Globals!PageNumber & " of " &
        Globals!TotalPages
```

The PageNumber and TotalPages variables are global variables that can be included by selecting them from the fields list.

Using tables for tabular display

A *table* is a data region linked to a report set. The table data region presents data row by row. Table columns remain fixed after they are defined. Table rows expand downward to accommodate the data. When the report is rendered, the table repeats rows based on the values from the dataset. The nice thing about tables is that they provide alignment within rows and columns that's easy to work with. The table control is located on the Layout tab of the Report Designer, as shown in Figure 5-4.

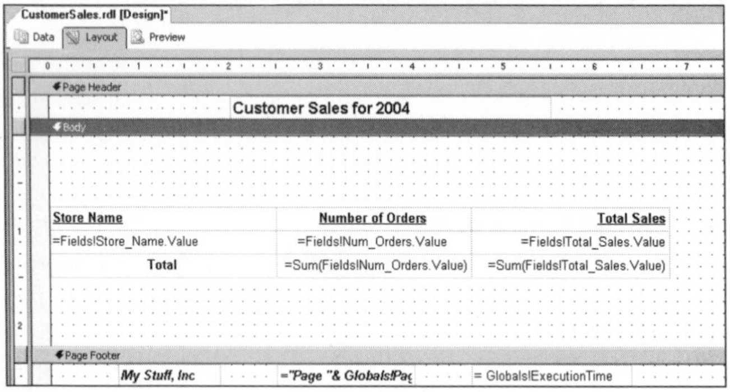

Figure 5-4: The table data region in the Report Designer showing totals.

To add a table to a report and populate it from a dataset you previously defined, follow these steps:

1. **In Layout view, click Table in the toolbox.**

2. **On the design surface, drag a box to the size you want the table to be.**

   Alternatively, click the design surface to create a table of a fixed size.

3. **Add items to the report by selecting fields from the Dataset window and dragging them into cells in the table.**

   When you begin with a blank table, you see three rows: header, detail, and footer. When you drag fields into the detail row, the names of the fields appear automatically in the header line. To create totals or subtotals for the table, drag a numeric field into a footer cell of the report. The Report Designer automatically puts a SUM or COUNT aggregate function on the field to indicate an aggregation will take place.

4. **Add or remove columns in the table by right-clicking on the control just above the header line corresponding to a column.**

   A pop-up menu appears where you can select Insert Column or Delete Column. You can insert detail lines by right-clicking on the detail symbol to the left of the detail line of the table. You can also merge cells by highlighting the cells and right-clicking and selecting Merge Cells. For reporting detail data, you can hide duplicates by right-clicking the cell, selecting Properties from the list that appears, and checking the Hide Duplicates check box.

The table data region is a versatile tool that you can use in most reports. If you're used to working with spreadsheets, this is a natural control to work with in building reports. To enhance their versatility, table cells can contain any report item. You can include a chart, image, or any report item in a cell. To insert multiple report items in a cell, begin with a rectangle. Then insert report items into the rectangle.

Using a matrix for cross tabs

The *matrix* is a data region linked to a report set. Like the table control, the matrix allows you to drag and drop fields into it. Unlike the table, you can also drop fields into the columns. The matrix enables you to create crosstab reports with report variables appearing on rows and columns. The crosstab puts multiple summaries in a single compact form. A matrix data region contains both columns and rows that expand to accommodate the data. A matrix can have dynamic columns and rows that are repeated with groups of data, or it can have static columns and rows that are fixed.

To add a matrix to a report and populate it from a dataset you previously defined, follow these steps:

1. **In Layout view, click Matrix in the toolbox.**

2. **On the design surface, drag a box to the size you want the matrix to be.**

   Alternatively, click the design surface to create a matrix of fixed size.

   If you've worked with pivot tables in Excel, the techniques for building a crosstab report are similar. After you place a matrix on the report body in the Layout tab of the Report Designer, you want to link it to a dataset. Incidentally, if you want to move the matrix after you have added it to the report body, just click the top-left corner of the matrix. Reporting Services gives you an outline of the matrix that you can click and drag to a destination.

3. **Add data to the matrix by dragging fields from the Fields window into the rows, columns, and data cells.**

   Figure 5-5 shows how a matrix looks when you add the product category to the rows and territory group to the columns.

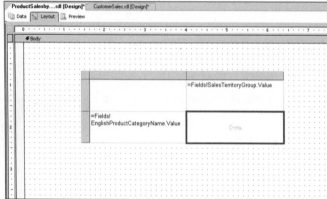

Figure 5-5: Matrix control in Report Designer.

4. **Drag in Sales as a field in the data cell.**

   If you want to add a subtotal, right-click the row cell and select Subtotal. Another row with the row heading appears. The actual amount of the total cannot be edited, so it will be grayed out. However, you can change the label of the Total field as you want it to appear in the report. You will see a green triangle in the top-right corner of the total row heading cell. If you click on this and view Properties, you can set the Layout Property Position to Before or After. That determines whether the subtotals come above or below the detail values. If you specify After for this property, the final matrix report is ready for preview.

Note that in a matrix, no detail level appears as it does in a table. You can add row groups and column groups, but that involves using features I talk about later in this chapter.

Using rectangles for separate reports

A *rectangle* is an independent report item where you can place and report items anywhere you like. As a container for items, a rectangle's size doesn't change with the data you put in it. In the Report Designer, if you move the rectangle in the Layout tab of Report Designer, all items within the rectangle move with it and keep their relative positions.

You can control whether page breaks happen before or after rectangles. You can use this property to do reports where the report header and footer are on separate pages from the report detail. This is a good way to produce reports requiring a title page prior to the detail data in the report.

To add a rectangle to a report, follow these steps:

1. **In Layout view, click Rectangle in the toolbox.**

2. **On the design surface, drag a box to the size you want the rectangle to be.**

   Alternatively, click the design surface to create a rectangle of fixed size.

Using lists

The *list* is a free-form data region that can contain multiple items, freely arranged, linked from a dataset. You can arrange report items to create a form, with textboxes, images, and other data regions placed anywhere within the list. The list is like a rectangle that repeats for each row in the dataset. Since it is free-form, you can put items anywhere within the list — you can even overlap them if you wish.

Using a list provides you with more flexibility than using a matrix or a table. For example, if you want to match the format of a W-2 or other IRS form, you may want to consider using a list data region to do it. However, more work may be involved in creating these special formats because you don't have columns to help with alignment.

If you're interested in creating a report with nested groupings with a special format that would be difficult to achieve with tables, this is a good option. Each nested level can be a set of report data in a rectangle, and each nested level would be contained in a rectangle nested within the next higher level rectangle.

The list is similar to bands in other report writers. The list allows only a single grouping, but you can nest lists within other lists. You can also use the list for complex repeating areas in a report.

To add a list to a report, follow these steps:

1. **In Layout view, click List within the toolbox.**
2. **On the design surface, drag a box to create a list the size you want.**

   Alternatively, click the design surface to create a list of fixed size.

Using subreports for containers

The subreport is not a data region; however, it looks like a data region because the referenced report is a data region. The subreport is essentially the referenced report placed within a rectangle in the host report. Note that page headers and footers of the referenced report will not appear in the subreport region in the host report.

Because you can have multiple data regions in a single report, you can avoid the use of subreports to show independent data elements on a report. Subreports become useful when you want to nest information in a data region that comes from a completely independent dataset. You can use an explicit parameter to define the values for the subreport within another data region.

To add a subreport to a report, follow these steps:

1. **In Layout view, click Subreport in the toolbox.**
2. **On the design surface, drag a box to create a subreport the size you want.**

   Alternatively, click the design surface to create a subreport of fixed size.

Using lines for formatting

The *line* is an independent report item. You can draw a line between any two points on a report. Your lines can be horizontal, vertical, or diagonal. Lines have attributes that control their location, color, thickness, and visibility. Lines are helpful for overall report formatting.

An alternative to the line report item is to use a border within a table. Borders will scale better if the column width is set to adjustable.

To add a line to a report:

1. **In Layout view, click Line in the toolbox.**

2. **On the design surface, drag a box to create a line that runs from the point where you pressed the mouse button to the point where you released the mouse button.**

Using images for logos

The *image* is an independent report item. However, the image can link to fields in a database, a URL, or a filename. Images can be one of a variety of image file formats such as BMP, GIF, JPG, PNG, or X-PNG. Images need to be cropped and sized prior to being added to the report. Some common uses of images include adding a graphic to a report or page header, showing a picture of a product in a catalog report, or filling the background of a report with a repeating image.

When you add an image to a report, you control how the image appears in the report body. You can autosize an item to match the size of the image, fit the image to the size of the item (with some distortion), or you can fit proportionally, where the image fits as close as possible to the size of the item without distortion.

You can add an image to a cell of a table. You can even specify an image as the BackgroundImage property of the report body to show some kind of watermark for the report — this may be an interesting effect for a Web report that will be run within a portal.

Follow these steps to add an image to a report:

1. **In Layout view, click Image in the toolbox.**

2. **On the design surface, drag a box to the size you want the image to be.**

   Alternatively, click the design surface to create an image item of fixed size. This starts the Image Wizard.

3. **On the Welcome page of the Image Wizard (see Figure 5-6), click Next.**

Figure 5-6:
The first page of the Image Wizard.

4. **On the Select the Image Source page, click Embedded, Project, or Database or Web (see Figure 5-7), and then click Next.**

5. **Select the image you want to add to the report.**

   Depending on which option you choose in Step 4, you see a slightly different version of the Choose the Image screen (see Figure 5-8).The four options give you the choice of embedding the image in the report (Embedded), storing the image within the project for use by all reports in the project (Project), obtaining the image from a field in the database (Database option — best choice for product catalog reporting), or referencing a URL or Web address to be retrieved when the report is run (Web). The following bullets provide more details on these options:

Figure 5-7:
Image Wizard prompts you to select the image source.

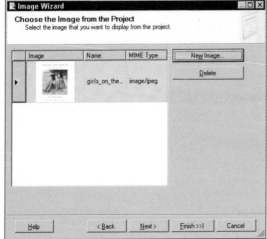

Figure 5-8:
Select an
image to
deploy.

- **Embedded:** Select an embedded image from the list. To add a new embedded image to the report, click the New Image button and then browse to the image.

- **Project:** Select an image. To add a new image to the project, click the New Image button and then browse to the image.

- **Database:** Select values for the Dataset, Image field in that Dataset, and MIME type of the image file (e.g. bmp, jpeg, gif). You are prompted for the dataset, image field, and format of the image file, as shown in Figure 5-9.

- **Web:** Specify the URL that corresponds to the image file (e.g., http://localhost/flename,jpg) .

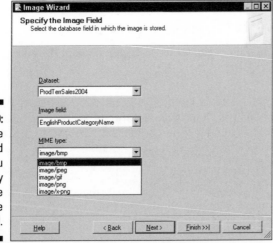

Figure 5-9:
The Image
Wizard
prompts you
to specify
the image
database
field.

6. **Click Next to review what the Image Wizard has created.**

   The Wizard prompts you to review the settings and then complete the wizard to add the image to the report in the manner you selected. I show the final step in Figure 5-10.

Figure 5-10:
Reviewing settings and finishing with the wizard.

Using charts for visualization

The *chart* is a data region just like the list, matrix, or table. A chart presents data graphically. You can determine trends and variances quickly and easily by looking at a chart. You also can use a chart to format data (numbers) to help an audience visualize information in a report.

To add a chart to a report, follow these steps:

1. **In Layout view, click Chart from the toolbox.**

2. **On the design surface, drag a box to create a chart the size you want.**

   Alternatively, click the design surface to create a chart of fixed size.

When you create a chart, you add at least one value to the chart. The values display as data points on the chart. Colors, formats, markers, labels, symbols, and 3-D effects are available for custom chart formatting. You can also choose from a variety of chart types. Similar to a matrix, there is no detail level in the chart.

The quickest way to see the variety of charting formats is by right-clicking on the chart data region and selecting Chart Type from the menu that appears. Here are some of your choices:

- ✓ **Column:** Simple, stacked, or 100% stacked. Column charts display data as sets of vertical columns.

- ✓ **Bar:** Simple, stacked, or 100% stacked. Bar charts display data as sets of horizontal bars.

- ✓ **Area:** Simple, stacked, or 100% stacked. Area charts display data as a set of points connected by a line, with a filled-in area below the line.

- ✓ **Line:** Simple or smooth. Line charts display data as a set of points connected by a line.

- ✓ **Pie:** Single or exploded. Pie charts display data as percentages of the whole.

- ✓ **Doughnut:** Single or exploded. Doughnut charts display data as percentages of the whole.

- ✓ **Scatter:** Simple, lines, or smooth. Scatter charts display data as a set of points in space.

- ✓ **Stock:** High, Low, Close; Open, High, Low, Close; or Candlestick. Stock charts display data as a set of lines with markers for high, low, close, and open values.

- ✓ **Bubble:** Bubble charts display a set of symbols whose position and size are based on the data in the chart.

If you want to create a basic columnar report that examines the quarterly trend of product sales in North America for 2003, you first need to write a query that provides some sample data with two variables, for example product and time.

To create such a report, follow these steps:

1. **Create a query using the AdventureWorksDW sample database.**

   The tables and columns I used to create this example chart appear in Figure 5-11.

   I selected only North America as the country and 2003 as the year. After creating the dataset and providing some aliases for each column to make the fields list simple to work with, you are now ready to work in the Layout view.

2. **In the Layout tab, add a chart to your report by dragging the chart control from the Toolbox onto the body of the report.**

3. **Add a column chart control to your report.**

   Click a chart control in the Toolbox and drag that to the report document. The chart will default to a column chart.

4. **Build a chart that has time on the x-axis (horizontal axis) and has a time series plotted for all product categories.**

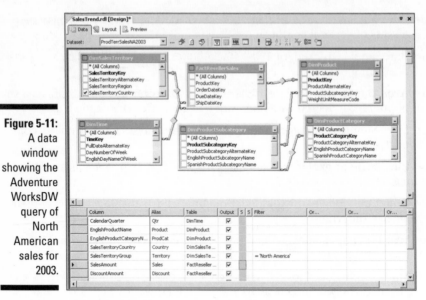

Figure 5-11:
A data window showing the Adventure WorksDW query of North American sales for 2003.

The sales revenue for each product subcategory for each quarter is shown as a column along the y-axis (vertical axis) of the chart. In order to do this, first click the Chart tool. This reveals a chart design area with a data area (the metric you want to chart), category area (for the variable on the x-axis), and series area (for the series to be plotted in the chart). In the Datasets window, select the Sales field to drag and drop into the data area, select the Qtr field to drag and drop into the category area, and select the ProdCat field to drag and drop into the Series area. You should see something similar to Figure 5-12.

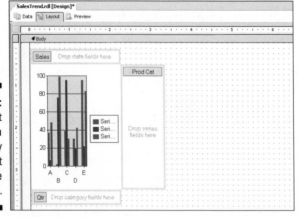

Figure 5-12:
A chart design area for quarterly product sales in the U.S. for 2003.

Now that you have a basic chart on a report, you may wonder how to further control the appearance of the chart. For example, you may want to add a title or change the scale on one of the axes to improve the readability of the chart. To further format the chart control, follow these steps:

1. **In Layout view, right-click the chart and select Properties from the menu.**

2. **On the General tab, provide the name and title of the chart.**

   I have named this chart 'US Sales Trend 2003'. On this tab I can also specify the chart subtype and set the styles for the chart and plot areas (see Figure 5-13).

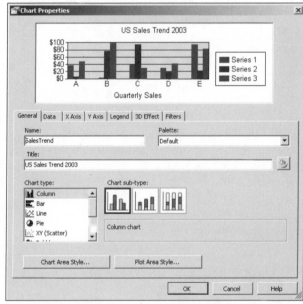

Figure 5-13: The General tab of the Chart Properties dialog box for a column chart of quarterly product sales in the U.S. for 2003.

3. **On the Data tab, specify the key aspects for the values (metrics) and report groups you are charting.**

   In this example, Values represent the sales amounts, Category groups are the quarters of 2003, and the Series group is the product category. This is shown in Figure 5-14.

4. **On the Y Axis tab, indicate format specifications for the vertical axis of the chart.**

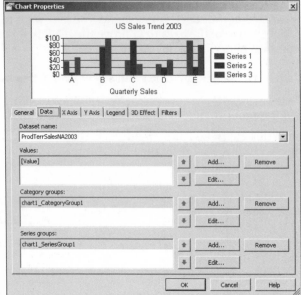

Figure 5-14:
The Data tab
of the Chart
Properties
dialog box.

You can provide the label for the Y axis. You can choose to show labels and use a custom format for the labeled values. In this example, I use the custom format c0, which shows currency with no decimal places. I can set the scale of the axis, where to place tick marks, and other aspects of the general appearance of the Y axis (see Figure 5-15).

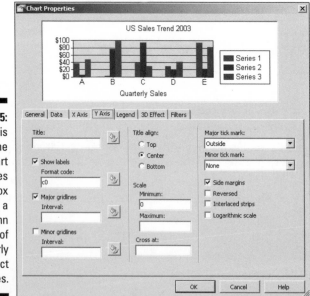

Figure 5-15:
The Y Axis
tab in the
Chart
Properties
dialog box
showing a
column
chart of
quarterly
product
sales.

5. Click OK in the Chart Properties dialog box to accept your specifications.

Click the Preview tab in the Report Designer to see what you created! Figure 5-16 shows the sales trend for U.S. product sales for 2003.

Figure 5-16:
The preview of the Column Chart of Quarterly Product Sales in the U.S. for 2003.

Chapter 6

Accessorizing Your Reports

*W*hen you think about home decorating, accessorizing is all about adding interesting items to a room to focus attention and establish a style. You can apply the same principles to displaying information on a report. You can think of using the various features and functions of Reporting Services to display information uniquely and focus attention. Accessorizing the information on a report is key to its usage and the user's understanding of the content presented. Examples of accessorizing include using filtering, derived functions, and special formatting options to draw attention to things like unfavorable variances or fantastic achievements beyond the expected.

In this chapter, I talk about how to produce interesting subtotals within a report and how to sort on various report columns to show a rank order of performance. I also talk about how to create formulas or report columns whose values are derived from several other column values on the same row of the report. The more advanced features that I cover include how to prompt the user for values of certain variables that are then used to filter the report at runtime. Finally, I review some advanced formatting options that will allow additional kinds of highlights to the report and make information jump out at the person reviewing the report. Each of these capabilities provides significantly more richness to the reports you create.

Sorting, Grouping, and Filtering

Have you ever seen a list of numbers on a report, such as sales by salesperson, that were arranged alphabetically by salesperson? Didn't you also want to see the information sorted by sales revenue from highest to lowest to see who was really pushing the envelope that period? This *sorting* is a natural need in the display of information on a report. Furthermore, have you noticed long reports that showed something like sales by office across all the regions, but you really wanted to see subtotals by region and by office? The subtotals are created based on types of groupings within a report. Furthermore, have you wanted to filter out extraneous information and focus on specific data that addresses your particular question about a general report? This *filtering* of report information is handy to know how to do. The following sections describe how you meet these common reporting needs.

Sorting and filtering report data

You can sort and filter the data within each data region (table, matrix, list, chart) by one or a combination of data field values. Remember that sorting is organizing the report data in a certain order and that filtering is about eliminating unwanted information within a report. You can sort data in ascending order or descending order. The sort order you request takes precedence over the order in which the query returns data in the dataset. Reporting Services also enables you to create nested sorts, where multiple columns are sorted together based on the values of the two columns considered together as a group.

To create a report showing key product information filtered for a single year of information and sorted on a column of information using data from a sample database, follow these steps:

1. **Add a report to a report project.**

   Within a report project, add a new report item to the Reports folder. Then click on this new report in the Reports folder to show the Report Designer dialog box. Refer to Chapter 3 for more details on how to set up the report project.

2. **Create a new dataset for your report. Then, click the Data tab and click the drop-down combo box showing the New Dataset Query tab.**

   The Dataset dialog box appears.

3. **On the Query tab in the Dataset dialog box, connect to your sample database.**

   I like to use the `AdventureWorksDW` sample database that ships with the product.

4. **Select the tables and columns of interest for your report.**

   You may want to focus on sales, cost, and volume for product categories and product subcategories. In order to do this, you need to find the tables in your database that contain these fields. You will find the tables FactResellerSales, DimTime, DimProduct, DimProductCategory, and DimProductSubcategory, which should be added to your query.

You will notice that there are three relationships between DimTime and FactResellerSales. These are represented by join lines between these two tables. Because you're interested only in the order date filtering, remove the joins for due date and ship date. You can do this by right-clicking on the lines joining the two tables for the respective fields.

5. **Filter your query for a single year of analysis.**

   The easiest way to do this is by using the Generic Query Designer. The Generic Query Designer view can be initiated from the toolbar presented when you are editing or creating a dataset. If you are interested in only values for the year 2003, you need to add a query filter for that year. You can enter this as text in the Filter column of the grid pane of the Generic Query Designer, as shown in Figure 6-1. The query filter eliminates unwanted rows from the result set to be reported. With a filter, the rows are eliminated after the dataset is created but before the data region is rendered in the report. The filter value refers to a column in the dataset. You can use any expression operator such as = or <= or >= when specifying the filter.

   Note the Alias column in Figure 6-1. The alias name is another name you can provide for the column to shorten the column names for the purposes of the query. For example, I used the alias Category instead of the full column name EnglishProductCategoryName.

6. **Create your report layout.**

   Click the Layout tab of the Report Designer. In the Toolbox window, click a table object in the toolbox and drag it into the report body section.

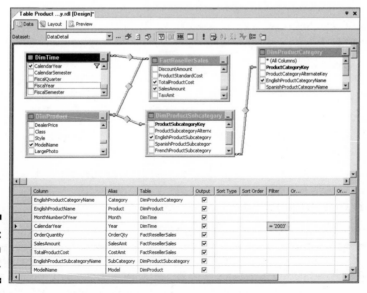

Figure 6-1:
Specifying a query filter.

7. **Populate your table with data fields from your query.**

   You want to create a report with some product information. To do this, drag the fields Product, SalesAmt, OrderQty, and CostAmt into the table columns in the detail section. The resulting layout should look like the one shown in Figure 6-2.

Figure 6-2:
Layout for
product
sales
information
in a table
control.

8. **Specify a sort on the data in the table.**

   Click anywhere inside the table to set the focus to the table and then click the top-left corner cell.

   The table control appears highlighted. Right-click on the border of the table control and select Properties from the menu that appears. You see the Table Properties dialog box, shown in Figure 6-3.

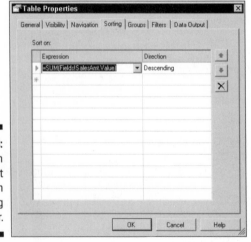

Figure 6-3:
Sort on
SalesAmt
Value in
descending
order.

9. **Click the Sorting tab, and type or select the expressions by which to sort the data and the sort direction for each expression.**

   For example, you want to select the SalesAmt field and sort in descending order, as shown in Figure 6-3. Click OK to accept the values entered in the dialog box.

10. **Preview the final report by clicking the Preview tab on the Report Designer.**

    You should see a report like the one shown in Figure 6-4.

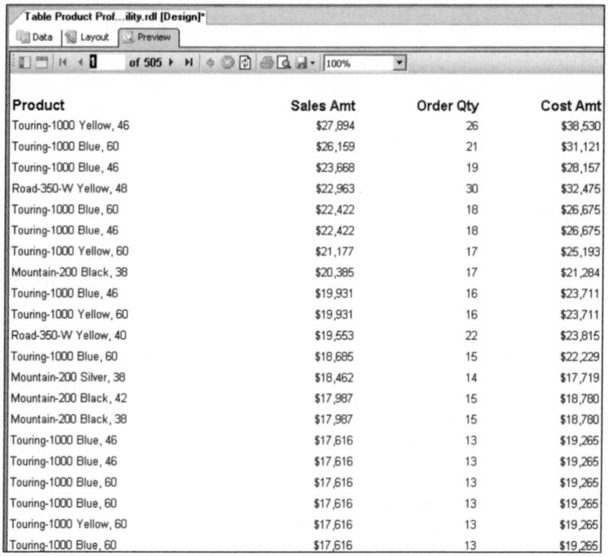

Figure 6-4: Tabular report of detail product information with SalesAmt sorted in descending order.

Product	Sales Amt	Order Qty	Cost Amt
Touring-1000 Yellow, 46	$27,894	26	$38,530
Touring-1000 Blue, 60	$26,159	21	$31,121
Touring-1000 Blue, 46	$23,668	19	$28,157
Road-350-W Yellow, 48	$22,963	30	$32,475
Touring-1000 Blue, 60	$22,422	18	$26,675
Touring-1000 Blue, 46	$22,422	18	$26,675
Touring-1000 Yellow, 60	$21,177	17	$25,193
Mountain-200 Black, 38	$20,385	17	$21,284
Touring-1000 Blue, 46	$19,931	16	$23,711
Touring-1000 Yellow, 60	$19,931	16	$23,711
Road-350-W Yellow, 40	$19,553	22	$23,815
Touring-1000 Blue, 60	$18,685	15	$22,229
Mountain-200 Silver, 38	$18,462	14	$17,719
Mountain-200 Black, 42	$17,987	15	$18,780
Mountain-200 Black, 38	$17,987	15	$18,780
Touring-1000 Blue, 46	$17,616	13	$19,265
Touring-1000 Blue, 46	$17,616	13	$19,265
Touring-1000 Blue, 60	$17,616	13	$19,265
Touring-1000 Blue, 60	$17,616	13	$19,265
Touring-1000 Yellow, 60	$17,616	13	$19,265
Touring-1000 Blue, 60	$17,616	13	$19,265

Note that the sales detail reflects all the transaction level of detail in the database.

Grouping related fields

Using groupings of data is the best way to summarize information within a report. The data within each of the data regions (table, matrix, list, and chart) can be grouped by fields and expressions. You can use groups inside a table to provide logical sections of data within the table. You can also add subtotals and other expressions to the group header or footer. In a table, you can have multiple grouping levels, but only on rows.

Suppose that you want to summarize the previous example product information by product subcategory. Begin with a report and follow these steps:

1. **Edit the grouping level of the rows in the report by right-clicking the Detail row in the table you created and selecting Edit Group from the menu that appears.**

   The Details Grouping dialog box appears.

2. **On the General tab, type or select the expression on which to group the data.**

   For example, if you want to group by product, enter the following expression in the Group On Expression text box in the Details Grouping dialog box:

   ```
   =Fields!SubCategory.Value
   ```

   You get a result that looks like the one shown in Figure 6-5.

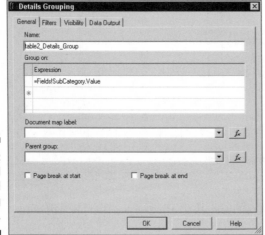

Figure 6-5:
The General
tab and
grouping
expression.

3. **Change the table sort properties to sort on the sum of the column in the new grouping. You need to sort on the SUM of the in the Table Properties dialog box. To do this, follow this sequence:**

   a. Highlight the table control by clicking the top-left corner cell. The table control appears highlighted.

   b. Right-click on the border of the table control and select the Properties menu option. The Table Properties dialog box appears.

    c. Click on the Sorting tab in the Table Properties dialog box.

    d. Insert a SUM function in the expression referring to the field value for SalesAmt. Then click OK to accept the entered data.

4. **Revise the textbox expressions for each numeric column to be the SUM of each field value.**

   Because each row is grouped by subcategory, you want to display the sum total for all products in that subcategory. Therefore, you need to explicitly state that you need to SUM these field values.

   For example, the textbox for the SalesAmt field should be:

   ```
   =SUM(Fields!SalesAmt.Value)
   ```

5. **Preview your report by clicking the Preview tab.**

   You should see a different grouping level than that shown in Figure 6-4.

   Notice that this report now shows only a single entry for each product category sorted in sales value in descending order.

Nested groupings

Another common requirement in reporting is to provide subtotals of detail information based on the natural groupings of the data. For example, if you are reporting product sales information and products are organized by sub-categories, you may want to see the detail product sales with subtotals by the subcategories these products are grouped within. The way to do this is to nest groupings within details or other groupings. To see how to do this, modify the report you just created to nest subcategory values within category values. Follow these steps to create a sample report.

1. **Insert another group in your report for product category. Follow these steps:**

   a. In Layout view, click the table so that column and row handles appear above and next to the table.

   b. Right-click the row handle for the detail row and select Insert Group from the menu that appears (see Figure 6-6). The Grouping and Sorting Properties dialog box appears.

   Note that selecting a detail row places the new group just outside the detail row. If you select an existing group row, the new group will be placed inside the selected group row.

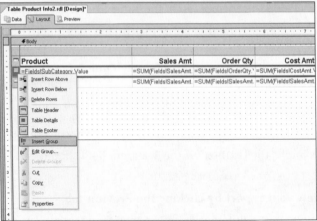

Figure 6-6:
Table
Layout view
showing the
menu items
available
when you
right-click
the detail
row handle.

2. **Enter the expression for the new grouping. On the General tab of the Grouping and Sorting Properties dialog box, type or select the expression on which you want to group.**

In my report, I select the Product Category field, indicated as `Fields!Category.Value`, as shown in Figure 6-7.

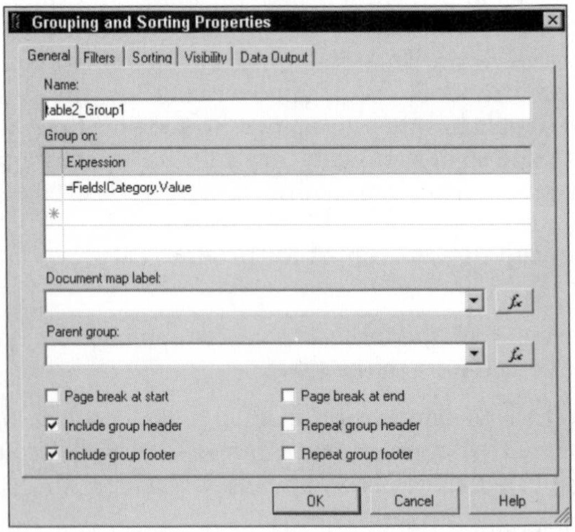

Figure 6-7:
The
Grouping
and Sorting
Properties
dialog box
for the
Category
group you
are inserting
into the
table.

3. **Click OK to accept what you have entered in the Grouping and Sorting Properties dialog box.**

   This will insert a group header and footer line into the table immediately above the detail line.

4. **Specify the information to display in the table grouping cells. You will want to display the group headings and footings in the table. Follow this sequence to accomplish this.**

   a. Drag the Category field from the Datasets window into the first column of the group header row. Next insert the following expression in the first column of the group footer:

      =Fields!Category.Value + "Subtotal".

   b. Copy the expressions in the report cells into the group subtotal row so that the report will show the subtotals for each Category report group.

   c. Select the report cells for the subtotal line and, using the Properties window, add a Border Style for the top border as Solid. You can see the result in Figure 6-8.

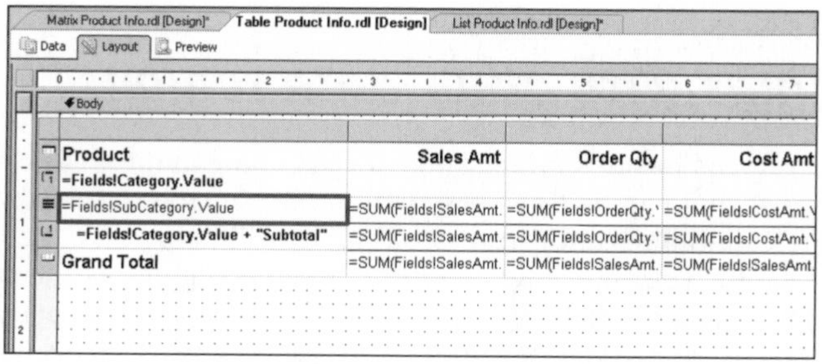

Figure 6-8:
Layout
View of the
table after
formatting
the group
header and
footer lines
and adding
the group
subtotal
fields.

Preview the report. Notice that the report is still sorted by SalesAmt in descending order within each SubCategory detail line within the Category group (see Figure 6-9).

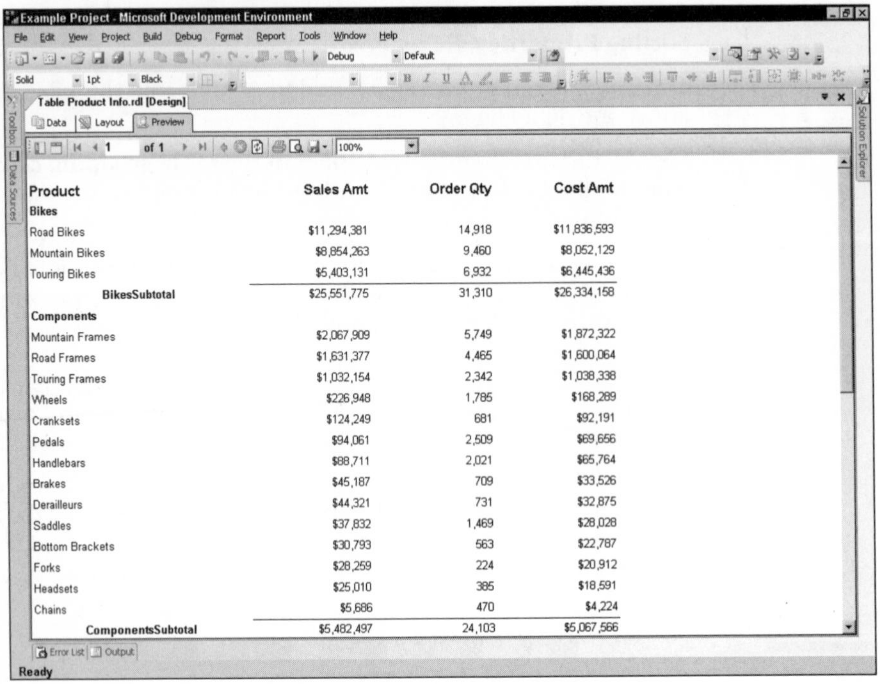

Figure 6-9: Preview of the report showing the table product information report using a table with Category report groups and SubCategory report detail sorted by sales in descending order.

Groupings with other data regions

Other data regions besides tables allow for grouping in different ways. So far, I've described what can be done only with table controls. Other data regions have unique capabilities and these capabilities will help you in deciding what control is best for your particular report. Table 6-1 highlights the capabilities for the major controls that support groupings. In the following sections, I show the difference between the table, matrix, list, and chart controls.

Table 6-1	Grouping Levels Supported by Data Regions
Data Region	*Grouping*
Table	Multiple grouping levels on the row axis
Matrix	Multiple grouping levels on rows and columns
List	Single grouping level (detail or grouped)
Chart	Multiple grouping levels

Note: While tables and matrices provide multiple levels of grouping within a single data region, lists have only one group. To create nested groups using lists, you place a list within another list.

Grouping with matrix controls

Unlike the table control where you can only group on rows of the table, the matrix control allows you to group detailed information along rows or columns or both. You can nest groups within other groups, and you can also add subtotals. You can have multiple grouping levels on both rows and columns.

To build a report similar to the Product Info report illustrated previously with a table control, follow these steps:

1. **Copy the table report by right-clicking the report in the Solution Explorer window and selecting Copy from the resulting menu. Click on the Reports folder and then press Ctrl+V.**

   A copy of the Product Info report is inserted in the reports folder. You can double-click this report to open it in Report Designer. This report will have the query already defined (refer to Figure 6-1).

2. **In the Layout view, delete the table control.**

   You can rename the report by right-clicking on the report in the Solution Explorer window and selecting Rename from the menu that appears.

3. **Insert a matrix control into the layout view by clicking on the matrix control in the Toolbox window and dragging that into the report body in the Layout view.**

4. **Create the initial matrix of rows and columns. Drag the Category field from the Data Sources window into the Rows cell of the matrix. Then drag the first column, SalesAmt, into the Data cell of the matrix.**

5. **To add the remaining columns in the matrix, right-click on the data cell farthest to the right (initially SalesAmt) and select the Add Column menu item. Then drag in the next column field for the report into the new data cell.**

6. **When you have all the columns set up on the detail line of the matrix, you need to edit the group to specify how the detail data should be sorted. Right-click the row heading cell containing the Product field and select the Edit Group menu item.**

   The Grouping and Sorting Properties dialog box appears (refer to Figure 6-7).

7. **On the Sorting tab, specify the field SalesAmt to be sorted in descending order and then click OK.**

8. **Insert a group into the matrix by right-clicking on the row heading cell containing the Category field and select the Add Row Group menu item. This is highlighted in Figure 6-10.**

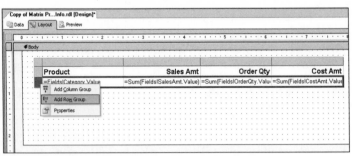

Figure 6-10:
Right-click
the menu on
the matrix
to add a
row group.

The Grouping and Sorting Properties dialog box appears (refer to Figure 6-7 for an example).

9. **Select the field Subcategory from the list of fields as the expression on which to group, and then click OK.**

The group subcategory is added to the right of the Category group. (This makes sense because you have inserted a subgrouping level in this process.)

10. **Check what you specified for your matrix control by highlighting the matrix (click on the top-left corner cell to show the control, right-click on the control, and select the Properties menu item.**

The Matrix Properties dialog box appears as shown in Figure 6-11. Note that this is similar to the Table Properties dialog box for the table control. You can use this to see all specifications for the control you are designing.

11. **Insert a subtotal into the matrix. To do this, right-click on the matrix cell for the row heading for which you want to create a subtotal.**

This will produce a subtotal line with the text "Total" as the row heading. Change the row heading for the subtotal to be

```
=Fields!Category.Value + " SubTotal".
```

Preview this report and compare this to the report you created previously for the table control in Figure 6-9. Except for the extra grand totals in the table report, you will notice some subtle formatting differences, but the reports are largely identical.

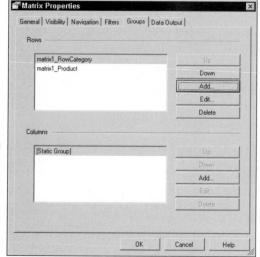

Figure 6-11:
Matrix
Properties
dialog box
for the
matrix.

Adding a column grouping to a matrix

After you master adding a row grouping to a matrix, you can find out how to add a column grouping to the same report. The process is very similar or analogous to the approach you used to build reports with grouping on rows. To demonstrate how column groupings are done in a matrix, follow these steps:

1. **Copy the previous matrix report by right-clicking the report in the Solution Explorer window and selecting Copy from the resulting menu. Click on the Reports folder and then press Ctrl+V.**

   This inserts a copy of the matrix product info report in the Reports folder. You can double-click this report to open it in Report Designer.

2. **In the Data view, add a query filter to limit the report to three months of data.**

   For the Month column, add the filter IN(1,2,3). This limits the months to January, February, and March of 2003.

3. **In the Layout view, delete all the data columns except SalesAmt.**

4. **Insert a column group by right-clicking on the SalesAmt column heading and selecting the Insert Group menu item. Select the Month field from the list as the expression on which to group.**

The last issue to address is the fact that the Month column has the value of the number of the month of the year. For example, January is 1, February is 2, and so on. You can use an expression to translate the value of a month number into a month name. To do this, right-click on the cell that was just added corresponding to the column group, and select Expression from the menu that appears. In the Expression Builder, enter the following expression for this column group header:

```
=IIF(Fields!Month.Value = 1 ."Jan".
IIF(Fields!Month.Value = 2, "Feb","Mar"))
```

For more on expressions, see the section on expressions in Chapter 7.

5. Preview the report.

Note that months have been converted to month names (although they are abbreviated) according to the expression entered in the previous step. If you compare this report to the report in Figure 6-9, you will notice that the report line for touring bikes within the bikes product category is missing. This is due to the fact that there were no touring bikes sold in the first three months of the year, which is the scope of the report.

Grouping with list controls

List controls have their own unique aspects compared to the table or matrix controls. According to Table 6-1, the list control supports only a single grouping level. You can control the grouping level with the List Properties dialog box.

To demonstrate how this works, I use the same general report style: the product info report. Follow these steps:

1. **Copy the table or the matrix report by right-clicking the report in the Solution Explorer window and selecting Copy from the resulting menu. Click on the Reports folder and then press Ctrl+V.**

   This will insert a copy of the product info report in the Reports folder. You can double-click this report to open it in Report Designer. This report will have the query as shown in Figure 6-1 already defined.

2. **In the Layout view, delete the table or matrix control in the report. Then insert a list control by clicking on it in the Toolbox window and dragging it onto the report body.**

3. **Create the columns similar to the table or matrix reports by selecting the appropriate fields from the Data Sources window and dragging them onto the list control. Then add text fields as columns above the actual list control.**

   Make sure that you specify the SUM function in the expression for each numeric field in the list control. Select the Product Category as the row heading column. Your layout should look similar to that in Figure 6-12.

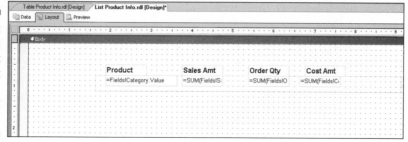

Figure 6-12:
Layout tab
for a report
of Product
Info using
the list
control.

4. **Select the list control, right–click, and select the Properties menu item.**

   The List Properties dialog box appears.

5. **(Optional) On the Sorting tab, specify the report be sorted on SalesAmt in descending order.**

   Make sure you specify the SUM function for SalesAmt as the sort expression.

6. **On the General tab, click the Edit Details Group button.**

   The Details Grouping dialog box appears, as shown in Figure 6-13.

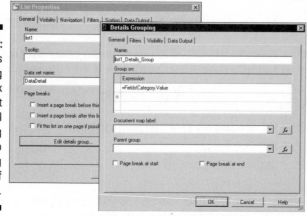

Figure 6-13:
Details
Grouping
dialog box
for the list
control
providing
access to
the grouping
level of
the list.

The General tab controls the level of summary displayed in the list. Because you want to see the category level of detail, select the Category field as the expression on which to group. This needs to match the row heading field selected for the report results to make sense. Otherwise, the report will display only the first occurrence of the row detail within each group. Click OK to accept your specifications.

Preview the report. The report should appear as shown in Figure 6-14.

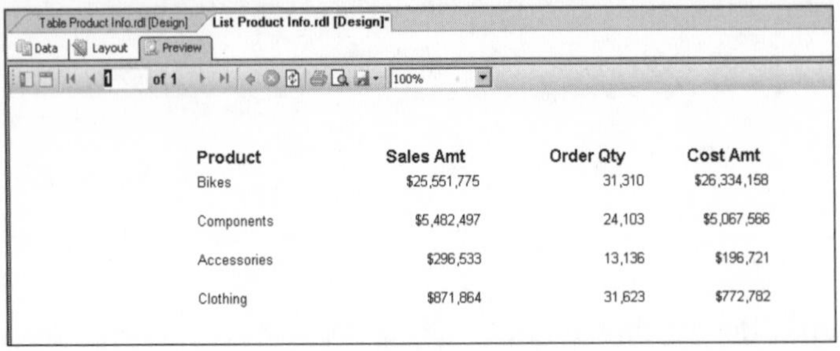
Table Product Info.rdl [Design]
List Product Info.rdl [Design]*
Data
Layout
Preview
of 1
100%
Product
Sales Amt
Order Qty
Cost Amt
Bikes
$25,551,775
31,310
$26,334,158
Components
$5,482,497
24,103
$5,067,566
Accessories
$296,533
13,136
$196,721
Clothing
$871,864
31,623
$772,782

Figure 6-14: Preview view of the Product Info report.

Using nested lists

The only way to create multiple levels of groupings in a report using lists is to nest the lists within each other. To illustrate this, let's see how to work with the layout to create a report similar to what we have seen with the table and matrix controls. Follow these steps:

1. **Create another list control that will be grouped by Category, the highest level group of the report.**

   Size this list so it can contain the list objects that you created previously, as shown in Figure 6-12. I refer to this as the larger list.

2. **Select all the fields in the initial list (grouped by SubCategory) and then click on the list control itself and drag it into the larger list.**

3. **Select the Category field and drag it into the larger list just above and left justified relative to the initial list.**

4. **Select the larger list and edit the list properties and insert a detail group on Category.**

   This will look similar to Figure 6-12.

5. **Construct the subtotal report line. First, add a textbox below the initial list (within the larger list) and type in** Subtotal **in this textbox. Then select the SalesAmt, OrderQty, and CostAmt fields and drag them into the larger list on the same line as the subtotal. Finally, add a line to the report just under the small list and just above the subtotal line.**

   The layout should now look like that shown in Figure 6-15.

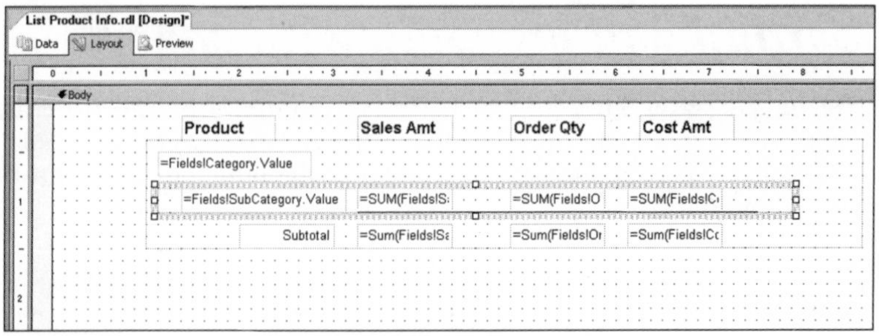
List Product Info.rdl [Design]*
Data
Layout
Preview
Body
Product
Sales Amt
Order Qty
Cost Amt
=Fields!Category.Value
=Fields!SubCategory.Value
=SUM(Fields!S
=SUM(Fields!O
=SUM(Fields!C
Subtotal
=Sum(Fields!S
=Sum(Fields!Or
=Sum(Fields!Cc

Figure 6-15: Layout view of the Product Info report using nested list controls.

If everything is nested properly, when you preview the report you will see what is shown in Figure 6-16.

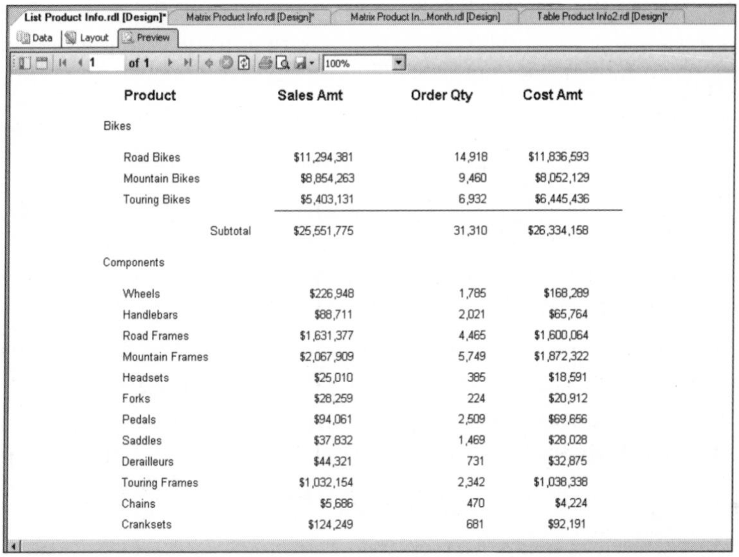
List Product Info.rdl [Design]*
Matrix Product Info.rdl [Design]*
Matrix Product In...Month.rdl [Design]
Table Product Info2.rdl [Design]*
Data
Layout
Preview
1 of 1
100%
Product Sales Amt Order Qty Cost Amt
Bikes
Road Bikes $11,294,381 14,918 $11,836,593
Mountain Bikes $8,854,263 9,460 $8,052,129
Touring Bikes $5,403,131 6,932 $6,445,436
Subtotal $25,551,775 31,310 $26,334,158
Components
Wheels $226,948 1,785 $168,289
Handlebars $88,711 2,021 $65,764
Road Frames $1,631,377 4,465 $1,600,064
Mountain Frames $2,067,909 5,749 $1,872,322
Headsets $25,010 385 $18,591
Forks $28,259 224 $20,912
Pedals $94,061 2,509 $69,656
Saddles $37,832 1,469 $28,028
Derailleurs $44,321 731 $32,875
Touring Frames $1,032,154 2,342 $1,038,338
Chains $5,686 470 $4,224
Cranksets $124,249 681 $92,191

Figure 6-16: Preview view of the Product Info report using nested list controls.

As you have seen, you can create reports that are very similar using either the table, matrix, or list control. With the list control, you have to do more work to align the columns and rows to ensure proper alignment. But this aspect of lists actually provides you with more flexibility in developing free-form reports.

Sorting and grouping with charts

Sorting and grouping with charts is very different from the other data regions we have explored this far. The chart does not contain other report items. The chart manages its own components, which include chart properties, types, and data.

There is no detail level in a chart (similar to the matrix). When you add a numeric field to the data area, the field automatically uses the SUM aggregation function. You can modify the field expression to use a different aggregate function if desired.

When you specify groupings for a chart, the aggregation function you specified in the data field is automatically used for the groupings. There are two types of groupings for a chart. The first type of grouping is known as a Category Group. The *category group* displays as additional slices in a pie chart, or groupings on the x-axis for column charts. If there are multiple category groups, each is nested within another category. The second type of grouping is known as a Series Group. The series group can be thought of as another dimension of the data. The *series groups* in a column chart create a column for each member in the series and are indicated by a different color in the legend.

Note: For the pie chart, you have a grouping that defines the pieces of the pie. If you have more than a single grouping level in the pie chart, only the first grouping displays on the pie chart. In future versions, you may have separate pie charts, one for each of the second grouping values.

Consider an example of how to represent the product info report information in our previous examples as a chart. Follow these steps:

1. **Copy the table or the matrix report by right-clicking the report in the Solution Explorer window and selecting Copy from the menu that appears. Click the Reports folder and then press Ctrl+V.**

   This places a copy of the Product Info report in the Reports folder. You can double-click this report to open it in Report Designer. This report will have the query, as shown in Figure 6-1, already defined.

2. **In the Layout view, add a chart control onto the report body.**

   The chart control defaults to a column display and shows you areas where you can add fields to construct the chart. You can drag and drop fields from the Data Sources window into these areas or drop zones. Follow these steps to produce a chart layout as shown in Figure 6-17.

   a. Data fields correspond to the numeric fields you are interested in. Values are plotted along the y-axis. Drag and drop the numeric fields SalesAmt, OrderQty, and CostAmt into this area.

b. Category fields correspond to x-axis values. When you add multiple fields in this area, you create category groups as described above. The chart groups on each field in this region and there will be a nesting of category groups within each other. Drag and drop the Category and SubCategory fields into this area.

c. Series fields can provide an additional dimension to the data. For example, if you want to examine product sales across region, bring in region as a series value. The series group, as described above, adds more complexity and data point to a chart, because each series value will be plotted at each x-axis (or category) value. I didn't add any information into the series fields.

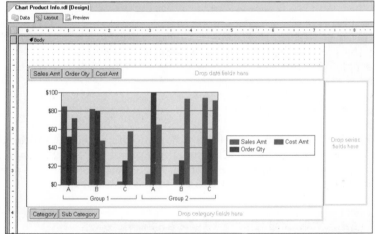

Figure 6-17:
Layout view of the Product Info chart.

3. **Right-click anywhere in the chart control and select Properties from the menu that appears.**

The Chart Properties dialog box appears, as shown in Figure 6-18.

4. **Add the sorting specification for SalesAmt in descending order. Select the first category group in the Data tab within the Chart Properties dialog box, corresponding to the product category grouping.**

The Grouping and Sorting Properties dialog box appears.

5. **Select the SalesAmt field and include the** SUM **aggregate function. Select the descending direction. Click OK to accept these values.**

You return to the Chart Properties dialog box.

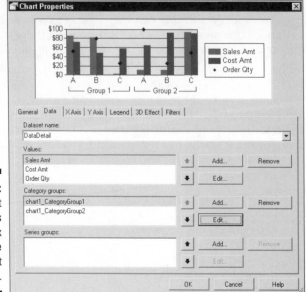

Figure 6-18:
Chart
Properties
dialog box
for the
Product
Info chart.

6. **To simplify the chart display, filter down to a single product category for reporting by clicking the Filters tab in the Chart Properties dialog box and specifying the expression Fields!Category.Value = 'Bikes' as shown in Figure 6-19. Click OK to accept these values.**

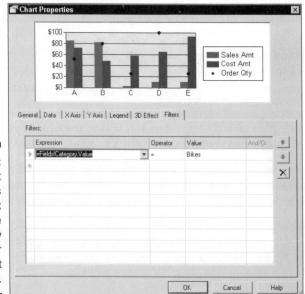

Figure 6-19:
Chart
Properties
dialog box
for the
category
filter for
the Product
Info chart.

7. **In the Chart Properties dialog box, click OK.**

You see the layout view similar to that shown in Figure 6-17. Preview this report and you should see something like what is shown in Figure 6-20. You will see that the chart only shows bike categories and all subcategories within it. It also shows the subcategories in order of sales in descending order.

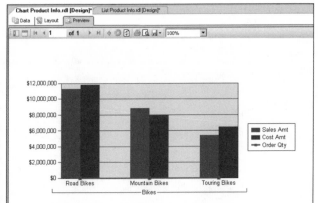

Figure 6-20: Preview of the product info chart.

Filtering data in reports

Filtering reduces the amount of data returned from the data query that is displayed in the report. I filtered data to simplify the chart. There are two ways to filter data in reports, and I explore these ways in the sections that follow.

Filtering queries

The first way to filter data is by doing it in the query. Figure 6-1 shows this capability. You can filter any field in the tables on which the query is based. The restriction here is that the filter must be made in the Data tab of the Report Designer.

Filtering reports

The second way to filter data is by specifying a filter in the Layout tab of the report. To build a report from the AdventureWorksDW sample database and show a territory product lines analysis report, proceed as follows:

1. **In the Query tab, connect to the** `AdventureWorksDW` **sample database and add the tables FactResellerSales, DimTime, DimProduct, DimSalesTerritory, DimReseller, DimProductCategory and DimProductSubcategory to your query.**

You're interested in 2004 and North America values only for metrics sales, sales volume for the product categories in rows and territories in columns. Notice that there are three relationships between DimTime and FactResellerSales. These are represented by join lines between these two tables. Because you're interested only in the order date filtering, remove the joins for due date and ship date. You can do this by right-clicking on the lines joining the two tables for the respective fields. The query designer for this example looks like Figure 6-21.

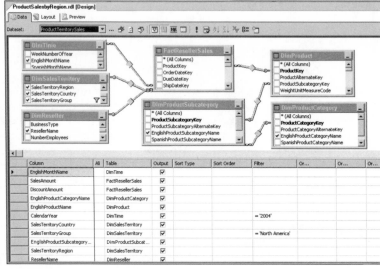

Figure 6-21:
Data view
for Product
Territory
Sales query
from the
`Adventure`
`WorksDW`
database.

2. **In the Layout window, click on a matrix object in the toolbox and drag it into the report body section.**

   You want to create a report with some product information. To do this, drag the ProductCategory field into the rows, the Territory field into the columns, and the SalesAmount field into the data area of the matrix. Title this report as North American Product Sales by Territory.

   Note: I referred to field names by their aliases in Step 2. The actual column name for ProductCategory is EnglishProductCategoryName and the actual column name for Territory is SalesTerritoryGroup.

3. **To filter the information presented in the report, you need to edit a group and work with the Grouping and Sorting Properties dialog box. If you want to show only two product categories in the report, right-click on the row and select Edit Group from the menu that appears. (See Figure 6-22).**

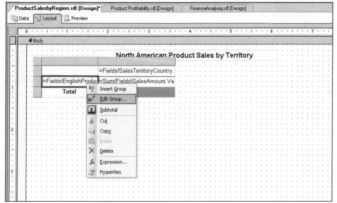

Figure 6-22:
Layout view
to edit the
row group
in the Sales
by Territory
report.

4. **Click the Filters tab and enter the product categories you would like to see in the report. Click the ProductCategory field and use the = operator and enter the value Bikes in the first filter expression. Enter another filter expression by clicking on the Expression column on the next row and select ProductCategory from the drop-down list. Then specify the = operator and the value Accessories. You will note that Reporting Services defaults to 'OR' to link the two filters.**

Click the Layout tab and view the completed report where you have filtered on bikes and accessories. Notice that there are only two territories in North America in the columns.

Top ten lists in a report

A popular need to filter revolves around seeing a top ten list or report. No, I don't mean a David Letterman Top Ten list, but rather a list of top ten customers or top ten products. Follow these steps to construct such a report:

1. **On the Layout tab, use the same query as shown in Figure 6-21 to create a matrix where Reseller Name is in the columns and Sales Amount and Sales Volume are the columns.**

   Make sure that the data fields indicate that you are summing the detail with the SUM function. Title the report as "Top Ten Reseller Sales."

2. **Add a filter on the rows. To do this, right-click the row and select the Edit Group on the pop-up menu.**

   The Grouping and Sorting Properties dialog box appears.

3. **Click the Filters tab and specify the** SUM **of the SalesAmount field. It should be subject to the** TopN **operator with a value of 10 (note the =10 in the Value column required to enable it to return as an integer).**

4. **Add a sort to the rows. To do this, click the Sorting tab in the Grouping and Sorting Properties dialog box and specify that the report should be sorted on the** SUM **of the SalesValue field in descending order.**

   Unless this is completed, the top ten list will not reflect a descending sort of the values.

5. **Preview the completed report.**

   Note that only the top ten resellers are listed in the report and that they are the top ones based on SalesValue and not Units.

Chapter 7

Reporting with Parameters and Format Options

. . . .

In This Chapter

▶ Using expressions in a report

▶ Using parameters

▶ Formatting reports

▶ Conditional formatting

. . . .

*1*n Reporting Services, you have tremendous flexibility in the way that the user can control the way a report looks when it is run. In order to do this, reports need to be defined with parameters that instruct the report to use information provided by the user to fine-tune the information shown within a report. Parameter values selected by the user can be dynamically passed into the report as filtering, sorting, or grouping commands. The parameter values selected can vary the information displayed within a report, not the overall format of the report.

In this way, a single report specification can generate hundreds of possible reports depending on what the user selects as parameter values when he runs the report. In order to understand how to get the most out of the parameters feature, I will explore some more elements of expressions that I have covered in previous chapters. With this background, I will be able to probe the depths of parameters much more easily.

In order to create reports that highlight information effectively, provide some statistical summaries, calculate values beyond the initial query results, and prompt the user for parameters at runtime to filter and sort according to any user demands, you must work through some of the examples in this chapter. This goes beyond report accessorizing (see Chapter 6) and provides you with capabilities that can turn a single report specification into a hundred possible reports depending on how the user wants to investigate the information.

Using Expressions

As you have seen in Chapter 6, report items that display data use expressions to retrieve data from fields and perform calculations. Expressions are like formulas used in Excel. For example, the value in a textbox or any other control in a report can be a constant or an expression, just like for any cell in an Excel spreadsheet. The most common expression in a report control refers to a database field. In addition to database fields, you can also reference other types of items. These items include global items (such as `PageNumber`, `TotalPages`), user items (`UserID`, `UserLanguage`), values from other textboxes (using the expression `=ReportItems!<textboxname>.Value`), aggregate functions (retrieving a single value from multiple detail rows), and parameters (covered later in this chapter). The global and user items can be created with the help of the Expression Editor.

Most properties of report items you would use in a report allow expressions to specify the value of a property. Expressions can include values from the datasets, values of other items on the report, and values of global properties and user properties. Expressions use Visual Basic .NET syntax, which means that field names are case-sensitive.

Aggregate functions

You can use functions within expressions to provide a summary number for a grouping of data. For example, you can calculate a sum of all values in a particular field by using the Sum function. Aggregate functions allow you to return a single value from multiple rows of a dataset. The aggregate functions are summarized in Table 7-1.

Table 7-1	Common Aggregate Functions
Aggregate Function	*Description*
Avg	The sum of all values divided by the count of non-NULL values
Count	The number of all non-null values, not just distinct values
CountDistinct	The number of distinct values for a field
First	The first value from a field over a defined scope
Last	The last value from a field over a defined scope
Max	The largest value from a field over a defined scope
Min	The smallest value from a field over a defined scope

Aggregate Function	Description
RowNumber	The number of the row of the dataset
RunningValue	Accumulates the results of any aggregate function except for RowNumber and RunningValue
StDev	The standard deviation based on a set that is a random sample
StDevP	The standard deviation based on a set that is an entire population
Sum	Simple summation for values that are additive
Var	The square of the standard deviation of a sample (StDev)
VarP	The square of the standard deviation of the entire population (StDevP)

Aggregate functions require you to specify two arguments: expression and scope. The expression defines the simple field reference on which to apply the aggregate function. Expression is typically a numeric field from the dataset, but it can be any valid expression. The scope is the name of a dataset, grouping, or data region that contains the report items to which to apply the aggregate function. In other words, the scope determines which detail rows from the dataset are accessed by the function. The aggregate applies only to rows that share a common value at the specified scope.

For example, if you want to use the AVG aggregate function, you would use the syntax:

```
=AVG(Expression, Scope)
```

To return the average of all costs contained in the outermost data region, you would use the expression:

```
=AVG(Fields!Cost.Value, Nothing)
```

The Scope argument allows three possibilities. First, if you omit the argument, you get the current level if the expression is on a group header or footer. If the expression is used in a detail row, you get the lowest available grouping. If you use the keyword Nothing, you get the entire dataset for the report. This allows you to create a percent-of-total calculation.

Finally, if you use the name of the grouping level as the scope, you get all the rows that have the same value for that grouping level. The grouping level name should be entered as a string, within quotation marks, from the current or higher level within the report and should be case sensitive. This also allows you to do percent-of-group calculations.

Adding calculated columns to a report

You can easily insert columns in report items such as tables and matrices. You can also create expressions using aggregate functions to create calculations that can be displayed in the newly inserted columns. I will show you how to do this with the report you've have already created. Suppose I start with a report I created in Chapter 6 as a table of product information. I want to add a column indicating Cumulative Sales and a column indicating Margin Pct. Proceed as follows:

1. **Insert a column in the table. Right-click a column handle and select Insert Column to the Right from the list that appears.**

2. **Name the column.**

   You can type the text for the column heading directly into the column header cell.

3. **Insert a column to the right of Sales Amount and call it Cum Sales.**

   Insert two columns to the right of Units called Margin$ and Margin%. To do this, right-click the column handle for the Sales Amount column heading and select the Insert Column to the Right menu item.

4. **Right-click an empty area within the Data Sources window and select Add New Field from the menu that appears.**

5. **Add the expression for Margin$ to the report. In the name field, type** MarginAmt.

   This calculated field will be used in the expression for the Margin$ column. Select the Calculated Field radio button and then click the fx button. The Edit Expression dialog box appears. Use the Expression Editor functions to select the SalesAmt field and subtract the CostAmt field. The expression for Margin$ is:

   ```
   =Fields!SalesAmt.Value - Fields!CostAmt.Value
   ```

6. **Rename the textboxes to make building the expression for Margin% and easy chore. Right click the SalesAmt column subtotal cell and select the Properties from the list that appears. Change the name of that cell to SalesTotal.**

   This is the process to change any table cell name. Similarly, change the Grand Total SalesAmt column cell to be SalesGrandTotal. Also change the Margin$ column cells for detail, subtotal, and grand total to be MarginAmt, MarginTotal, and MarginGrandTotal respectively.

7. **Add the expression for Margin% to the report. Right-click the cell in the detail row in the Margin% column and select Expressions from the list that appears.**

   The Edit Expression dialog box shown in Figure 7-1 appears. The expression for the Margin% detail field is:

```
= ReportItems!MarginAmt.Value /
      ReportItems!SalesAmt.Value
```

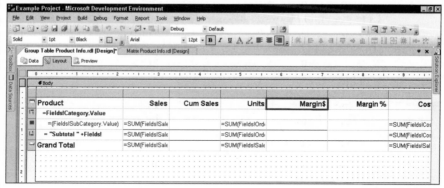

Note that you are referring to the cell name in the table to get the value of the SalesAmt and Margin% columns at the product subcategory level (summing appropriately from the detail rows in the query). Similarly, specify the expressions for the subtotal and grand total rows of the Margin% columns. The expression for the Margin% Subtotal field is:

```
= ReportItems!MarginTotal.Value /
      ReportItems!SalesTotal.Value
```

The expression for the Margin% Grand Total field is:

```
=ReportItems!MarginGrandTotal.Value/
      ReportItems!SalesGrandTotal.Value
```

8. Add the expression for CumSales to the report.

The `RunningValue` aggregate function is designed to handle showing cumulative values within a report. Right-click the cell in the detail row in the Cum Sales column and select the Expressions menu item. Use the `RunningValue` aggregate function (see Table 7-1 for an explanation). Specify the scope as the ProductCategory grouping that the detail line is contained within, which in this case is table2_Group1. The resulting expression for CumSales is as follows:

```
=RunningValue(Fields!SalesAmt.Value,
      Sum, "table2_Group1")
```

9. Hide the Margin and CostAmt columns.

To do this, change the properties for these columns in the report. Right-click the table column handle for the Margin$ and CostAmt columns and select Properties from the list that appears. In the Properties window for each column, set the Visibility Hidden property to False.

10. **Add a report title by selecting Page Header on the Report menu.**

    A page header region will appear in the report. Then drag a textbox into the page header region. In the textbox, add a report title such as Product Profitability. Save this report as a new report file.

11. **Preview the newly created Product Profitability report.**

    You see a report similar to the one shown in Figure 7-2.

Figure 7-2:
Preview of
the newly-
created
Product
Profitability
report.

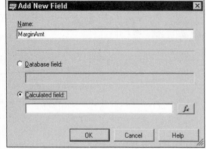

Discovering How to Use Parameters

Parameters restrict results, dictate the sort order of the result set, or control how a report is filtered when it executes. Parameters may be the most powerful aspect of reporting because they offer so much flexibility in reporting potentially large datasets. They also enable a single report to serve many different purposes and can reduce the number of reports you need to meet all the informational requirements you need in business.

Report parameters

You can add parameters to a report to manipulate data that the report contains. Report parameters can be used to pass values to an underlying query, to pass values to a filter, or as variables for calculating data within the report. A report parameter textbox is usually presented to the user when they run the report, but a report can also use a default parameter without presenting the choice to the user.

You define report parameters when you create your report, but the values of the parameters are provided by the user when the report is executed. Parameters can be hand-typed into the report or they can be selected from a drop-down list of values.

Report parameters can be optional. If a non-optional parameter is required and not specified, the report will not run. You can specify a default value and you do not necessarily have to show the parameter to the end user.

You can use report parameters to

- ✔ Provide a value to an SQL parameter in a query that generates a dataset for a report.
- ✔ Control a filter that limits rows after they are retrieved in a dataset.
- ✔ Control the dataset that feeds the possible values of another report parameter to create a dynamic parameter list.
- ✔ Control the appearance of report items or textboxes by changing color schemes.
- ✔ Set different limits for exception reporting.

In the following sections, I cover how to use report parameters in your reports.

Query parameters

Query parameters are different from report parameters in that they filter the rows of a dataset and are always linked to report parameters to get a value.

When specifying a query parameter in a query, the notation that must be used is the @ sign followed by the parameter name. To manually create a map between the query parameter and a report parameter, select the dataset in the Data view, click the Edit Selected Dataset button, and select the Parameter tab.

Using parameters in a report

To see how this works in Reporting Services, you can modify the report I create in Chapter 6. You can start with the Data window and progress through the steps to create a parameter in the report. You will notice that I have modified the report somewhat to show margin results in the report. To use parameters in a report, you create a report and follow these steps.

1. **In the Data view, add a query parameter for year. For the column CalendarYear, enter the filter value of** `=@year`.

   This produces a parameter-based query as shown in Figure 7-3.

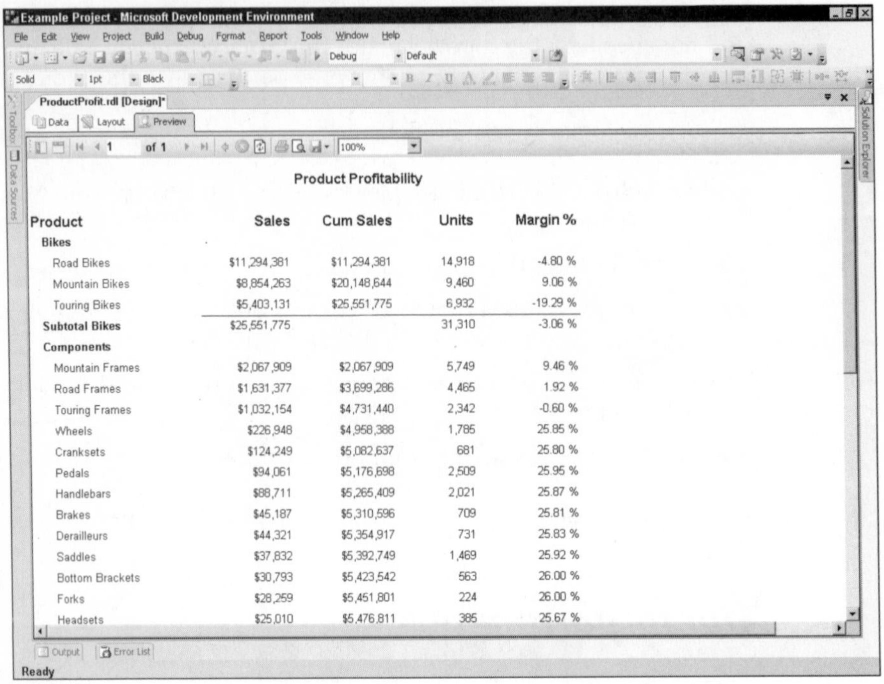

Figure 7-3:
Data view of
the modified
Top 10
Customers
report.

If you try to execute this query, the Query Parameters dialog box will appear to prompt your for a value of `CalendarYear` to use in the query (see Figure 7-4).

2. **In the Layout view, edit the `CalendarYear` parameter.**

   To do this, click on the Report menu and select the Report Parameters menu item. You will see the Report Parameters dialog box. Note that the parameter `year` has already been created for you.

3. **Set how you want the parameters to be prompted. From the Report menu, select the Report Parameters menu item.**

   This will pop up the Report Parameters dialog box box.

   The available values have been preset to Non-queried, and the default values have been preset to None. If you would like to have a query provide you with values, you need to define another dataset specifying how you will query these values from the data source.

4. **Define the default value of the parameter, if needed, in the Report Parameters dialog box.**

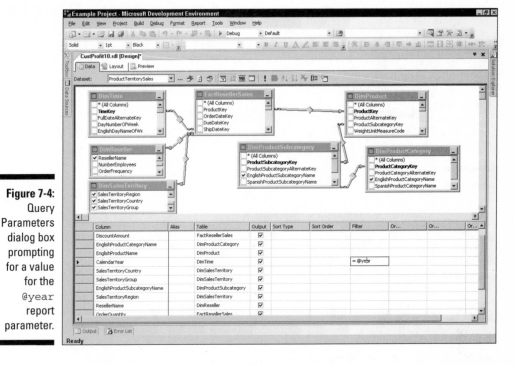

Figure 7-4:
Query
Parameters
dialog box
prompting
for a value
for the
`@year`
report
parameter.

If you would like the default value of year to be set to the current year,
check that the current year is in the available values table and that there
is data for the current year. The expression `=Year(Now)` will specify the
current year. Using this approach, Figure 7-5 shows how this dialog box
would look.

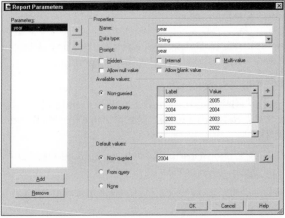

Figure 7-5:
Report
Parameters
dialog box
with para-
meter value
list and
default val-
ue for the
`@year`
report
parameter.

5. Preview the result by clicking the Preview tab (see Figure 7-6). Notice that parameter year appears just above the Report toolbar in the form of a drop-down list box. You can select from the list and then click the View Report button on the Report toolbar to see a refreshed report based on the new parameter value substituted in the dataset query.

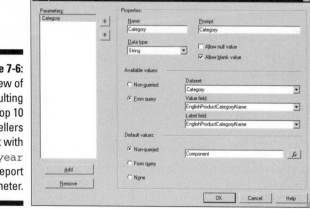

Figure 7-6:
Preview of
the resulting
Top 10
Resellers
report with
the @year
report
parameter.

Each time the SQL query is changed, the query must be executed and the dataset regenerated. Such was the case in the previous example. This happens each time you change a parameter that modifies the SQL query. It is possible to get better reporting performance by pulling a larger set of data into the dataset and then filtering the rows that will appear in the report.

You can modify a report I created earlier in this chapter on Product Profitability (refer to Figure 7-2). To create a report that will query all report categories and present a parameter to the user to select which category should be filtered when the report is run, follow these steps:

1. Create a new dataset. In Data view, click on the dataset combo box and select New Dataset from the list that appears.

The Dataset dialog box appears.

2. Enter your query specification in the Dataset dialog box. Name your dataset, select the database to use (AdventureWorksDW) and enter a query string like:

SELECT DISTINCT EnglishProductCategoryName FROM DimProductCategory

The resulting Dataset dialog box should look like that shown in Figure 7-7.

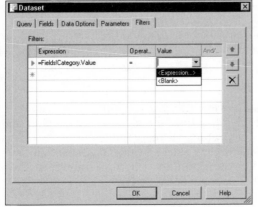

Figure 7-7:
Dataset
dialog box
for the new
Category
dataset in
the Product
Profitability
Report.

3. Create the Category parameter.

In the Layout view, click on the Report menu and select the Report
Parameters menu item. In the Report Parameters dialog box, click on
the Add button to create a New parameter. Then enter the values as
shown in Figure 7-8.

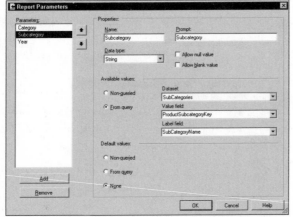

Figure 7-8:
Report
Parameters
dialog box
for the
Category
parameter
for the
Product
Profitability
report.

4. Add a filter to the DataDetail dataset.

You can filter either the data region in the Layout tab or the dataset in
the Data view because they're equivalent. Go to the Data view, and from
the Dataset drop-down list box, select the DataDetail dataset. Click the
Edit Selected Dataset button and the Dataset dialog box appears. Click the

Filters tab and then, in the Expressions drop-down list, select =Fields. Category.value. Then select = for the operator and click on Expression. In the Edit Expression dialog box, expand the Parameters in the Fields list and insert Category into the expression. The resulting expression should read =Parameters!Category.Value.

5. **Preview the report.**

First, go to the Layout view. To make the report more relevant to the filtering, right-click the group header and footer report lines and select the Properties menu item. Set the Visibility Hidden property to True for both. Then click the Preview view, select a value for Component in the parameter and then click the View Report button. Your result should look something like what appears in Figure 7-9.

Using cascading parameters in a report

You can define a set of parameters where the list of values for one parameter depends on the value chosen in another parameter. For example, the first parameter could be a list of product categories. When the user selects a category, the second parameter is updated with a list of subcategories within the selected category.

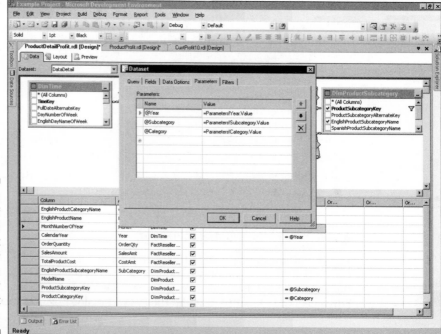

Figure 7-9: Preview of the revised Product Profitability report with a parameter on Product Category.

If you want to create a report based on Product Profitability that will report the product detail within a selected `SubCategory`, follow these steps. The process involves prompting first for Year and for Product Category and then subsequently prompting for the Product `SubCategory` within the selected Product Category. Here's how to do this:

1. **Create a dataset called Categories that will return product category information. The SQL for this dataset is:**

```
SELECT EnglishProductCategoryName AS CategoryName
       ProductCategoryKey
FROM DimProductCategory
```

2. **Create a dataset named Subcategories that returns a list of subcategories filtered by category. The SQL for this dataset is:**

```
SELECT  ProductSubcategoryKey,
        EnglishProductSubcategoryName AS
        SubCategoryName FROM   DimProductSubcategory
        WHERE (ProductCategoryKey = @Category)
```

3. **Create a dataset named Products that retrieves a list of products filtered by Subcategory. The SQL for this dataset is:**

```
SELECT ProductKey, EnglishProductName AS ProductName
FROM DimProduct
WHERE (ProductSubcategoryKey = @Subcategory)
```

4. **Edit the Category report parameter.**

   This parameter already exists because the `@Category` query parameter was used in the Subcategories dataset. Specify a queried available values list that uses the Categories dataset, setting the label to `CategoryName` and the value to `ProductCategoryID`.

5. **Edit the Subcategory report parameter.**

   This parameter already exists because the `@Subcategory` query parameter was used in the Products dataset. Specify a queried available values list that uses the Subcategories dataset, setting the label to `SubcategoryName` and the value to `ProductSubcategoryID`.

6. **Use the values from the parameters to filter the data in the report to the relevant year, Category and Subcategory.**

   You can do this in the Data view by specifying that the parameter values come from selections from the user when the report is executed, as shown in Figure 7-10.

7. **Preview the report.**

   As shown in Figure 7-11, the report prompts the user for Year, Category, and Subcategory and shows the relevant product detail based on these parameters.

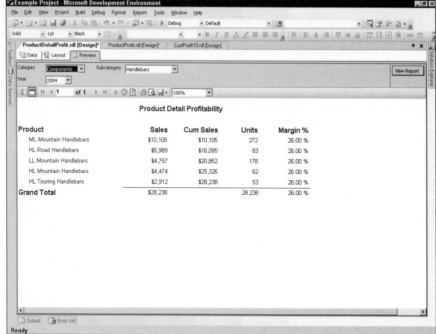

Figure 7-10: Dataset dialog box showing the mapping from query parameter and user specified parameter.

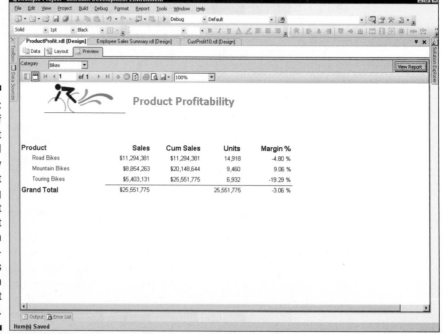

Figure 7-11: Preview of the Product Detail Profitability report showing the result of product information after applying the filters specified in the report parameters.

Formatting Reports

Reporting Services gives you ample resources to fine-tune your report formats to meet most requirements for enterprise reporting. I covered its capabilities in sorting, grouping, and filtering in Chapter 6. In this chapter, I cover the remaining capabilities Reporting Services offers in the way of putting some final touches on a report's look and feel.

Headers and footers

Page headers and footers provide you with additional context in reports. Occasionally, you need to deal with the top and bottom (first and last) pages of the report differently than the other pages. You need to be aware of several levels of headers and footers:

- **Report Level.** A report header appears only on the first page, and a report footer appears only on the last page of the report. To create report headers and footers, just place report items above or below your data region(s).

- **Page Level.** Page headers and footers appear on all pages, and can exclude the first and last pages as an option. The options PrintOnFirstPage and PrintOnLastPage can help you control how you want the page header to behave. You can add a page header or footer to any report by clicking the Report menu and selecting the Page Header or Report Header menu items. To select the option of printing on first page and/or last page, click on the Report menu and select the Report Properties menu item. Check boxes are available on the General tab of the Report Properties dialog box. Note that the Print on First Page and Print on Last Page options are only enabled if there is a page header or footer, respectively.

- **List/Table/Matrix Level.** List, table, or matrix headers and footers are available for the beginning and end of a table. In this way, you can create headers an footers that are the same for all pages. You also have control of whether the report header or footer shows on each new page. To do this, simply right-click on the handle for the list, table, or matrix table header or footer and select the Properties menu item. Then in the Property window, set the `RepeatOnNewPage` property to True or False.

- **Group Level.** Group headers and footers are available at the beginning and end of grouping levels in a table. You can cause these group headers and footers to repeat on each page. To do this, right-click on the handle for the group header or footer and select the Properties menu item. This will display the Grouping and Sorting Properties dialog box that you have seen before. In the General tab, you can click on the check boxes to include and repeat the group headers and footers.

As an example of using a page header to put some final touches on a report, see how you can spice up the Product Profitability report originally shown in

Figure 7-9. If you want to add a company logo and put in a larger font for the report title and change its color, follow these steps:

1. **Add a page header to the report.**

   Use the Report menu and Report Properties menu item to add this section above the body.

2. **Move the title to the page header by clicking the title and dragging it into the page header section. Then change its font to something interesting.**

   I like an 18 point Tahoma font with a color of Slate Blue.

3. **Add the company logo onto the page.**

   Here I borrowed the AdventureWorks logo from the Employee Sales Summary report in the sample reports that ship with Reporting Services. I just copied it from the source report and pasted it into this report. I also added a line underneath the logo to represent the beautiful track on which the cyclist is performing. The result is shown in Figure 7-12.

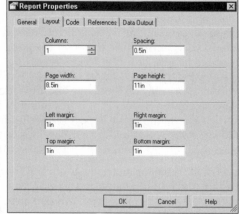

Figure 7-12: The Layout view for the Product Profitability report with a page header section.

4. **Right-click the handle for the entire report (upper-left corner of the entire report document) and select Properties from the menu that appears.**

   The Report Properties dialog box appears. Select the check box for Print on First Page. Alternatively, you can click on the Page Header handle and in the Property window on the left side, and set the property `PrintonFirstPage` to True.

   Do the same for Printing on the last page.

5. **Preview your work.**

   The final report should look like the one shown in Figure 7-13.

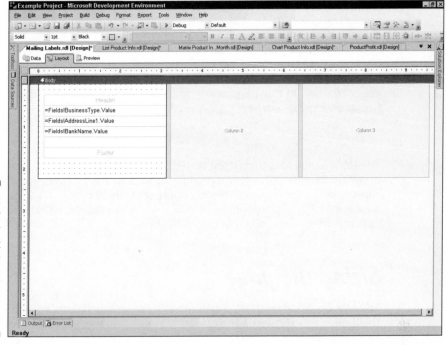

Figure 7-13:
The Preview view for the Product Profitability report with the page header section.

Paginating reports — Is that legal?

A page break introduced at a certain point within a report will make the report advance one page before continuing the reported information. It's both legal and interesting in that it enables you to introduce different kinds of page breaks.

- ✔ **List/Table/Matrix/Chart/Rectangle Level.** For a list, table, matrix, chart, or rectangle, you have the ability to insert a page break before or after the control. You also have an option to fit the control on one page if possible. You need only select the control and view the Properties window or right-click the control and select the Properties menu item. Charts have the `PageBreakAtEnd` and `PageBreakAtStart` properties you can set in the Properties window.

- ✔ **Group Level.** When you edit a group of a list, matrix, or table control, the General tab of the Grouping and Sorting Properties dialog box provides options to page break at the start and page break at the end of the group.

- ✔ **Detail Level.** You can edit a detail line in a matrix or a table control and the General tab of the Grouping and Sorting Properties dialog box provides options to page break at the start and page break at the end of the detail line.

You also have the option of placing a page break at the end of a specified number of rows. To do this, create a group in a data region immediately outside the detail, add a page break to the group, and then add an expression that you want to group on that is based on a certain number of rows in the General tab of the Grouping and Sorting Properties dialog box. As an example of the group expression to use, suppose you want to break a report after every 30 rows. In this case, you would use the following expression in the Group on Expression list:

```
=Int((RowNumber(Nothing)-1)/30)
```

The RowNumber function used here displays the row number for each instance of the textbox in which the expression appears. The Nothing keyword indicates that the function will begin counting at the first row in the outermost data region. To begin counting within child data regions, use the name of the data region in place of the keyword Nothing.

Sizing the page

You can set the size of the pages of your report by clicking the Layout tab in the Report Properties dialog box box. There, you can set Page Width, Page Height, and all the margins for the report. This is equivalent to selecting the report by clicking in the upper-left corner square and viewing the Properties window to set the respective report properties. These size settings will affect how the report is rendered in production.

Creating multi-column reports

Reporting Services supports multiple columns in a report. When you define more than one column in a report, Report Designer calculates the width of the columns in the report based on the number of columns, the width of the report, and the width of the space between columns. It then displays a decreased design surface so that you can place report items on the report that will fit within the column.

Columns can snake within the report. For example, a list box placed within a multi-column report will display data from the top left of the page to the bottom left of the page, and then continue the list in the adjacent column at the top of the page. You can define as many columns you want.

For example, suppose that you want to create mailing labels. The trick is to line up the report with the mailing labels on the page. But in principle, all you need to do is define a report with three columns through the use of the Layout tab in the Report Properties dialog box, accessible from the Reports menu. Within the table control, you can show the name and address fields and insert a blank line or two based on the spacing between the labels so that the next occurrence starts at the next label.

Using expressions in formatting reports

You can utilize expressions in your reporting in many ways. In this section, I highlight some of the capabilities of string functions, data functions, and conditional formatting expressions in better controlling your report format needs.

String functions

You can format dates and numbers within a string with the Format function. The following expression displays values of the StartDate and EndDate parameters in long date format.

```
=Format(Parameters!StartDate.Value, "D") & " through " &
        Format(Parameters!EndDate.Value, "D")
```

Note: If the textbox contains only a date or number, you should use the Format property of the textbox to apply formatting rather than the Format function within the textbox.

Date functions

The following expression contains the Today function, which provides the current date. This expression can be used in a textbox to display the date on the report, or in a parameter to filter data based on the current date.

```
=Today()
```

The DateAdd function is useful for supplying a range of dates based on a single parameter. The following expression provides a date that is six months after the date from a parameter named StartDate.

```
=DateAdd(DateInterval.Month, 6,
        Parameters!StartDate.Value)
```

The following expression contains the `Year` function, which displays the year for a particular date. You can use this to group dates together or to display the year as a label for a set of dates. This expression provides the year for a given group of order dates. The `Month` function and other functions can also be used to manipulate dates. For more information, see the Visual Basic .NET documentation.

```
=Year(Fields!OrderDate.Value)
```

Conditional formatting expressions

You can use Visual Basic functions to evaluate an input value and return another value depending on the result. Specifically, the `IIF` function returns one of two values depending on whether the expression evaluated is true or not. To use the `IIF` function to return a Boolean value of True if the value of `SalesAmt` exceeds 100, or False otherwise, use the expression:

```
=IIF(Fields!SalesAmt.Value > 100, True, False)
```

You can use expressions to vary the appearance of report items in a report. For example, you can set the Color property of a textbox to change based on the value of the Profit field by using the expression:

```
=IIF(Fields!Profit.Value < 0, "Red", "Black")
```

To make it easier to copy the same expression to multiple textboxes, you can use the special word *Me* to refer to the current report item. Suppose that you want to conditionally format a textbox named *Sales* and set the `Backcolor` property to be green if the value is > 10 and red otherwise. To do this, use the expression:

```
=IIF(Sum(ReportItems!Sales.Value)>10, "green", "red")
```

If you need to copy this expression to a textbox named Sales Total, you would need to change the expression. To get around this, use the Me word for the control so you can copy the expression for the `Backcolor` property of the textbox to the `Backcolor` property of any textbox as:

```
=IIF(Sum(ReportItems!Me.Value)>10, "green", "red")
```

To make matters more interesting, suppose that you want to format SalesAmt to be one of three colors depending on its value. In this case, you use nested `IIF`s to return one of three values depending on the value of SalesAmt:

```
=IIF(Fields!SalesAmt.Value >= .8, "Green", IIF(
        Fields!SalesAmt.Value >= .5, "Amber", "Red"))
```

A last example for using conditional formatting expressions is to set the `BackgroundColor` property of a detail line in a data region, alternating the background color of each row between pale green and white to make it look like the old greenbar report. You would use the following expression to achieve this effect:

```
=IIF(RowNumber(Nothing) Mod 2, "PaleGreen", "White")
```

Custom code

You can use Visual Basic functions to evaluate an input value and return another value depending on the result of the function. To use code within a report, you add a code block to the report. This code block can contain multiple methods. Methods in embedded code must be written in Visual Basic .NET and must be instance based.

Suppose that you want to write a function that will change the `BackgroundColor` property of the cell based on the values of that cell. you know our target Margin% in the Product Profitability report (see Figure 7-9) is 8.5%. The following function pasted into the Code tab within the Report Properties dialog box will change the color based on the values specified:

```
Public Shared Function GetColor(ByVal Value As Decimal) As
        String
        Select Case Value
                                        Case Is > 0.085

        Return "Transparent"
                                        Case Is > 0.080

        Return "Yellow"
                                                Case Else

        Return "Red"
        End Select
End Function
```

This new function, or method, is now in embedded code and is available for reference in an expression through a globally defined Code member. You access these by referring to the Code member and method name. Therefore, in order to set the `BackgroundColor` property of the MarginPct field in the Product Profitability report based on the values specified in the `GetColor` function above, use the following expression:

```
=Code.GetColor(Me.Value)
```

The resulting report looks like the report shown in Figure 7-14.

Figure 7-14:
Product
Profitability
report
usingthe
`GetColor`
function
as Custom
Code used
to set the
`Back
ground
Color`
property of
the Margin%
cell.

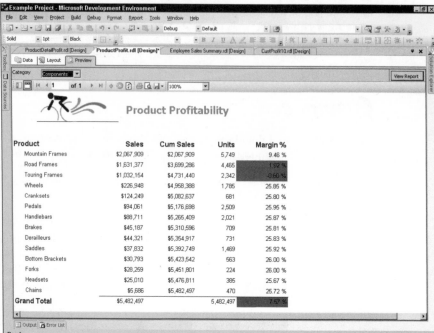

Chapter 8

Using Report Builder

*I*f you have a license for the Enterprise version of SQL Server 2005, you have access to an ad hoc report building tool called Report Builder. Using Report Builder, you can create table, matrix, and chart reports. Report Builder is a powerful but easy-to-use tool that enables business people to explore and find information without having to understand the underlying data source structures. The Report Builder tool is built using familiar Microsoft Office paradigms so that users can get started quickly. You can quickly drag and drop data elements onto a report template to create reports. Clickthrough reports are generated automatically so that report viewers can follow natural navigation paths to explore the data. You can continue clicking and drilling through the data as long as there is a relationship to follow from the data element of interest. You can also customize your report by filtering, grouping, and sorting, or adding formulas to calculate values.

While designing your report, you are working with the report layout. Like other Reporting Services reports, Report Builder uses Report Definition Language (RDL) to design report layouts. Therefore, the actual data isn't visible when you're working on your report layout. In order to see your data within the report layout, you need to run the report. When you run the report, the report server combines the data with the report layout. You can view the results in the Report Builder preview area. After creating and saving your report, you can continue to open the report and edit the report layout as often as you want. Report Builder can only open reports created using Report Builder.

The Report Builder interface is simpler than the Report Designer interface I examine in previous chapters. However, Report Builder provides less control over formatting and control breaks compared to Report Designer. Whereas Report Designer is designed for the serious report developer, Report Builder is designed for business people who don't understand the underlying data source structures.

Creating a Report Model

Report Model Designer is a new Reporting Services tool within Business Intelligence Development Studio that enables you to view, design, edit, and refine report models. A *report model* is an abstraction of the database's contents and connection information. Report Model Designer uses a new Extensible Markup Language (XML), called Semantic Model Definition Language (SMDL), to create models. SMDL is a set of information that describes what data is available, how the data is related, and where the data is located. These models are used in Report Builder to create reports.

Creating a model project

You can create a report model project using Business Intelligence Development Studio. In order to create reports in Report Builder, at least one model needs to be available. A report model project contains the definition of the data source (a .ds file), the definition of a data source view (a .dsv file), and the model (an .smdl file).

To create a new report model project, follow these steps:

1. **Start the Business Intelligence Development Studio.**
2. **Choose File⇨New.**

   A menu appears.
3. **Select Project.**
4. **In the Templates list, click Report Model Project.**
5. **In the Name field, type AdventureWorksModel, as shown in Figure 8-1.**
6. **Click OK to create the model project.**

   The AdventureWorksModel solution appears in Solution Explorer.

Defining a data source

After creating a report model project called AdventureWorksModel, you need to define one data source from which you'll extract business intelligence data and metadata. Begin by defining the AdventureWorksDW sample database as your data source.

Figure 8-1:
Creating a
report
model
project
within the
Business
Intelligence
Develop-
ment Studio.

To define a data source for a report model project, follow these steps:

1. **In Solution Explorer, right-click Data Sources and choose Add New Data Source from the menu that appears.**

2. **On the Welcome to the Data Source Wizard page, click Next.**

   The Select How to Define the Connection page appears. On this page, you can define a data source based on an existing connection or on a previously defined data source object (from within the current solution or within another report model project), or define a new connection.

3. **Verify that Create a Data Source Based on an Existing or New Connection is selected, and then click New.**

   A Connection Manager dialog box appears. In this dialog box, you define connection properties for the data source.

4. **In the Provider list box, select .NET Providers/SQL Client Data Provider (not the OLE DB provider) and then click OK.**

5. **In the Server name text box, type** localhost.

6. **In the Select or Enter a Database Name list box, select AdventureWorksDW.**

7. **Specify any credentials you need for the database connection.**

   When you publish your report model project, a connection to the specified database will be established using the credentials you provide here.

8. **To verify that the connection works, click the Test Connection button.**

   If you receive a message confirming your connection, click OK to accept the properties. If the connection doesn't work, verify that the information you entered is correct.

9. **Click Next.**

The Select How to Define the Connection page reappears.

10. **Verify that the Create a Data Source Based on an Existing or New Connection option is selected, verify that localhost.AdventureWorksDW is selected in the Data Connections list box, and then click Next.**

11. **In the Data Source name box, type AdventureWorksModel, and then click Finish.**

The name you selected appears by default. You can, however, use a different name to name the connection. (The connection name can contain spaces.) The .ds file is created and displayed in the Data Sources folder in the AdventureWorksModel project.

Creating a data source view

A data source view is a single, unified view of the specified tables and metadata from the data source defined in the project. Reporting Services generates the report model from the data source view.

Data source views facilitate the model design process by providing you with a useful representation of the data that you specified. Because metadata is stored in the data source view, you do not need to be connected to the underlying data source to work with the objects. You can rename tables and fields, as well as add aggregate fields and derived tables, in a data source view without changing the underlying data source. For an efficient model, only add the tables to the data source view that you intend to use.

To define a data source view based on the tables in the AdventureWorksModel data source, proceed as follows:

1. **In Solution Explorer, right-click Data Source Views and choose Add New Data Source View from the menu that appears.**

2. **On the Welcome to the Data Source View Wizard page, click Next.**

The Select a Data Source page appears.

3. **In the Relational Data Sources window, verify that the AdventureWorksModel data source is selected, and then click Next.**

Only one data source can be referenced when creating a data source view for a model project. The Select Tables and Views page appears.

4. **Select the tables from the data source that you want to use in the data source view. Add the FactResellerSales table. Then click all related tables so all related dimensions are added for this fact table.**

5. **Click Next.**

6. **Type** AdventureWorksModel **in the Name text box and then click Finish.**

   The AdventureWorksModel.dsv data source view appears in the Data Source Views folder in the AdventureWorksModel project. The View Designer window appears in Business Intelligence Development Studio displaying the contents of this data source view. This is shown in Figure 8-2.

Define a report model for ad hoc analysis

A report model is a layer on top of a physical database that identifies business entities, fields, and roles. Sometimes people refer to this layer as a metadata layer, where metadata is "data about data". This means that the report model describes the information that exists within the data source on which it has been built. When published, the report model enables Report Builder users to develop reports without having to be familiar with database structures or understand and write queries.

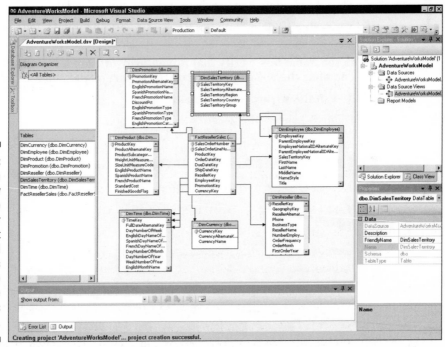

Figure 8-2:
The Data Set View (dsv) for the FactReseller Sales fact and related dimensions in the Adventure Works database.

Models are comprised of three major components: Entities (which are sets of related report items that are grouped together under a familiar name), predefined relationships between these business entities, and predefined calculations. When you create and save a model, you are creating an object that uses an XML language called Semantic Model Definition Language (SMDL). The file extension for saved report model files is .smdl.

To define a report model:

1. **In Solution Explorer, right-click Report Models and select Add New Report Model from the menu that appears.**

   The Report Model Wizard appears.

2. **In the Available Data Source Views list, verify that AdventureWorksModel is selected and click Next.**

   The Select Report Model Generation Rules page appears. These rules determine how the metadata is generated from the data source.

3. **Accept all the defaults.**

   The metadata will be combined into objects called entities.

4. **Click Next.**

   The Update Statistics page appears.

5. **Verify that Update Statistics Before Generating is selected, and then click Next.**

6. **In the Name box, verify that AdventureWorksModel is selected. To complete the wizard and create the report model, click Run.**

7. **To exit the wizard, click Finish.**

   Figure 8-3 shows the wizard's last dialog box.

Figure 8-3:
The Report
Model
Wizard
screen
showing
what is
generated
when you
create a
Report
Model.

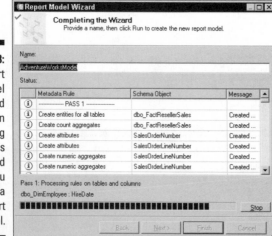

In the AdventureWorksModel - Microsoft Development Environment window, the entities and folders within the model are displayed. Selecting an entity displays the list of fields, folders, and roles that are contained within that entity. When the model name is selected, you can right-click to add entities, perspectives, and folders. When an entity is selected, you can right-click to add a folder, source field, expression, and role.

Publish a report model project

In order to build reports using the model you create, you must publish the model to the report server. The data source and data source view are included with the model when it is published.

To publish a report model to a report server, in Solution Explorer, right-click the AdventureWorksModel project and then select Deploy.

The model is saved to the report server using the Target Server URL that you specified when setting up Business Intelligence Development Studio. If any errors or warnings are encountered, they are displayed in the Output window.

Business Intelligence Development Studio defaults to the report server URL automatically. However, if you want to change or view the report server information, you can right-click the AdventureWorksModel project name and view the properties. The report server URL is specified in the Target Server URL area. By default, the value is `http://localhost/report server`.

To verify that the published model project uploaded successfully to the report server, you can use Report Manager to view items on the server. Figure 8-4 shows the folders created in Report Manager for the objects in the report model. When publishing a model project, the model is published to the Models folder and its corresponding data source is published to the Data Sources folder. Figure 8-5 shows what the report model publication process writes to the Models folder.

Figure 8-4: The Report Manager shows new folders populated.

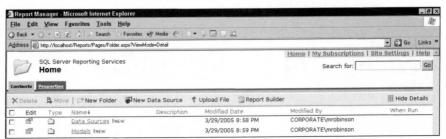

Figure 8-5:
The Models
folder within
the Report
Manager
shows the
new report
model
created
in the
publishing
process.

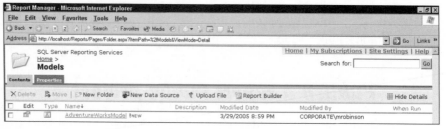

To use the published model as a basis for a Report Builder report, you must have access to the model. In the role-based security model that is implemented for Reporting Services, users who are assigned to the Content Manager role or Publisher role have automatic permissions to publish the model and data source. In addition, users who are assigned to the Content Manager role can create and edit reports in Report Builder. Local administrators are automatically assigned to the Content Manager role. If you want other users to be able to edit and interact with a Report Builder report, you must create a role assignment for them that includes the default Report Consumer role. You can also create a custom role definition. As long as the role includes the Consume Reports task, users who are assigned to that role will have sufficient permission to create and modify reports using Report Builder.

When the model is published, and you have configured role assignments for the users who want to use the model, you can run Report Builder to create a report. To launch Report Builder, click the New Report link on the Report Manager toolbar. To create a report in Report Builder, you begin by selecting a model, referred to as a data source in Report Builder, and a template for the report layout you want (for example, a table). You can then drag and drop the model items to the report.

Working with the Report Builder

After you create a report model, you can start building reports with the Report Builder. Start the Report Builder directly from the Report Manager, which I talk about in more detail in Chapter 9. Report Manager was designed to be a natural place for business users to go to find reports.

Launching Report Builder

To start the Report Manager, specify the following Report Server home page URL in your browser:

```
http:// WebServerName/reports
```

`WebServerName` is the name of the server on which Reporting Services is running. If Reporting Services is actually running on your own machine, `localhost` is usually the name you specify for the `WebServerName`.

Notice that on the toolbar within Report Manager, the Report Builder icon appears. You can see this in Figure 8-5. Click on this toolbar button to start Report Builder.

Creating reports in Report Builder

You can use Report Builder to create ad hoc reports. Ad hoc reports enable end users to view data immediately for review and analysis. You don't need to understand how to use databases or programming languages to use Report Builder. You can simply drag fields to the design area where you can arrange, format, filter, group, sort, and preview them.

After launching Report Builder, you see a splash screen while the WinForms application loads. After the program has loaded, you see a dialog box showing all the report models you have published. This is shown in Figure 8-6.

Figure 8-6:
The initial display after launching the Report Builder is a prompt for you to select the report model you wish to work with.

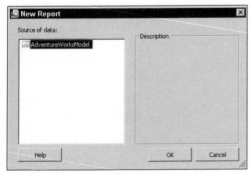

After you select the report model you want to work with, you see a display of the design surface of the Report Builder, as shown in Figure 8-7. To build a table, matrix, or chart report, select a report layout template (on the right side of the design interface, entitled Report Layout) that contains predefined data regions. On the left side, you see the components of the report model that you have selected in the section entitled Explorer. You see in the Explorer at the top all the dimensions and the key facts available from the model. When you click on a dimension, for example, Dim Customer, the Explorer displays all the attributes and counts associated with that dimension in the Fields list below it. When you click on a fact, you may see some dimensions that are carried on the fact table in the model as well as aggregates (generally Sum, Min, Max, and Avg) computed on the underlying metrics in the fact table.

To begin developing a report, proceed as follows:

1. **Select a predefined report model containing items such as data fields, then drag and drop the report items onto the data regions within the template.**

   I recommend that you select the fact table first to get the metrics of interest on the report. After you do this, you will see all the dimensions in the Explorer list on the top left that are available for exploration based on the metrics in the report. This is shown in Figure 8-8.

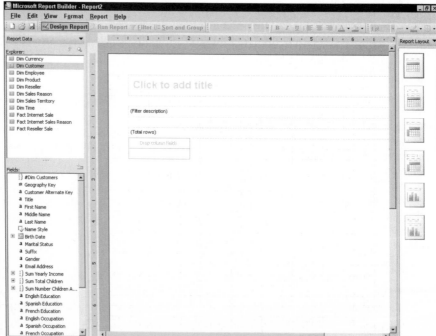

Figure 8-7: Report Builder's design interface lets you select layout templates or chart report styles as well as drag items into your report.

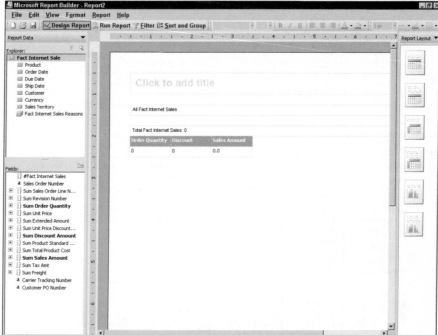

Figure 8-8:
The report
layout after
dragging a
few metrics
from the
Internet
Sales fact
table.

2. **Select a dimension and drag the attribute to the first column of the report. Then add a title.**

3. **Click the Run Report button on the toolbar beneath the menu to see the report (see Figure 8-9).**

You can interactively explore the related data within the report because click-through reports are automatically generated. A *clickthrough* report is a report that is automatically generated by clicking on some data element within the Report Builder to show a detail report on the data element you selected. As long as there is a relationship to follow from the current item, you can continue clicking through the data. In this way, users can follow the report model's navigation paths to explore the data. If the report model is robust, there are many areas to explore within a high-level report such as the one shown in Figure 8-9. When clicking through the data, queries are generated automatically by passing information about the context of the current data location within the report. There is a clickthrough report available when you hover over the data and the icon of a hand appears at the mouse pointer.

Within the preview interface, you can right-click anywhere on the report to see options you have for zooming in on the detail and exporting to another format (XML, CSV, TIFF, Acrobat or PDF, Web Archive, and Excel options). You can also preview and print within the Report Builder.

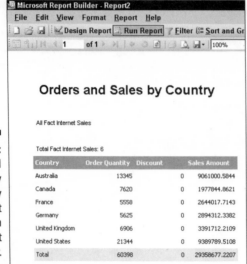

Figure 8-9:
Orders and
Sales by
Country
report
created in
Report
Builder.

Sorting, grouping, and totaling with Report Builder

Filtering information assists in reviewing a large data source. Instead of generating and clicking through a large report of perhaps 100 pages, you can filter on a column to greatly reduce the length of the report.

You can filter data interactively. Just click the Filter button and the Filter Data dialog box shown in Figure 8-10 appears. For example, if you filter to see the sales based on promotions only, you can use the Filter Data dialog box to specify these conditions.

You can also sort and group the report by clicking the Sort and Group button on the toolbar. You will see the Sort dialog box (see Figure 8-11), which walks you through your options for sorting and grouping the report.

How do you change the format or a formula for a cell in the report? To do this, simply right-click on a cell and you see a menu of options. This is shown in Figure 8-12.

Figure 8-10:
Filter Data
dialog box
illustrating
how to build
multiple
groups of
filters which
can be
combined
into a
complex
filter for any
Report
Builder
report.

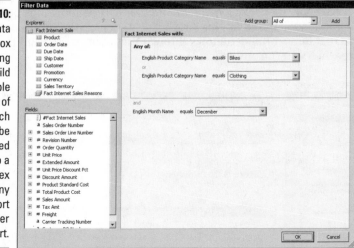

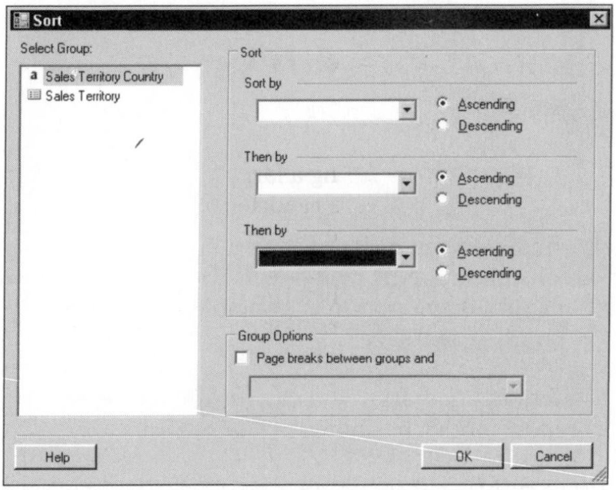

Figure 8-11:
Specifying
the sorting
and
grouping
options for a
report.

Drill-down analysis with Report Builder

Another special capability with Report Builder is that you can drill down on some of the information within your original report design without additional coding! Microsoft refers to this capability as infinite drill down, but, of course, there are finite levels of hierarchies and relationships in a data model. The report model knows the hierarchies and relationships between tables in the model. Based on this knowledge, there are drill-down paths available that Report Builder knows through the report model and that are available when you run any report.

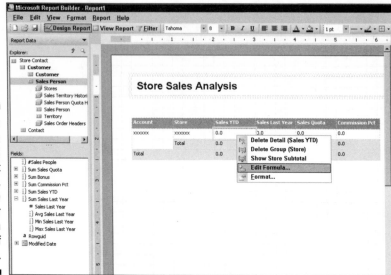

Figure 8-12: Interface showing how to edit formulas, delete columns, or change a format of any column.

How can you tell where you can drill down on a Report Builder report? To ask Report Builder which cells support drill-down, hover your mouse over any cell in the report; if a drill-down option is available, the mouse pointer will change to a finger pointing to the cell.

To see how this functionality works, you can create a basic report with the AdventureWorks report model, as shown in Figure 8-13.

Each of the metrics on this report supports a drill-down analysis. The initial view when a cell is clicked is for a specific product on the report. This drill-down level shows all sales orders for that particular product. This detail level is shown in Figure 8-14. This report is not formatted well out of the box. In the next section, I talk about how to refine the format of this report.

If you click on any column of the drill-down default report in Figure 8-14, you can view the entire set of information for a specific sales order. This default format for the second-level drill-down (lowest level of detail in the AdventureWorks database for this information) is shown in Figure 8-15.

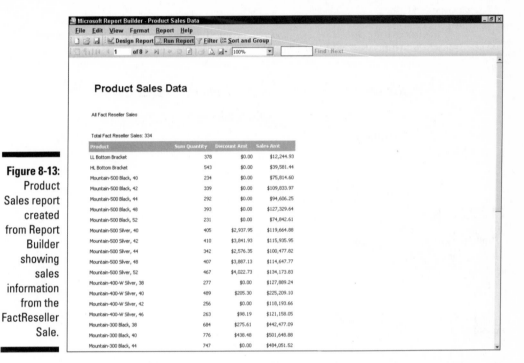

Figure 8-13:
Product
Sales report
created
from Report
Builder
showing
sales
information
from the
FactReseller
Sale.

Figure 8-14:
Drill-down
report from
Product
Sales
showing all
sales orders
for the
selected
product.

Through this drill-down analysis, you are navigating through the natural drill-down levels available from the FactInternetSale table, which does contain the sales order as an attribute of the table. Knowing how Report Builder provides drill-down navigation can give you some insight into how to design the data model to enable intuitive report navigation.

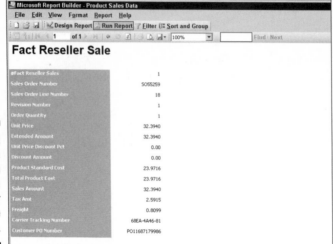

Figure 8-15:
Drill-down report from clicking on a sales order in the report.

Publishing Report Builder Reports to Report Manager

Publishing a Report Builder report to the Report Manager is simply a matter of saving the report to a specific folder. To publish a report to a folder on Report Manager, proceed as follows:

1. **On the Report Builder menu bar, choose File⇨Save.**

2. **Select the folder where you want the report to be stored.**

   This appears on the Save Report dialog box. You can select from all the folders that have been defined within Report Manager.

3. **Type a report name in the box provided.**

4. **Click the Save button.**

Report Builder is a work in progress. Microsoft acquired this technology in the summer of 2004 and there are still considerable features that can be included in this product. I look at Report Builder as a first version release that is only going to get better. You will undoubtedly see these features in future releases. This provides a great platform for adding more functionality and it is a great leverage strategy for Microsoft SQL Server 2005.

Part III
Publishing, Accessing, and Subscribing to Reports

The 5th Wave — By Rich Tennant

"The top line represents our revenue, the middle line is our inventory, and the bottom line shows the rate of my hair loss over the same period."

In this part . . .

*P*ublishing your report to an audience is an important final step in the report development process. Besides being a great tool for creating reports, *Microsoft Reporting Services 2005* makes publishing and distributing reports on the Web easy.

Many methods of report distribution exist, including printing, e-mailing, and running them on the Web on demand. There are so many formats that reports can be exported to that you can conceive of a single report serving so many more purposes than just the paper reports you may be used to. Making your work visible to so many more people is well within your reach.

Chapter 9

Publish or Perish —
Getting the Report Out

*Y*ou've got a report design that you're happy with. You've coddled it, refined it, massaged and aligned it, lined it up, and ironed it out. Now is the time to figure out how to publish the report, how to get it in the correct format for distribution, and how to put it on a directory for others to access. In this chapter, I tell you everything you need to know (and perhaps more) about how to deploy your report to the Report Server so that you can publish the report for other people to use. Publishing functionality requires the Report Manager, which is a great interface for accomplishing this as well as rendering reports in a variety of output formats.

Deploying Reports

Reporting Services is designed from the ground up to provide intuitive report access and distribution from the Web. After you complete the report design, you need to deploy the report to the Report Server. In this chapter, you begin from the point of finalizing and saving a report (I developed several reports in Chapters 5, 6, and 7). You can do this from either Report Designer (for people who develop in the Visual Studio environment) or from the Report Builder. In the following sections, I walk you through these two environments for deploying a report.

Deploying a report from Report Designer

Report Designer runs within the Visual Studio environment. If you used Report Designer to develop your report, you developed a reporting project and saved this project. Now it's time to deploy the report project content to your report server. Follow these steps to get the report to the Report Server:

1. **Check the project's properties to know where you are deploying the report.**

   This information is commonly referred to as *deployment properties*.

   a. To set the report project's deployment properties, start at the Solution Explorer window.

   b. Right-click the report project, and then click Properties from the menu that appears.

   You see the RS Demo Property Pages dialog box shown in Figure 9-1.

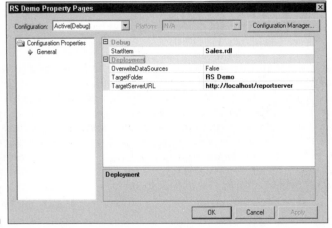

Figure 9-1:
A list of report project deployment properties.

2. **Click TargetServerURL and enter the URL to your report server:**

   ```
   http://localhost/reportserver
   ```

   where *localhost* is the name of your report server.

3. **Click TargetFolder and enter the name of your project.**

4. **Click OK.**

5. **Deploy the report to the Report Server by choosing Build⇨Deploy<Project Name>.**

Saving a report from Report Builder

If you created your report using Report Builder, you need to use a different technique to deploy a report to the Report Server. Follow these steps to get the report to the Report Server:

1. **From the Report Builder menu, choose File⇨Save Report.**

   A dialog box appears.

2. **Enter the report name.**

3. **Identify the folder in which this report should be saved, entering this information in the dialog box provided.**

Introducing the Report Manager

After you deploy the report to your report server, you can use the Report Manager for all other activities related to publishing your report. Report Manager is a Web-based tool used for viewing and managing reports. Report Manager is the user interface for the Report Server, and it comes with Reporting Services out of the box, meaning that you don't have to pay extra for it! This is a great tool for viewing and navigating to reports made available on the Report Server. It also has other capabilities that I explore in future chapters.

One of the great aspects of the Report Manager is that it leverages the capabilities of the client browser accessing it. Report Manager requires Internet Explorer 6.0 with Service Pack 1 (SP1) or Internet Explorer 5.5 with Service Pack 2 (SP2). You need to have scripting enabled within your browser to have this work. This is done by modifying your security settings for your IE browser through Tools⇨Internet Options⇨Security. On the Security tab, click the Custom Level tab. Make sure that Active Scripting is enabled.

Accessing the Report Manager

To start the Report Manager, specify the following Report Server home page URL in your browser:

```
http://WebServerName/reports
```

WebServerName is the name of the server on which Reporting Services is running. If Reporting Services is installed on your local computer, you can also start it from the Start⇨Programs menu from the SQL Server program group. This is the link to your Report Manager. Using either method of start-ing Report Manager, you see a listing of all report folders, data sources, and resources in the root of the Report Server, as shown in Figure 9-2. After you have access to the home page for Report Manager, you have access to pro-ject folders within Report Manager.

Figure 9-2:
The Report
Manager
startup
page, which
is the home
page for
your report
server.

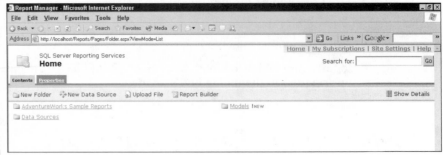

If the Report Server home page does not start, you might not have the Report Server service started and running on your server. In order to ensure that this is running, on your server machine, choose Start⇨Programs⇨ Administrative Tools⇨Services. Then scroll to the listing for Report Server and ensure that this service has started and is running. If this service is stopped, click the Start button. Then start your browser and navigate to the Report Server home page URL.

Uploading a report to Report Manager

From the list of folders in the home page for Report Manager, you can quickly navigate to the folder where you published your reports. After clicking that folder, look for the Upload File icon which will take you to the Upload File screen shown in Figure 9-3. This is yet another alternative for publishing a report to the Report Server. The Report Manager provides some great admin-istrative capabilities as well as a way to publish and render your reports. Your completed report design creates a Report Definition Language (RDL) file that represents a report. To upload the RDL file via Report Manager, follow these steps:

1. **Start from the Report Server home page (refer to Figure 9-2) in the folder in which you would like to upload a report.**

   You can create a new folder by clicking the New Folder icon.

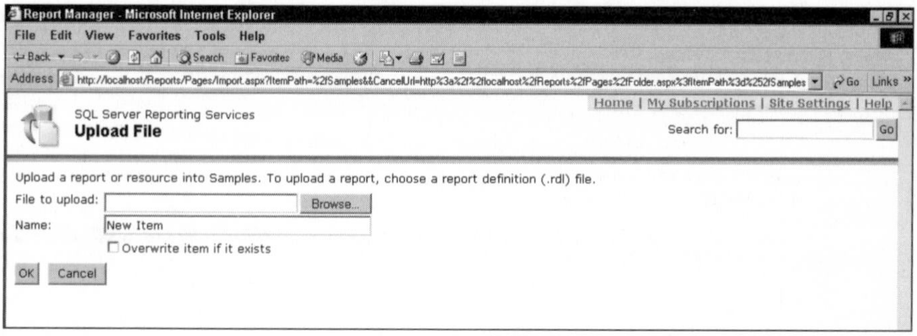

Figure 9-3:
Upload
File Web
page for
uploading a
file into
Report
Manager.

2. Complete the upload.

a. Enter or browse to the upload filename.

b. Enter the name of the item as it should appear in Report Manager.

c. Select the Overwrite Item If It Exists radio button if this entry should replace the existing entry for the name you entered.

d. Click OK.

Report Manager shows the folder contents, which includes the new report name that you just uploaded.

After you upload the report, you can begin interacting with the report.

Viewing a report in Report Manager

The Report Manager provides a report viewer capability. Viewing a report is as simple as clicking the report hyperlink from the appropriate folder. To begin, navigate to the report folder in Report Manager. You see any report content that you uploaded from RDLs that you created or Report Projects that you deployed. Your reports folder will look similar to what's shown in Figure 9-4.

Click the hyperlink to any of the reports in this folder to view a report. For example, I clicked the Product Line Sales link to bring up what you see in Figure 9-5.

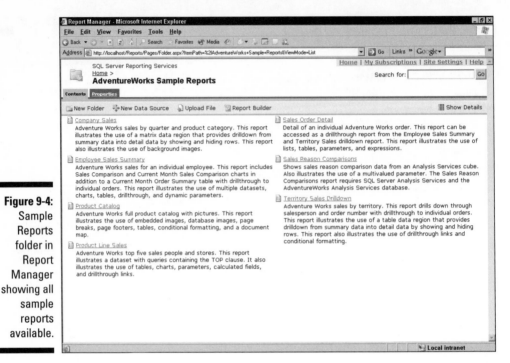

Figure 9-4:
Sample
Reports
folder in
Report
Manager
showing all
sample
reports
available.

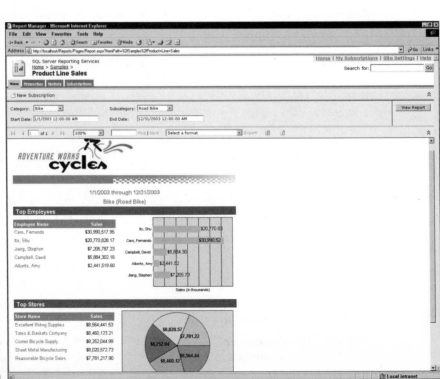

Figure 9-5:
Viewing a
report in
Report
Manager.

Getting Around in Report Manager

Report Manager offers an HTML viewer so that reports can be viewed in a Web format. The HTML viewer, which runs over a Web connection, contains many features for working with your reports, including the Report toolbar. After I walk you through the nuances of this toolbar, I show you how to use the Report Manager to print a report.

The Report toolbar

This HTML viewer includes a Report toolbar, a parameter section, and a Document Map. The Report toolbar (see Figure 9-6) is the uppermost control shown in the report preview screen.

Figure 9-6:
The Report
toolbar.

The Report toolbar provides some great features to work with your report. Here is a brief description of each of the features within the Report toolbar:

- ✔ **Scroll:** These controls look like your VCR buttons and enable you to scroll to the top, scroll to the bottom, page down, page up, and go to a page number within the report.

- ✔ **Zoom:** This control allows you to magnify or reduce the size of the page by adjusting the percentage displayed.

- ✔ **Search:** This control allows you to search for content. It is a text search control that scans the complete report data for matching text entered into this control. Click the Find button to begin the search and the Next button to find the next occurrence of the search term.

- ✔ **Export:** This drop-down list box lets you select the export format in which you would like to render your report. (See detailed coverage of this in the following section.)

- ✔ **Show/Hide Document Map:** For reports with Document Maps, this control allows you to show or hide this map.

  A Document Map acts as an outline for specific report values that are contained within the scope of the report.

- ✔ **Show/Hide Parameter Fields:** This control allows you to show or hide the report parameters for reports with parameters.

✔ **Refresh:** This control allows the user to refresh the data in the report. Cached reports are merely reloaded from the cache, but live reports are refreshed from the data source.

✔ **Help:** This control opens Help.

Printing a report

You can use the Report Manager to print a report. After you open the report within Report Manager, you can print the report directly by clicking the printer icon on the toolbar above the report.

Alternatively, you can export the report to another format that has more print options available. Exporting a report actually places the report in a different viewer. You can then leverage the print capabilities of the viewer to print your report. The export formats that have viewers to support printing are PDF, TIFF, and Web archive formats.

To use the Report Manager to print a report, proceed as follows:

1. **From Report Manager, navigate to the report that you want to print.**

2. **Open this report by clicking the link for the report.**

   This reveals a report (refer to Figure 9-5).

3. **Click the Export button on the Report toolbar.**

   You see the export drop-down list options, as shown in Figure 9-7.

Figure 9-7:
Report export options of the drop-down list box.

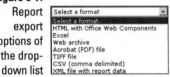

Select a format	▼
Select a format.
HTML with Office Web Components
Excel
Web archive
Acrobat (PDF) file
TIFF file
CSV (comma delimited)
XML file with report data

4. **Select the PDF, TIFF, or Web archive format.**

5. **Choose File⇨Print in the selected viewer to print to a specific printer.**

Exporting Reports to Other Formats

When you create a new report, you are creating it in a neutral format within your authoring tool. The preview facility merely renders the report in a panel where you can see relative formatting. You have explicit control over what format to render the information for distribution to the report consumer.

Reporting Services provides support for a number of rendering extensions. A *rendering extension* controls the type of document that is created when the report is processed. Report Manager displays the report in a neutral output format. The export option allows you to select an appropriate rendering format.

In future releases of Reporting Services, Microsoft allows any developer to create a custom rendering extension.

The rendering extensions that are supported include

- **PDF (Acrobat):** This extension produces reports in the Adobe PDF file format. This is the most popular document format on the Web because it's clean as well as easy to read, and it also has printing capabilities. It appears in the viewer that same way it would appear if printed. You must have Adobe Acrobat Reader to use this format.

    Pro: Neat format that allows the best print capability after distribution.

    Con: File sizes can be large.

- **TIFF File:** This extension produces the Tag Image File Format (TIFF), which takes the report definition and data and transforms it into this specific file that can be viewed. For some Microsoft Windows clients, this is the Windows Picture and Fax Viewer. Choose this format to a view a report in a page-oriented layout.

    Pro: This is the default format for rendering an image. This format has the best viewer for report printing.

    Con: File sizes can be large.

- **HTML with Office Web Components:** View the report using client-side Office Web Components to support charts or controls embedded in the report. You must have Office Web Components to use this format.

    Pro: This format will render a matrix as a pivot table with its ease of use in pivoting rows and columns to do analysis.

    Cons: Not available unless user has OWC. Also, this format does not render data regions, images, or rectangles within the matrix.

✔ **HTML:** HTML is, of course, the standard format for showing information in any browser. Because this is not in the list box for rendering extensions options in the Report toolbar, the only way to create this is via URL access, where you specifically name the format as HTML4.0 or HTML3.2. Any report can be rendered in either HTML 4.0 (dynamic HTML) or HTML 3.2 (for old browsers). The .NET Framework supporting Reporting Services functionality examines the user request, determines which browser is being used, and renders it into the appropriate format.

Pro: Good format for viewing in a Web-based portal.

Con: Requires URL access and not a standard export option from the Report Manager.

You can tell what type of HTML is being rendered by choosing the View⇨Source menu item in Internet Explorer and reading the header information at the top of the document.

✔ **Web Archive:** For HTML documents, this format encodes all images into the document. This is a MIME-encoded HTML format that keeps images and linked content together with a report. It increases the document size but more easily allows offline viewing of the content. In this manner, it supports disconnected viewing of the report HTML.

Pros: Can be sent as an attachment in an e-mail; captures all formatting on the Web page and is great for offline viewing.

Con: If the MHTML is a fragment, the HEAD, HTML, and BODY tags of the MHTML document are removed.

✔ **Excel:** This format is really an Excel-specific MHTML (MIME Encapsulation of Aggregate HTML). Excel is a common user interface for analysts and other professionals who use report information frequently.

Pro: Great for structured reports for users who naturally work in Excel.

Con: Is not well suited for free-form report layouts.

✔ **CSV:** Short for comma-separated values, this extension creates data fields separated by a delimiter (like a comma or tab or | character). The first row of the CSV result contains the field names for the data.

Pros: Can be imported directly into a database; good for symmetric data content.

Con: This format ignores page headers and footers, images, and lines.

✔ **XML File with Report Data:** This extension produces the eXtensible Markup Language (XML), which is a structured markup language. The XML file structure is becoming the lingua franca or common file format for file transfer applications. This is due to the structured nature of the file that supports easy transformation into other formats.

Pros: This format can be imported directly into a database; asymmetric data content is handled.

Con: Images and lines are ignored.

Software vendor SoftArtisans (`http://support.softartisans.com`) is developing renderers for Excel and Word that can be added as new export formats available in Reporting Services.

Design Considerations for Each Rendering Extension

Although the title of this section might make you think that this is advanced material, it's really fundamental. I remember the first time that I tried rendering a report in a PDF format. I was totally unimpressed with the fact that the page margins were set at seemingly unorthodox values so that half of the report content was abruptly cut off and shown on the next pages. After a few choice words and a few hours of research with the manuals, I was able to discover a straightforward solution to the problem: You need to be aware of the properties specific to each export format while you design and build your report so that the rendering extension is set up perfectly. Enough said; it's just that simple. I outline these considerations and properties in the following sections.

One other thing to keep in mind: You can access the report server by using a URL directly in the browser. URL requests can contain multiple parameters that are listed in any order. Parameters are separated by an ampersand (&), and name/value pairs are separated by an equal sign (=). For example, to render a report in a particular folder as a PDF would be:

```
http://<servername>/reportserver?/<Folder>/<reportname>&rs
        :Command
=Render &rs:format=PDF
```

Note: Any space characters in the URL string are replaced with the characters "%20," according to URL encoding standards. Similarly, a space character in the parameter portion of the URL is replaced with a plus character (+), and a semicolon in any portion of the string is replaced with the characters "%3A." Browsers should automatically perform the proper URL encoding.

Finally, to use URL access correctly, you must also know how to use parameters in the URL string. Parameter prefixes are used with URL parameters to access the report server. You can specify multiple parameter prefixes in a URL. For example:

✔ Prefix=rc means that you will supply a rendering extension with specific device information settings.

✔ Prefix=rs means that you will target the report server with specific parameters.

✔ Prefix=dsu means that you will specify a username with which to access a data source.

✔ Prefix=dsp means that you will specify a password with which to access a data source.

As an example, if you decide to hide the Report toolbar in the rendering of the previous report URL example, you would use the syntax:

```
http://<servername>/reportserver?/<Folder>/<reportname>&rs
         :Command
=Render &rs:format=PDF &rc:Toolbar=false
```

Notice that you just append to the end of the html string the text

```
"&rc:Toolbar=false"
```

where the `rc` prefix indicates you are providing the rendering extension with specific device information settings.

Setting up the PDF format

The Portable Document Format (PDF) is probably the most widely used document format on the Web. It can be printed and appears the same for all users because it's viewed in the free, downloadable Acrobat Reader viewer provided by Adobe (`www.adobe.com`). PDFs, however, cannot be edited by end users because their content is fixed. For documents that you do not wish to be altered — such as invoices, weekly sales summaries, or financial statements — PDF is a suitable format. PDFs also support the Document Map functionality, which allows you to define bookmarks within the report to quickly navigate to areas of the report by clicking links.

Make sure that you preview your report exported to PDF format before you distribute the report. The default settings might not render your content how you expect. You can adjust the Report Layout Properties in the Properties window within Visual Studio, as shown in Figure 9-8.

Check the settings on the Layout tab of the Report Properties dialog box. For example, to render the report in landscape mode for letter-size paper, set the PageWidth to 11 inches and the PageHeight to 8.5 inches. You can also adjust the margins (left, right, top, and bottom) so that you have more control over the screen real estate.

Check the Body properties of the report to make sure that pagination and column settings are correct. To access these properties, click in the body section of the report or select the Body object from the drop-down menu of objects in the Properties window in Visual Studio (see Figure 9-9).

Figure 9-8:
Report
Properties
window in
Report
Designer.

Figure 9-9:
Adjust the
report body
properties
within this
Properties
window in
Report
Designer.

For example, make sure that

```
Body:Width <= (Report:PageWidth - Report:LeftMargin -
          Report:RightMargin)
```

If you don't use this setting, extra blank pages appear in the exported report. You can also set the Columns properties in the Body Properties window to override the report's original settings. The Columns property refers to the number of columns for the body of the report, and the ColumnSpacing property references the column spacing for the report.

You can set other device settings as parameters in the URL to render the report to the browser. Use the `rc` prefix to interact with the report output format. For example, if you would like to render only page 5 of a multi-page report, use

```
&rc:StartPage=5&rc:EndPage=5
```

Table 9-1 shows other settings that you have access to for PDF rendering.

Table 9-1	PDF Rendering Settings
Settings	**Explanation**
StartPage	The first page of the report to render. Default value is 1. A value of 0 indicates that all pages are rendered.
EndPage	The last page of the report to render. Default value is the value for StartPage.
DpiX	The resolution of the output device in x-direction. Default value is 300.
DpiY	The resolution of the output device in y-direction. Default value is 300.

Setting up the TIFF format

The TIFF (Tag Image File Format) export format renders a report in a page-oriented format. TIFFs are widely used to store document images. If you need to store documents in a document management system, this is an appropriate format to use. Transferring TIFFs of reports into a document management system allows you to remove historical snapshots from the Report Server and also take advantage of common document management features, such as indexing. The TIFF viewer allows you to print locally, just like the PDF viewer. Refer to the earlier section on PDF for the properties to consider setting while you design the report so that you get the report that you expect. Table 9-2 shows other settings that you have access to for TIFF rendering.

Table 9-2	TIFF Rendering Settings
Setting	*Value*
StartPage	The first page of the report to render. A value of 0 indicates that all pages are rendered. Default value is 1.
EndPage	The last page of the report to render. Default value is the value for StartPage.
OutputFormat	One of the Graphics Device Interface- (GDI) supported output formats: BMP, EMF, GIF, JPEG, PNG, or TIFF.
ColorDepth	The pixel depth of the color range supported by the image output. Valid values are 1, 4, 8, 24, and 32. Default value is 24. ColorDepth is supported only for TIFF rendering and is otherwise ignored by the Report Server for other image output formats.
DpiX	The resolution of the output device in x-direction. Default value is 96.
DpiY	The resolution of the output device in y-direction. Default value is 96.

Setting up the HTML format

The HTML export format is great for interactive reports to users in Web sites, intranets, and portals. Whether you select HTML3.2, HTML4.0, or HTMLOWC, you have the same interactivity that you would when you access the report within Reporting Services. The key difference is that you do not have access to the Report Manager menu of options nor access to the Report Properties, History, and Subscription capabilities. HTML rendering also supports dynamic visibility so that you can drill down to detailed information. Additionally, it supports Document Maps for easier navigation.

Office Web Components (OWC) allow even greater capability. If your Web browser cannot load OWC, you are prompted with an option to download OWC or to view the report without the control. The download location of OWC is a Microsoft Web site. If your report includes a matrix (see Chapter 5 for what a matrix is), the matrix is rendered in an OWC PivotTable control. However, PivotTable controls cannot display all items that can appear in a matrix. A matrix that includes the following does not display as a pivot table:

✔ Any data region (table, chart, matrix, or list)

✔ Image

✔ Subreport

✔ More than one group expression in a grouping

✔ Static columns and static rows

✔ Dynamic columns or rows nested inside static columns or rows

✔ Data size larger than 262,144 rows

Tables, charts, and lists are not rendered in OWC. OWC is a set of ActiveX controls. Keep these points in mind:

✔ If OWC is rendered on the client, the Web browser used to display reports must support ActiveX.

✔ The device information setting for ActiveX controls must not be set to False.

✔ OWC must be on the client, or the client must be able to download OWC.

The Find function on the Report toolbar searches the report only. It does not search the contents of an OWC control.

Table 9-3 shows other settings that you have access to for HTML rendering.

Table 9-3	HTML Rendering Settings
Setting	*Value*
BookmarkID	The bookmark ID to jump to in the report.
DocMap	Indicates whether to show or hide the report Document Map. Default value is True.
DocMapID	The Document Map ID to scroll to in the report.
EndFind	The number of the last page to use in the search. For example, a value of 5 indicates that the last page to be searched is page 5 of the report. The default value is the number of the current page. Use this setting in conjunction with the StartFind setting.
FallbackPage	The number of the page to display if a search or a Document Map selection fails. Default value is the number of the current page.
FindString	The text to search for in the report. Default value of this parameter is an empty string.
GetImage	Gets a particular icon for the HTML viewer user interface.
Icon	The icon of a particular rendering extension.

Setting	Value
JavaScript	Indicates whether JavaScript is supported in the rendered report.
LinkTarget	The target for hyperlinks in the report. You can target a window or frame by providing the name of the window (`LinkTarget=window_name`), or you can target a new window (`LinkTarget=_blank`). Other valid target names include `_self`, `_parent`, and `_top`.
Parameters	Indicates whether to show or hide the parameters area of the toolbar. If you set this parameter to a value of True, the parameters area of the toolbar is displayed. Default value is True.
Section	The page number of the report to render. A value of 0 indicates that all sections of the report are rendered. Default value is 1.
StartFind	The number of the page on which to begin the search. The default value is the number of the current page. Use this setting in conjunction with the EndFind setting.
StreamRoot	The path used for prefixing the value of the `src` attribute of the `IMG` element in the HTML report returned by the report server. By default, the report server provides the path. You can use this setting to specify a root path for the images in a report (for example, `http://myserver/resources/companyimages`).
StyleStream	Indicates whether styles and scripts are created as a separate stream instead of in the document. The default value is False.
Toolbar	Indicates whether to show or hide the toolbar. If the value of this parameter is False, all remaining options (except the Document Map) are ignored. If you omit this parameter, the toolbar is automatically displayed for rendering formats that support it. Default of this parameter is True. The Report Viewer toolbar is rendered when you use URL access to render a report.
Type	The short name of the browser type (for example, *IE5*) as defined in `browscap.ini`.
Zoom	The report zoom value as an integer percentage or a string constant. Standard string values include Page Width and Whole Page. This parameter is ignored by versions of Microsoft Internet Explorer earlier than Internet Explorer 5.0 and all non-Microsoft browsers. Default value of this parameter is 100.

Setting up the Web Archive (MHTML) format

The MHTML (MIME Encapsulation of Aggregate HTML) export format encapsulates all externally referenced information, such as images, into one document. This format is great for including report content inline within e-mail messages without having to attach another document to your message. Consider using this format for sending out subscriptions. Users are able to view reports through e-mail without opening an attachment.

Not all e-mail clients support this format.

Table 9-4 shows other settings that you have access to for MHTML rendering.

Table 9-4	MHTML Rendering Settings
Setting	**Value**
JavaScript	Indicates whether JavaScript is supported in the rendered report.
MHTMLFragment	Indicates whether an MHTML fragment is created in place of a full MHTML document. An MHTML fragment includes the report content in a `TABLE` element and omits the `HTML` and `BODY` elements. Default value is False.

Setting up the Excel format

Excel is a common format for many users, especially financial users. This format enables further analysis on the exported information. The Excel exporting capability is more sophisticated than that for other competing reporting tools. By using table and matrix controls in your reports, you can create report layouts that are very compatible with Excel spreadsheets. Table 9-5 shows other settings that you have access to for Excel rendering.

Table 9-5	Excel Rendering Settings
Setting	**Value**
OmitDocumentMap	Indicates whether to omit the Document Map for reports that support it. Default value is False.
OmitFormulas	Indicates whether to omit formulas from the rendered report. Default value is False.

Setting	Value
RemoveSpace	Indicates whether to omit rows or columns that do not contain data and are smaller than the given size. Use this setting to remove extra rows or columns that do not contain report items. You must include an integer or decimal value followed by `in` (for example, `0.5in`). Default value is 0.125in.

Setting up the CSV format

The CSV (comma-separated values) format takes the report definition and converts it into a flat file. This is not suitable for reading, but it is suitable for data interchange. Mainframe computer-based systems might be good at parsing and consuming flat files. CSV is also a common format for applications to import data. For example, Excel or Access support the CSV format for both import and export.

Table 9-6 shows other settings that you can use for CSV rendering.

Table 9-6	CSV Rendering Settings
Setting	**Value**
Extension	The file extension to put on the result. Default value is .CSV.
FieldDelimiter	The delimiter string to put in the result. Default value is a comma (,).
NoHeader	Indicates whether the header row is excluded from the output. Default value is False.
Qualifier	The qualifier string to put around results that contain the field delimiter or record delimiter. If the results contain the qualifier, the qualifier is repeated. The Qualifier setting must be different from the FieldDelimiter and RecordDelimiter settings. Default value is a quotation mark (").
RecordDelimiter	The record delimiter to put at the end of each record. Default value is <cr><lf>.
SuppressLineBreaks	Indicates whether line breaks are removed from the data included in the output. Default value is False. If the value is True, the FieldDelimiter, RecordDelimiter, and Qualifier settings cannot be a space character.

Setting up the XML format

The XML (eXtensible Markup Language) format renders a report in XML and opens the XML in a browser. This format is designed specifically for the exchange of information, similar to the CSV format. (See the preceding section.) As more applications are being written to receive XML format, this format enables more options for how information can be exchanged between applications. Table 9-7 shows other settings that you can use for XML rendering.

Table 9-7	XML Rendering Settings
Setting	**Value**
XSLT	The path in the report server namespace of an XSLT (XSL Transformation) to apply to the XML file: for example, `/Transforms/myxslt`. The XSL file must be a published resource on the report server, and you must access it through a report server item path. The value of this setting is applied after any XSLT that is specified in the report. If the XSLT setting is applied, the OmitSchema setting is ignored.
MIMEType	The Multipurpose Internet Mail Extensions (MIME) type of the XML file.
UseFormattedValues	Indicates whether to render the formatted value of a text box when generating the XML data. A value of False indicates that the underlying value of the text box is used.
Indented	Indicates whether to generate indented XML. Default value of False generates non-indented, compressed XML.
OmitSchema	Indicates whether to omit the schema name from the XML and to omit an XML Schema Definition (XSD). Default value is False.
Encoding	One of the character encoding schemas: ASCII, UTF-8, or Unicode. Default value is UTF-8.
FileExtension	The file extension to use for the generated file.
Schema	Indicates whether the XSD is rendered or whether the actual XML data is rendered. A value of True indicates that an XSD is rendered.

Archiving Reports

Although there are no specific features in Reporting Services for archiving reports, you might require an electronic copy of a report that is identical to a report that you distributed. This section provides two options for accomplishing this: saving reports and using reporting history.

Saving reports to create an archive

If you have a small number of reports to archive, consider saving a report as a file in a fixed format. Earlier in this chapter, I cover the page formats available to you (such as PDF or TIFF). You can export to these formats and save to a protected shared directory on the network. Alternatively, you can upload a PDF or TIFF report that you saved as a resource item if you want to keep all copies of a report, regardless of the format, in the report server database.

Saving report history

Report history is a collection of previously run copies of a report. You can create a report history to maintain a record of a report over time. Think of a report history as an extension of a report: If you move a report, its report history moves with it. However, if you modify a report or delete its data source, existing report history is preserved.

Report history is available to all users who have access to the report. You cannot selectively enable nor disable report history for a subset of users.

Report history consists of report snapshots, instances of a report that contain layout information, and data obtained from an external data source at specific points in time. Each snapshot in report history captures a report as it was when the snapshot was created. If you change the layout or delete the data source, snapshots in report history remain intact.

When you create a report snapshot, a few types of information are stored along with the report snapshot in the report server database:

- **The result set,** or data in the report.
- **The underlying report definition,** as it exists at the time the snapshot was created. Changing a report layout subsequent to a snapshot does not affect the snapshot.

✔ **Parameter values** that are used to obtain or filter the result set.

✔ **Embedded resources,** such as images.

External resources that are linked to a report are not stored with the report snapshot.

To create a snapshot in report history, the report must be able to run *unattended*. This means that the report must use stored credentials or no credentials at all. Furthermore, if the report uses parameters, you must specify default values to use when the report runs. You can specify stored credentials and parameter values for the report in the Data Source and Parameters Property pages, respectively. This will be covered in detail in Chapter 12.

Here's how you create report history:

1. **In the Report Manager, select the report for which you want to create history and view the report.**

2. **Click the Properties tab for that report.**

3. **Click the History link in the left margin.**

   This provides a view similar to Figure 9-10. Make sure that the Allow History to Be Created Manually check box is marked.

Figure 9-10:
History properties page in Report Manager.

```
Report Manager - Microsoft Internet Explorer                                    _ 8 X
File   Edit   View   Favorites   Tools   Help
← Back  ▼  →  ▼  ⊗  ⊠  ⌂   ⊗Search  ⊛Favorites  ⊗Media  ⊗  ⊠▼ ⊕ ⊠ ⊠
Address  http://localhost/Reports/Pages/Report.aspx?ItemPath=%2fSamples%2fProduct+Line+Sales&SelectedTabId=PropertiesTab&SelectedSubTabId=HistoryPropertiesTab   ▼  ⊘Go   Links »
              SQL Server Reporting Services              Home | My Subscriptions | Site Settings | Help
  ⊞         Home > Samples >
              Product Line Sales                          Search for:                        Go
  View  Properties  History  Subscriptions
   General        ☑ Allow history to be created manually
   Parameters     ☐ Store all report execution snapshots in history
   Data Sources   ☐ Use the following schedule to add snapshots to report history.
   Execution         ⦿ Report-specific schedule    Configure
   History           ○ Shared schedule             No shared schedules ▼
   Security
                  Select the number of snapshots to keep:
                     ○ Use default setting
                     ○ Keep an unlimited number of snapshots in report history
                     ⦿ Limit the copies of report history:  2
                  Apply
```

4. **After you set your report history settings, select the History tab.**

   This displays all history for the report.

5. **To create an instance of report history, click the New Snapshot icon.**

   This produces a link that you can click to retrieve the report history, as shown in Figure 9-11.

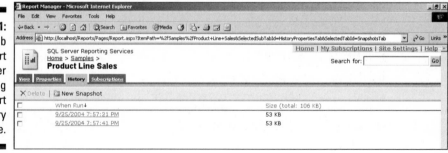

Figure 9-11:
History tab
in Report
Manager
showing
report
history
available.

Out of site: Server-level properties

Notice a reference to the default settings when you are at the History properties page. You can set properties at the server level or for individual reports that become defaults in other property pages within Report Manager. To get to the Site Setting page from the Report Manager, simply click the Site Settings hyperlink on the top right. The Site Settings page displays, as shown in Figure 9-12.

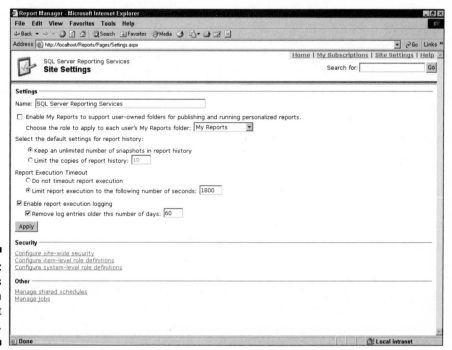

Figure 9-12:
Site Settings
page in
Report
Manager.

Server properties for report history are located on the Site Settings page. These settings determine default values that set an upper limit on how many snapshots can be stored in report history. The values apply to all reports that use default settings.

Report-specific properties for report history are located on the History properties page of each report. Properties that you set at the report level override the default values that are set at the server level. In addition to report history storage limits, you can set properties that determine how report history is created.

You can then back up the report server database and store the backup in a safe location for future use. All report history (along with reports, shared data source items, folders, subscriptions, and shared schedules) is stored in the report server database. You can create a backup to maintain a permanent copy of report history and metadata, such as subscription information that indicates the recipients of a report.

Chapter 10

Executing and Accessing Reports on Demand

*P*eople can be downright demanding about having current information at their fingertips. Can you imagine big decisions that are made without key information because it's not immediately available?

When the data is available you want to get it to users in an efficient manner. That's what this chapter is all about. I consider the options you have in executing reports. Reports sent on demand show information as it exists in the data sources at the time of execution. On-demand reports aren't stored anywhere because they execute at the time you seek the information. You can specify that a report be stored in some manner so that the processing time is greatly reduced. In this chapter, I describe how these report properties can be specified, and I offer several scenarios of executing reports.

Understanding the Pull Model

The *pull model* describes the way you access on demand reports within Reporting Services. In the pull model, a user specifies when he wants the report run and how it is managed in memory. Other users will be exploring the same reports. This leads to topics on how the report server manages versions of reports served up to users.

Types of reports: published, intermediate, and rendered

In Chapter 9, I discuss how publishing a report consists of posting the RDL to the report server. *Execution* of a report is the process of turning a published report into a rendered report. The execution of a report is a two-phased process:

1. Execution of a report takes a published report and performs required data retrieval and processing. In this initial phase, the report server combines the layout definition with the source data to produce an intermediate format of the report.

2. Delivery of a report to end users in a format they can understand consists of the report server sending the intermediate report to a rendering extension where it is rendered in a specific format. Using Report Manager and the SQL Server Management Studio, you can manipulate settings to specify whether steps occur at the time of the user browsing the report or before. I cover that in more detail later in this chapter.

Executing with the latest data

If you specify that a report should execute on demand, it means that the report should always execute with the most up-to-date data. This is helpful when you're reporting from a dynamic source data that is frequently updated.

To tell Reporting Services to execute a report on demand, after running a report in the Report Manager, click the Properties tab and then click the execution properties link in the left margin. The Execution Properties page appears, as shown in Figure 10-1.

You can perform the same process within the SQL Server Management Studio by following these steps:

1. **Connect to the report server within the Management Studio by clicking Start and choosing SQL Server Management Studio from the pop-up menu.**

2. **Open the Reports folders within the Home folder to see specific reports.**

   You can expand each folder to navigate to the report of interest.

3. **Show the Properties of the report by right-clicking the report and selecting the Properties menu item from the pop-up menu, as shown in Figure 10-2.**

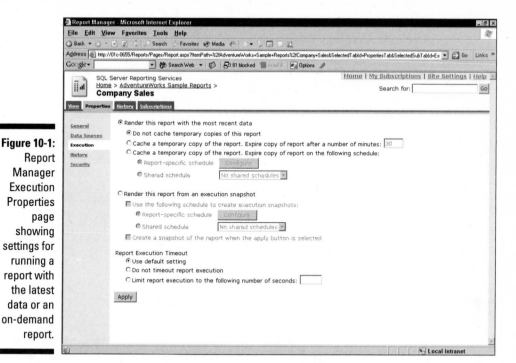

Figure 10-1:
Report
Manager
Execution
Properties
page
showing
settings for
running a
report with
the latest
data or an
on-demand
report.

Figure 10-2:
SQL Server
Manage-
ment Studio
showing
how to get
to the
properties
of any
report in the
report
server
(current
connection
shown).

4. Click Execution.

The Execution Properties page appears, as shown in Figure 10-3.

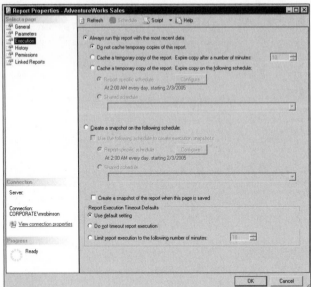

Figure 10-3:
Report
Properties
dialog box in
SQL Server
Manage-
ment Studio
showing the
properties
for a
particular
report and
the on
demand
setting.

Note: For an on-demand report, the report server follows the same process for each user who opens the report. So if ten users execute the report, there will be ten queries issued to the source database.

Considering the execution properties in Figures 10-1 and 10-3, notice that you have options to control report execution time limits. You can apply the default (which is set in Site Settings), you can limit execution to a certain number of seconds, or you can specify that there are no limits. This can be helpful to limit runaway queries on the report server and better provide responsiveness to your user population.

Saving Your Cache

The report server can store a copy of a processed report in memory and return that copy when a user opens the report. This report server memory is called *cache*. The process of storing a copy of the report in this manner is called *caching*.

Caching can shorten the time required to retrieve a report if the report is large or is accessed frequently. The contents of the cache are volatile and can change as reports are added, replaced, or removed. If the server is rebooted, all cached instances are reinstated when the report server Web service comes back online.

Reporting Services provides you with capabilities for managing how the cache works with your reported information. Upon each request for a specific report, Reporting Services leaves the report in the cache during the user's computer session.

In the following sections, I explore some of the forms of cache.

Working with the session cache

For every user and client application running on the server, there is a unique session. Reporting Services stores temporary files to support user sessions and report processing. These files are cached for internal use and to support a consistent viewing experience during a single browser session.

When you browse a report, it's added to the session cache, which is stored in ReportServerTempDB. The lifetime of a session starts when a user navigates to a browser and selects a report to view. The session ends when the user closes the browser.

During the time the report is in session, the underlying report stored in the ReportServer database can change. The administrator could be making some changes to the report, or the report could even be moved or deleted. If the report is in an active session, it is not affected by changes made to the underlying report. You do have a choice to manually refresh the report while you are viewing it to see report or data changes.

Creating with the cached instance

To enhance the performance of report execution, you can enable caching of the report to create a cached instance. A cached instance of a report is based on the intermediate format of a report. The report server caches one instance of a report based on the report name.

When a user requests a report, the report is available in cache for other users who request the same report. So, if a hundred users open the report, the request from the first user results in report processing. The report is subsequently cached, and the remaining 99 users view the report that is retrieved from cache.

To create a cached instance of a report, you would specify this behavior as part of the Report Properties page in the Report Manager. You have the option to expire the copy of the cached instance after a certain time interval or based on a schedule.

Another way to specify that a report be cached on the Report Server is by using the Report Properties window in the SQL Server Management Studio.

Note: Not all reports can be cached. If a report includes user-dependent data, prompts users for credentials, or uses Windows Authentication, it cannot be cached.

Considering query parameters with cached instance

Because a report can contain different data based on query parameters, multiple versions of the report may be cached at any given time. Suppose you have a parameter-based report that takes a product category as a parameter value. If another user specifies another category other than the one you selected, another cached copy of the report is created.

The first user who runs the report with a unique product category creates a cached report that contains data for that category. Subsequent users who request a report using the same product category get the cached copy. Each time a user specifies a different parameter value for this report, a new cached instance will be created if one does not already exist.

Considering filters with cached instance

Unlike query parameters, which are applied when a cached instance is created, filters are applied to the cached instance each time the report is browsed. The filtered cached instance is not available to other users. It is recreated on demand for each subsequent user who requests it. For different report parameter values, the current cached instance is filtered.

Because other users cannot access a filtered cached instance produced by other users, the performance advantage is not as great as cached instances resulting from query parameter selections that produce new cached instances available to all users.

Configuring a cached instance

To complete the configuration settings required to create a cached instance, you need to configure the data source settings to use stored credentials. You must do this in addition to setting the report properties, or Reporting Services will return an error.

To store the login credentials securely in the ReportServer database, follow these steps:

1. **Select a report.**

   You can use either Report Manager or SQL Server Management Studio to do this.

2. **Change the data source properties in the Report Manager settings. For cached instances, the credentials for the report must be specified. Within the Report Manager, proceed as follows:**

   a. View the report by clicking on the report in its folder.

   b. Click on the Properties tab and select the Data Sources option on the left panel of the Web page.

   c. Click the Credentials Stored Securely in the Report Server radio button and specify the user ID and password required to run the report.

   d. Click the Apply button at the bottom of the Web page. These selections are shown in Figure 10-4.

Figure 10-4:
Data
Sources
Properties
window in
Report
Manager
showing the
settings
required for
creating a
cached
instance of
the report.

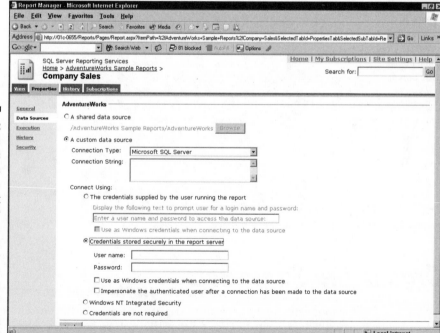

3. **Alternatively to Step 2, you can change the data source properties in the SQL Server Management Studio. For cached instances, the credentials for the report must be specified. This is an alternative way to do what is described in Step 2. Within the Management Studio, proceed as follows:**

   a. Select the data source for the report in question and right-click to select the Properties menu item on the pop-up menu.

   b. In the Data Source Properties window, select the Connection option in the left margin.

   c. Click the Credentials Stored Securely in the Report Server radio button and specify the user ID and password required to run the report.

   d. Click OK at the bottom of the Web page. These selections are shown in Figure 10-5.

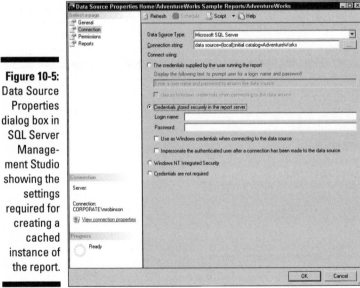

Figure 10-5:
Data Source
Properties
dialog box in
SQL Server
Manage-
ment Studio
showing the
settings
required for
creating a
cached
instance of
the report.

Organizing Snapshots

For the moment when you want to capture a report in the current state, you can actually take snapshots of reports that can be accessed later. This section will show you how to create snapshots and how to manage them.

Creating a snapshot

A *report snapshot* is a report that contains layout information and a dataset that was retrieved at a specific point in time. Unlike on-demand reports, which get up-to-date query results when you select them, you can request report snapshots, at which time the report server creates an intermediate report (data and report) and stores it as a snapshot in the ReportServer database. When you request a report, Reporting Services merely retrieves and renders the snapshot. You then see the data and layout that were current for the report at the time the snapshot was created.

Report snapshots are not saved in a particular rendered format. Instead, report snapshots are rendered in the requested viewing format (such as HTML) only when a user or an application requests it. Deferred rendering makes a snapshot portable.

Report snapshots have many purposes. Here are a few:

- Capturing report data at a specific point in time. Sometimes this is referred to as keeping a report history. By creating a series of report snapshots, you can build a history of a report that shows how data changes over time. Report snapshots are used in report histories because they contain the essential elements of a report (query results and layout).

- Providing multiple people with access to the same data at the same time. For example, finance and marketing and sales want the monthly financial reports when they are produced. You can specify that financial reports be set up as snapshots that execute each month.

- Preventing arbitrary report execution. For example, an invoice report requested during business hours slows overall system performance. In order to alleviate the system load and avoid inconsistent results, execute the invoice report as a snapshot every evening.

- Controlling long-running reports with queries that take a long time. For example, the weekly sales report runs a long time and each salesman wants to know results the first thing Monday morning. You can specify that the weekly sales report run every Sunday evening so it is ready to go on Monday morning.

You can schedule snapshots to be generated at specific times (for example, during off-peak hours when system resources are not in heavy use). You can also schedule how often the snapshot is refreshed. For example, if you want to refresh the data on a daily basis, you can schedule a snapshot to be generated every night at 11 p.m. Finally, you can create a snapshot immediately at any time.

You need to utilize the Execution Properties page to control the creation of snapshots. Figure 10-1 shows that you have an option to render any report as an execution snapshot. You have a choice to create the snapshot on a schedule or create the snapshot immediately when you click the Apply button to apply the selected execution properties.

Refreshing a report snapshot replaces the previous version. If you want to keep all copies of a report snapshot, set report history Properties to Copy Report Execution Snapshots to Report History.

Using query parameters in your snapshots

When you create snapshots for reports that have query parameters, the query parameters are applied at the time the snapshot is created. This means that the snapshot contains a restricted dataset. The query parameters used to create the snapshot are the default parameter values that have been set in Report Manager or in SQL Server Management Studio. This is illustrated in Figure 10-6 (for Report Manager) and Figure 10-7 (for Management Studio).

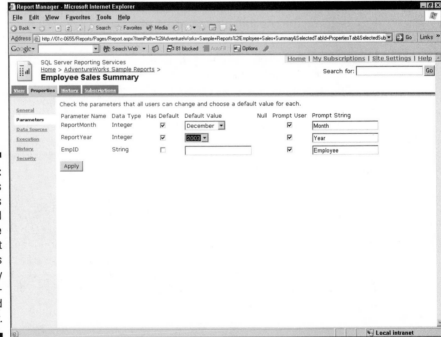

Figure 10-6: Parameters Properties page used to set the default parameters for any parameter-based report.

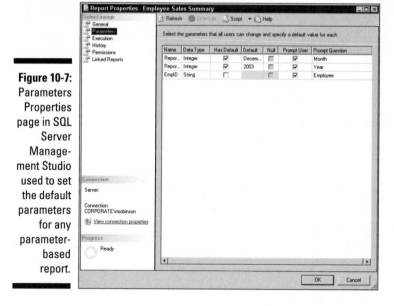

Figure 10-7:
Parameters
Properties
page in SQL
Server
Manage-
ment Studio
used to set
the default
parameters
for any
parameter-
based
report.

For example, if you want to provide one version of your company's monthly financial report and don't want users to change the report's view, use the query parameters month and year and then create a snapshot that freezes the data. Then each user would see the same view of the report until the snapshot is refreshed.

If you need to create a report snapshot for another set of parameter values, you can use the technique of *linked* reports. A linked report is a report with another name that is based on another report whose unique difference is the default parameters used to create the report. You can link a report in Report Manager by navigating to the General Properties page and clicking the Create Linked Report button (see Figure 10-8).

Not all parameters may be visible in the report at run time. A report author, report server administrator, or content manager can specify which values to use and then hide the input fields on the report. You can use the Parameters Properties page shown in Figure 10-6 or Figure 10-7. Simply uncheck the check boxes in the Prompt User column to hide this parameter from your user. As long as the parameter has a default value, the report can be run with the default parameter value (if you so choose) without a selection from your user.

Figure 10-8:
General
Properties
page in
Report
Manager
enabling
you to
change a
report
description,
move it, edit
it, or create
a linked
report with
different
default
values
of the
parameters.

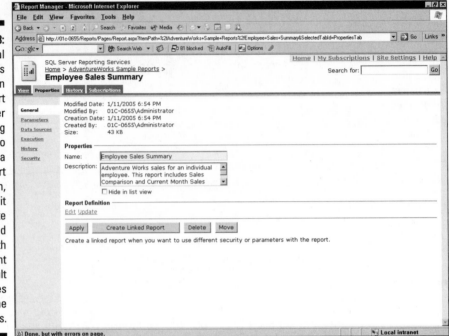

Using filters in your snapshots

Filters offer greater flexibility because changing the filter values only filters the current snapshot of a particular report. The flexibility provided with using filters is that you are filtering a single snapshot rather than creating multiple snapshots from which to select as you change filters.

For example, if you want to provide to users monthly financial information that pertains only to their departments, you can create a snapshot for all departments and add a report filter based on department to filter the snapshot down to the department you are interested in.

Configuration guidelines on snapshots

Snapshots can be executed manually, according to a report-specific schedule, or on a shared schedule that is used for multiple reports. Only a single snapshot is executes at a time. Also, like cached instances, snapshots require that data source credentials be stored securely in the report server.

Creating a Historical Perspective

Report history is a collection of previously run copies of a report. You can use report history to maintain a record of a report over time. Report history can be saved only for those reports that query a data source using a single set of credentials (either stored credentials or credentials used for unattended report execution) that are available to all users who run a report. As a result, report history is not intended for confidential or personal information.

Keep in mind that report history is an extension of a report, so if you move a report, its report history moves with it. The report and its history are attached at the hip. What happens to report history if you modify a report or delete its data source? It turns out that report history is preserved in the format and with the data sources that were in place when the report history was created.

Creating report history

You must save the report as a snapshot to create *report history*. Report history is stored in the ReportServer database. Report history enables you to keep a record of all snapshots that are generated over time.

There are many methods to request that a report history instance be created. The most popular way to do this is to add a snapshot to report history on the creation of the snapshot. To do this, follow these steps:

1. **Ensure that the credentials are stored securely in the ReportServer database.**

   You can do this in the Data Sources Properties page (refer to Figure 10-4).

2. **Execute a report normally.**

   You can do this either in Report Manager or the SQL Server Management Studio.

3. **In Report Manager, click the Properties tab and then click on the History view (see Figure 10-9).**

   You have many ways to create report history. You can specify that you want to create report history manually, or that each execution automatically creates history, or that you want to create history according to a schedule. You also can select the number of snapshots to keep.

4. **If you want to create report history according to a regular schedule, click the Configure button.**

   The Schedule details page, shown in Figure 10-10, appears. You can enter the start and end dates as well as the frequency of snapshot production.

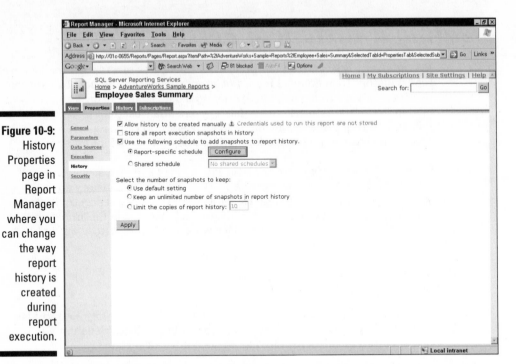

Figure 10-9:
History
Properties
page in
Report
Manager
where you
can change
the way
report
history is
created
during
report
execution.

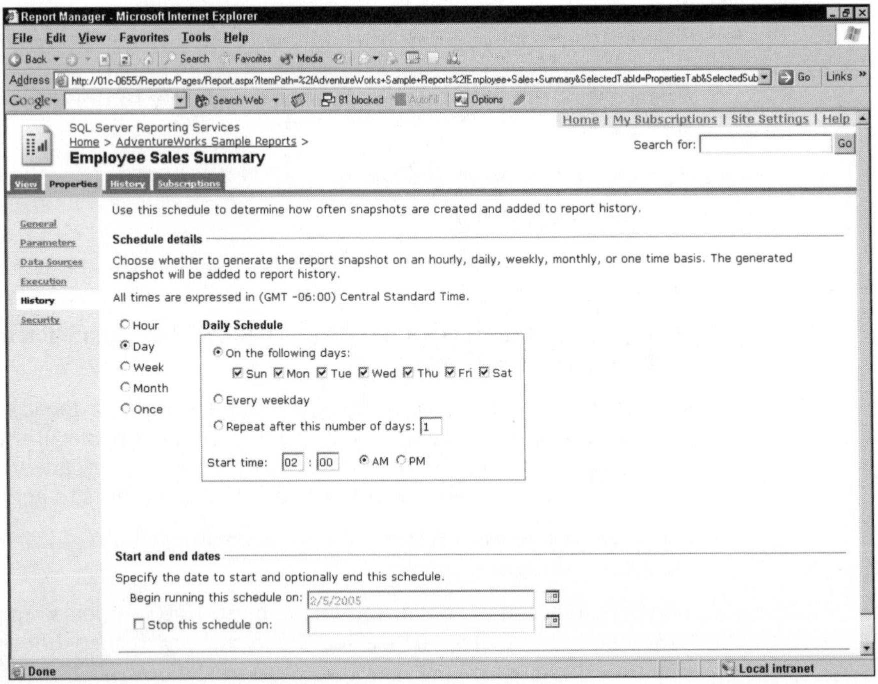

Figure 10-10:
Schedule
Details page
from the
History
Properties
page in
Report
Manager
where you
can set your
schedule for
creating
report
history.

Alternatively, you can use the SQL Server Management Studio and right-click on the report of interest to bring up the Report properties page and select the options on the History view, as shown in Figure 10-11.

Figure 10-11:
The History
tab of the
Report
Properties
dialog box
in the
Manage-
ment Studio
provides
options for
creating
report his-
tory during
report
execution.

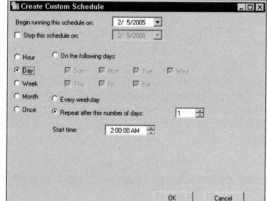

Creating snapshots in report history

To create a snapshot in report history, the report must be able to run unat-tended. That means the report must use stored credentials or no credentials at all. In addition to this, if the report uses parameters, you must specify the default values to use when the report runs.

You may ask what information is stored in the ReportServer database for any snapshot. Well, the result set, the underlying report definition, and the param-eter values used to create the snapshot, as well as any embedded images, are stored in the database. External resources that are linked to a report are not stored with the report snapshot.

You can add snapshots to report history through a schedule or by creating snapshots manually. To create a snapshot manually using Report Manager, follow these steps:

1. **Ensure that the credentials are stored securely in the ReportServer database.**

   You can do this in the Data Sources Properties page (refer to Figure 10-4).

2. **Execute a report normally.**

3. **Click the History tab in Report Manager.**

   The History page appears, as shown in Figure 10-12.

4. **Click the New Snapshot icon.**

   The snapshots currently in report history appear, as shown in Figure 10-13.

If you're using SQL Server Management Studio to administer your reports, expand the folder navigation tool for report server to locate the report of interest. Then expand the explorer to show the History folder. In this folder, all report history snapshots available will be listed, as shown in Figure 10-14.

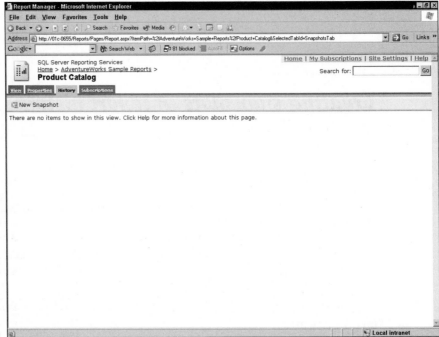

Figure 10-12:
History tab in the Report Manager where you can create a snapshot.

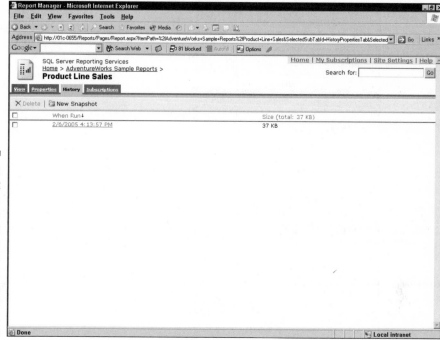

Figure 10-13:
Snapshot History page in the Report Manager showing all snapshots available in report history.

Modifying properties and deleting report history

After you create report snapshots and report history, you cannot modify them. However, you can modify the properties and settings that affect report history. In some cases, modifying report history limits can cause deletion of report snapshots. Report history is also deleted when you delete a report. Report history can be deleted in any of the following ways:

✔ **Manually delete snapshots.** You can delete snapshots by using the History page. Select the check box next to the snapshot that you want to delete, and then click Delete.

✔ **Lower the report history limit to reduce the number of snapshots that are stored.** If report history uses the default report history limit, lowering the value for the server reduces report history to the new limit. If report history uses a report-specific setting, lowering that value reduces excess report history for that report. When the report server deletes report history to conform to lowered limits, older reports are deleted first.

Note: To delete snapshots, you must access report history for each report individually. You cannot delete all report history stored on a report server in a bulk operation.

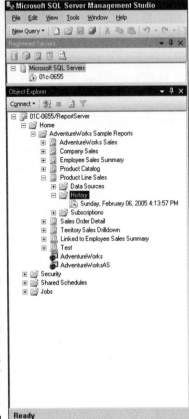

Figure 10-14:
View of
report
history in
the SQL
Server
Manage-
ment Studio.

Rendering history as a URL

You can render a specific snapshot in report history through a URL reference. This is useful when you need to view snapshots separately or send them to a recipient through e-mail. To do this, you must access the report through its URL and attach a rendering parameter that identifies the snapshot you want. The following example URL illustrates the syntax:

```
http://<servername>/ReportServer?/My%20Reports/
employee%20Directory&rs:Command=Render
&rs:historyID=03/20/2005%2011:02:06
```

The `rs:historyID` rendering parameter specifies that the specific report history snapshot be retrieved from report history. The value indicates which report snapshot to return. The date is in the format MM-DD-YYYY%THH:MM:SS

Summary of Report Execution Methods

In this chapter, I describe the options for executing and accessing reports in Reporting Services. Only on-demand reports do not require credentials to be stored securely on the report server. On-demand reports are created when the report is opened. Cached instances are created the first time the report is opened. In contrast, snapshots and report history are created sometime in advance of the actual viewing of the report, either according to a schedule or when the report is executed for the first time. Therefore, you must specify the credentials to properly run the report so that the server can automatically create the snapshot or report history.

For all report execution strategies, it is the intermediate report that is stored in the report server. For cached instances, only one version of the report exists for any combination of parameter values, and the cached instance expires. Report history will allow multiple versions of the report to be stored up to a limit that you can impose on report history. On demand reports are temporary and exist only in the session cache. Finally, report snapshots are replaced according to a schedule or when you decide to create another snapshot to replace the current one.

Chapter 11

Delivering Your Reports

. . . .

In This Chapter

▶ Automating report delivery through subscriptions

▶ Delivery methods: E-mail, fileshare, and null

▶ Specifying execution conditions and parameters for subscriptions

▶ Creating standard subscriptions

▶ Creating data driven subscriptions

▶ Common scenarios for using subscriptions

▶ Maintaining your subscriptions

▶ Configuring subscriptions

. . . .

*W*ould you like to open your e-mail tomorrow and find all the information you need to start your day right out of the chute? This is the vision of delivering your reports by subscription. Just as you can subscribe to magazines, you can sign up to receive reports with the latest data on the topics that inquiring minds need.

Subscriptions are the means of delivering reports automatically to users via e-mail or writing files to a shared directory. Subscriptions are great for getting the right information to the right people at the right time. Subscriptions are the other model for reporting — the push model where reports are pushed to users based on conditions and schedules.

In this chapter, I cover the nuances of subscriptions and show how you can use them to establish sophisticated report delivery solutions where users can access a specific file or receive them automatically in the mail. Reporting solution administrators may want to read closely because they're typically the people implementing subscriptions for their business users.

Automating the Delivery of Reports

With Reporting Services, you can request delivery of a report at a specific time or in response to a specific event. This is called *subscribing* to a report. You can also define the way you want the report presented to you. For example, the *push* method involves sending a report to a user on a scheduled or time event basis.

In Chapter 10, I describe how on-demand reporting requires that you actively select the report each time you want to view it. Subscriptions, on the other hand, are used to schedule and then automate the delivery of the most up-to-date report. When you subscribe to reports, you specify how the reports will be distributed to you.

A subscription consists of a report that can run unattended (that is, a report whose data source uses stored credentials or requires no credentials) as well as a delivery method (for example, e-mail) and settings for the mode of delivery (such as an e-mail address or a file location). The conditions for processing the subscription are either time-based or when the data changes. For example, you may want to run a particular report every Sunday at 11:00 p.m. CST. If, however, the report runs as a snapshot, you can specify that the subscription is "executed" whenever the snapshot is refreshed.

Subscriptions are executed according to *schedules*. You control when and how frequently the subscription will be processed. You may want a weekly report at a time when the data is expected to be updated in the source database. Reporting Services gives you a lot of flexibility in how you schedule your subscriptions.

For reports that require parameters (see Chapter 7 for more on parameters), the parameter values need to be specified. Because a subscription is typically owned by a specific user, the parameter values that are specified will vary across subscriptions. As an example, sales managers for different divisions will use parameters that return data for their division. All parameters must have a value explicitly defined, or have a valid default value.

Subscription information is stored with individual reports in a report server database. You cannot manage subscriptions separately from the report to which they are associated. You cannot search for subscriptions by name, and you cannot search for subscriptions based on trigger information, status information, and so forth.

Note: Unlike reports that are hosted and managed by a report server, reports that are delivered to a file are static documents. The file type is the application format that corresponds to the rendering format selected for the subscription. Interactive features that are defined for the report are represented as static elements in a file. A matrix report shows the top-level view of the report; you cannot expand rows and columns to view supporting data. If the report includes charts, the default presentation is used. If the report links through to another report, the link is rendered as static text.

It's important to remember that the report is delivered as a static file. If the report includes interactive features (for example, links to additional rows and columns), those features will not be available after delivery from a subscription.

Accessing subscriptions

The most logical place to start in creating a subscription is the Subscriptions tab for a report in Report Manager or the Subscription folder within a specific report within the SQL Server Management Studio. Figures 11-1 and 11-2 show how this looks in Report Manager and SQL Server Management Studio, respectively.

Figure 11-1: Report Manager Subscriptions tab showing the two buttons for creating subscriptions.

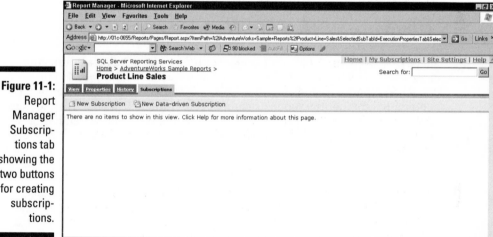

Figure 11-2: SQL Server Management Studio showing the menu options for subscriptions within a specific report.

For reports that support subscriptions, you can click the New Subscription button on the toolbar immediately after you execute a report.

Getting Familiar with Subscription Components

Subscriptions use delivery extensions to distribute a report in a specific way and format. When you create a subscription, you can choose one of the available delivery extensions to determine how the report is delivered. Reporting Services includes support for e-mail delivery and delivery to a shared folder. An additional delivery method is called the null delivery provider. This method is not available to users. Null delivery is used by administrators to improve report server performance by preloading the cache. In the following sections, I describe the two main delivery methods in more detail.

Working with e-mail delivery

Report Server e-mail delivery can deliver reports by sending a notification and a hyperlink to the generated report or by sending an embedded or attached report. For embedded reports, the rendering format and browser determine whether the report is embedded or attached. If your browser supports HTML 4.0 and MHTML, and you choose the Web archive rendering format, the report is encapsulated as part of the message. All other rendering formats (CSV, PDF, and so on) deliver reports as attachments. You can disable attachment and embedding in the configuration file.

Reporting Services does not check the size of the attachment or message before sending the report. If the attachment or message exceeds the maximum limit allowed by your mail server, the report will not be delivered. Use the URL or notification delivery options if the report is large.

Also, the Report Server does not validate e-mail addresses or obtain e-mail addresses from an e-mail server. You must know in advance which e-mail addresses you want to use. By default, you can e-mail reports to any valid e-mail account within or outside of your organization. Configuration settings can be used, however, to restrict e-mail delivery to hosts that you identify by name. If you want to guarantee that e-mailed reports are delivered only to e-mail accounts of the host computer of your organization, you can specify the host name in a configuration setting. You can specify additional hosts if you want to support e-mail delivery to people that are not members of your organization.

The most effective way to control report distribution is to configure a report server to send only a Report Server URL. Report Server uses Windows Authentication and a role-based authorization model to control access to a report. If a user accidentally receives through e-mail a report that he or she is not authorized to view, the report server will not display the report.

Working with fileshare delivery

Reporting Services includes a file share delivery extension so that you can deliver a report to a folder. The file share delivery extension is available by default and requires no additional configuration. File share delivery is used to send a report to a file on a hard drive. After the file is saved to disk, it is no longer subject to the role-based security model that the report server uses to control the user.

You must specify an existing folder as the target folder. The report server does not create folders on the file system. The file share location must be specified in Uniform Naming Convention (UNC) format that includes the computer's network name. Do not include trailing backslashes. The following example illustrates a UNC path:

```
\\localhost\SQLServer2005\ReportDirectory
```

Reports can be rendered in a variety of file formats, such as HTML or Excel. The rendering format that you select for the subscription is used to save the report in a specific file format. For example, choosing Excel saves the report as a Microsoft Excel file. Although you can choose from any supported rendering format, some formats work better than others when rendering to a file.

Selecting a rendering format

When you create a subscription, you can choose which rendering format to use with the delivered report. If you are using file share or e-mail delivery, choose a format that delivers the report in a single file, where all images and related content are included in the report. Suitable formats include Web archive, Acrobat (PDF), TIFF, and Excel.

Avoid the formats HTML 3.2, HTML 4.0, and HTML with Office Web Components. If your report includes images, the HTML3.0 and 4.0 formats will not include them in the file. HTML with Office Web Components is not recommended because it is designed for user interaction, which cannot be supported in a report that is delivered as a static file. Note that when you use Report Manager to create a standard subscription, HTML formats are excluded automatically.

Specifying execution conditions

You can specify how you want your subscription to be run. For e-mail and fileshare delivery methods, this is the execution schedule of the subscription. Reporting Services provides a schedule creation and maintenance capability. You can schedule a report to run on any frequency between start and end date ranges. You can create shared schedules that many subscriptions can utilize if that is a requirement. These schedules can be managed, paused, and resumed centrally. You can also create a report-specific schedule. These schedules can be used when shared schedules don't provide the frequency or recurrence needed. Note that report-specific schedules cannot be centrally managed.

Note: Schedule processing is based on the local time of the Report Server owning the schedule, with the time format following the Windows standard.

Specifying execution parameters

For reports containing parameters, specify parameters to use for the report generated by this subscription. The parameters can be different from those used to run the report on demand or in other scheduled operations. You can only specify parameters in a subscription to reports that run on demand. If you are subscribing to a report containing parameters that runs as a report execution snapshot, your subscription must use the parameter values defined for the snapshot.

Creating Standard Subscriptions

Two types of subscriptions exist: standard, which are end-user driven, and data-driven, which are driven by the administrator. I talk in the following sections about how you can use these two subscription types.

Creating a standard subscription

Standard subscriptions are created and managed by individual users. A standard subscription delivers one rendered report to one destination. The destination can be an e-mail address or a shared file directory commonly called a *fileshare*. For standard subscriptions for report snapshots (see Chapter 10), you can select a null delivery method to provide a way for the system to create pre-cached reports for a variety of parameters to improve processing performance. For each standard subscription, there is one set of report presentation options, delivery options, and report parameters.

To create a standard subscription, follow these steps:

1. **Click the New Subscription button.**

   The New Subscription page appears, prompting you to select a method of delivery (see Figure 11-3).

2. **Select a method of delivery.**

   You have choices of e-mail or file share delivery (or Null delivery for report snapshots). E-mail delivers an e-mail, whereas file share deposits a file on a shared directory. Choose one of the options in the following list based on the delivery method of the subscription:

   • **Complete the delivery specification for the e-mail subscription.** The e-mail delivery subscription page is shown in Figure 11-4. You will note that you need to specify the key information for an e-mail (which user, who is copied or blind copied, the text of the e-mail, and how the file is added to the message).

   • **Complete the delivery specification for a Fileshare subscription.** The fileshare subscription page is shown in Figure 11-5. Options you need to define include the filename, the path at which the file should be saved, the credentials used to access the file, and any overwrite options.

   • **Complete the delivery specification for a NULL delivery.** This amounts to caching a snapshot.

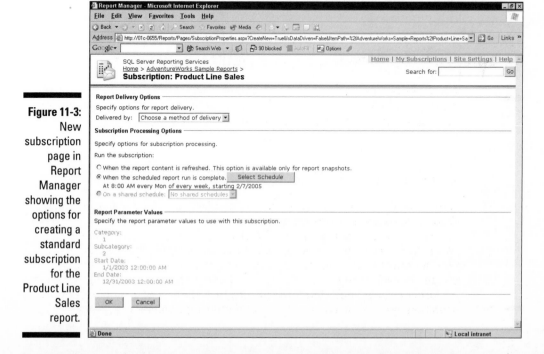

Figure 11-3: New subscription page in Report Manager showing the options for creating a standard subscription for the Product Line Sales report.

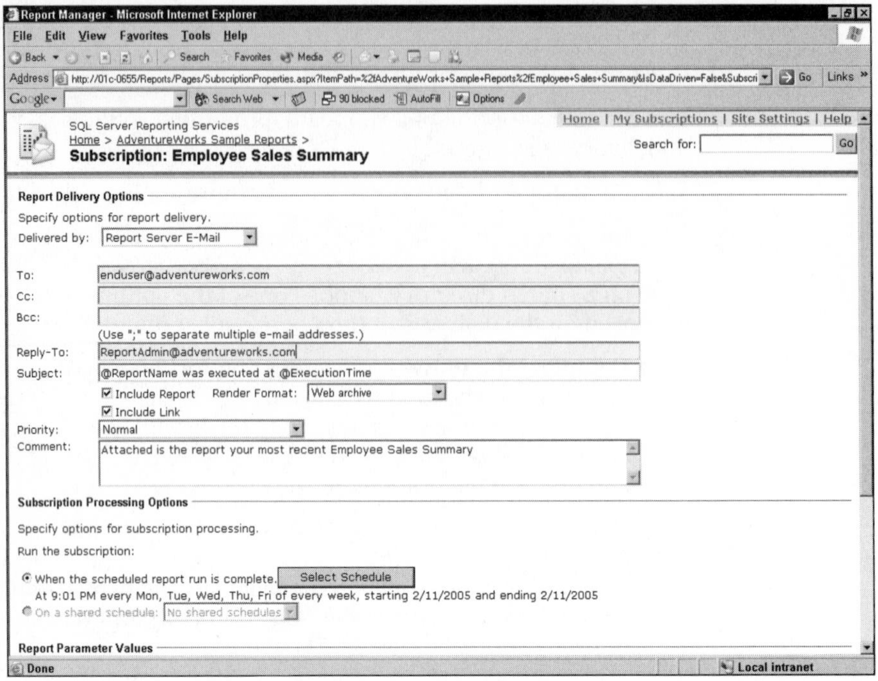

Figure 11-4:
New
Subscription
page in
Report
Manager to
define a
Report
Server
E-mail to be
delivered for
the
Employee
Sales
Summary
report.

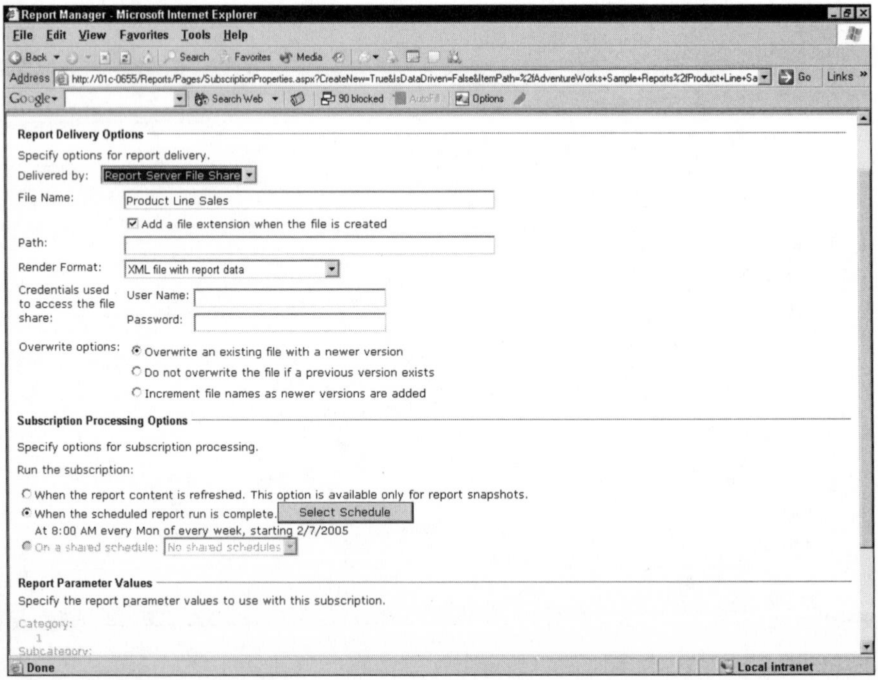

Figure 11-5:
New
Subscription
page in
Report
Manager to
define a
Report
Server
Fileshare to
be delivered
for the
report.

3. **Select the subscription processing option.**

   You can choose between when the report is refreshed (for snapshots only) and processing according to a schedule that you either create or specify a shared schedule.

   a. **For snapshots when report content is refreshed.** If you prefer this method, click the radio button to indicate the that you want to run the subscription when the report content is refreshed. This subscription processing option is available only for snapshots that are already associated with an update schedule.

   b. **Scheduled Subscription.** If you prefer this method, click the radio button to creating a schedule; then click the Select Schedule button and define a specific delivery schedule. This will bring up the Schedule page as shown in Figure 11-6. The schedule used to update a report snapshot determines when your subscription is processed. For reports that run only on demand or from cache, schedules are the only option for subscription definition.

4. **Specify any parameters required by the report.**

   For reports with parameters, you must specify the values to provide the parameters when the subscription executes this report.

Figure 11-6: Subscription schedule page for specifying on what regular basis a subscription report will run.

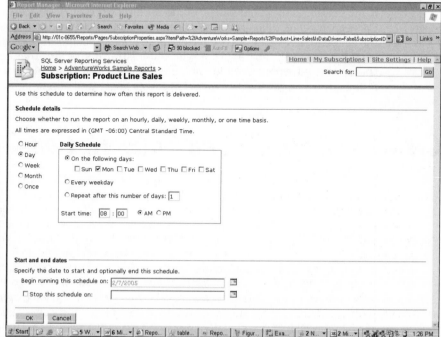

5. Click OK.

You get a subscription and return to the Subscriptions tab with your subscription listed on the page, as shown in Figure 11-7.

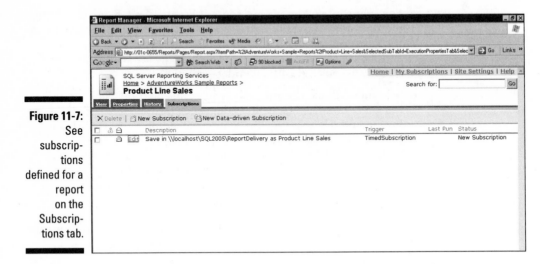

Figure 11-7:
See subscriptions defined for a report on the Subscriptions tab.

If you create a scheduled subscription for a report that runs as a snapshot, the report will be delivered at the time you specify in the subscription, but the snapshot delivered will be based on the most recent refresh of the snapshot. For example, if a Report Server administrator specifies that a report snapshot is refreshed at midnight, subscriptions that schedule that same report for 6 a.m. receive the report that was generated at midnight.

Creating Data-Driven Subscriptions

You may notice the Data-driven Subscription button on the toolbar. Data-driven subscriptions deliver a single report in many rendered formats to many destinations. They are dynamic in that the values used for specifying presentation, delivery, and parameter values are retrieved at run time from a data source, and then used to complete subscription processing. You can use data-driven subscriptions if you have a very large recipient list (for example, all employees in an organization), or if you want to vary report output for each recipient. Data-driven subscriptions generate subscription data from a data source. To use data-driven subscriptions, you must have expertise in building queries and an understanding of how parameters are used. Report server administrators typically create and manage these subscriptions.

A data-driven subscription provides a way to deliver reports to a list of sub-scribers that is determined when the subscription executes. You can use data-driven subscriptions to customize report output for each recipient of a delivery.

A data-driven subscription gets some settings from a data source at run time, and other settings from the subscription definition. Fixed aspects of a data-driven subscription include the report that is delivered, the delivery extension, connection information to an external data source that contains subscriber data, and a query. Dynamic settings of the subscription are obtained from the row set produced by the query that includes the subscriber list and user-specific delivery extension preferences or parameter values. This data is retrieved from a data source each time the subscription is processed.

To create a data-driven subscription, follow these steps:

1. **In Report Manager, navigate to the report for which you want to create a subscription and then click the report to open it.**

2. **Click the Subscriptions tab.**

   If the report you selected uses a data source configured to use stored credentials or one requiring no credentials you will see a New Data Driven Subscription button. Click this button.

3. **Select the method of delivery.**

   You can select from three options: Report Server File Share, Report Server E-mail, or Null Delivery Provider, as shown in Figure 11-8.

4. **Click Next.**

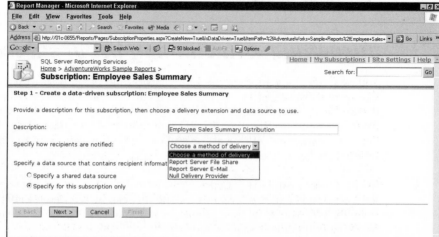

Figure 11-8:
Create a
data-driven
subscription
page.

5. **Select a shared data source to use with the report. Expand the folders to find the shared data source appropriate to your report.**

For the Employee Sales Summary report, you would select the shared data source AdventureWorks, as shown in Figure 11-9.

6. **Click Next.**

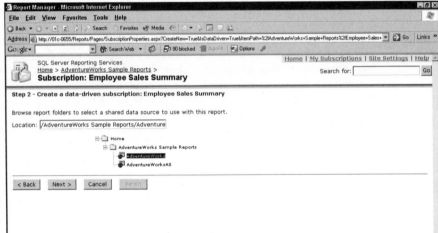

Figure 11-9: Navigating to a folder in Report Manager containing the shared data source for a report.

7. **Create a data-driven subscription.**

Based upon the selection of the method of delivery, you will have a different sequence of steps to complete the data-driven subscription setup. I consider each option in the sections that follow.

Supporting a fluctuating list of subscribers

You can effectively support the wide distribution of a report with a fluctuating list of subscribers. For example, you can use data-driven subscriptions to distribute a report throughout a large organization where subscribers vary from one month to the next, distribute a report on retirement benefits to all employees who are retiring at the end of the month, or use other criteria that determines group membership from an existing set of users.

In order to best support data-driven subscriptions for a changing subscriber list, you should consider creating a table that can be queried for particular subscriptions to provide all the parameters required to get your information in the hands of the people who need it quickly when the information is available. By creating a table-driven approach to specifying your subscriptions, you can merely edit (or modify) the subscriptions information table to make any changes in the process rather than editing the subscription definition. Furthermore, this is the only technique for truly specifying multiple parameter values across a diverse group of users requiring unique views (and even rendering formats) of a single report.

As an example, a data-driven subscription that will send an e-mail on a schedule basis to a variety of users requires the following information: To e-mail address, CC address(es), BCC address(es), ReplyTo address, include the report flag, rendering format specification, priority, subject text, comment text, include a link flag, send e-mail to a user alias flag and the parameters appropriate to the report. One approach is to create a table for which you can populate all these parameters to ensure good maintainability. The create table statement could be as follows:

```
CREATE TABLE [SubscriptionEMailReport]
( [ReportID] [smallint]
  [To] [nvarchar] (50) NULL,
  [CC] [nvarchar] (50) NULL,
  [BCC] [nvarchar] (50) NULL,
  [ReplyTo] [nvarchar] (50) NULL,
  [IncludeReport] [bit] NULL ,
  [RenderFormat] [nvarchar] (50) NULL,
  [Priority] [bit] NULL,
  [SUBJECT] [nvarchar] (50) NULL,
  [COMMENT] [nvarchar] (50) NULL,
  [IncludeLink] [bit] NULL ,
  [ReportYear] [nvarchar] (50) NULL,
  [ReportMonth] [nvarchar] (50) NULL,
  [EmpID] [nvarchar] (10) NULL
)
```

This provides the delivery extension methods for all reports like the Employee Sales Summary report where there are three parameters (ReportYear, ReportMonth, and EmpID). Then in the data-driven subscription process for a report with ReportID of 10, you can simply use the SQL statement:

```
SELECT *
FROM SubscriptionEmailReport
WHERE ReportID = 10
```

For a fileshare delivery, the expected columns are FILENAME, FILEEXTN, PATH, RENDER_FORMAT, USERNAME, PASSWORD, WRITEMODE, and the parameter values. The Create Table statement for this delivery method would be as follows:

```
CREATE TABLE [SubscriptionFileshareReport]
( [ReportID] [smallint]
  [Filename] [nvarchar] (50) NULL,
  [FileExt] [nvarchar] (5) NULL,
  [Path] [nvarchar] (50) NULL,
  [RenderFormat] [nvarchar] (50) NULL,
  [UserName] [nvarchar] (50) NULL,
  [Password] [nvarchar] (50) NULL,
  [Writemode] [bit]  NULL,
  [ReportYear] [nvarchar] (50) NULL,
  [ReportMonth] [nvarchar] (50) NULL,
  [EmpID] [nvarchar] (10) NULL
)
```

Then in the data-driven subscription process 3 for a report with a ReportID of 20, you can simply use the SQL statement:

```
SELECT *
FROM SubscriptionFileshareReport
WHERE ReportID = 20
```

Fileshare delivery of data-driven subscriptions

Beginning with Step 5 of the data driven subscription process, I review the steps to complete a fileshare subscription delivery. For this method, the server will refresh the report located somewhere on the network directory that is usually referenced by some intranet page hyperlink to display the report. Follow these steps:

1. **Define the query for the fileshare delivery method.**

   You should enter a query that will return all the key fields required for the remaining specification of the subscription. If you use the definitions outlined in the previous section, you can enter the query

   ```
   SELECT * FROM SubscriptionFileshareReport WHERE
          ReportID = 20.
   ```

   This is shown in Figure 11-10. Then click Next.

2. **Define delivery settings.**

   Configure the properties required by the fileshare data driven specification as shown in Figure 11-11. All the values you need to provide come from the database and should be available from the drop-down list box for each field you need to specify. Then click Next.

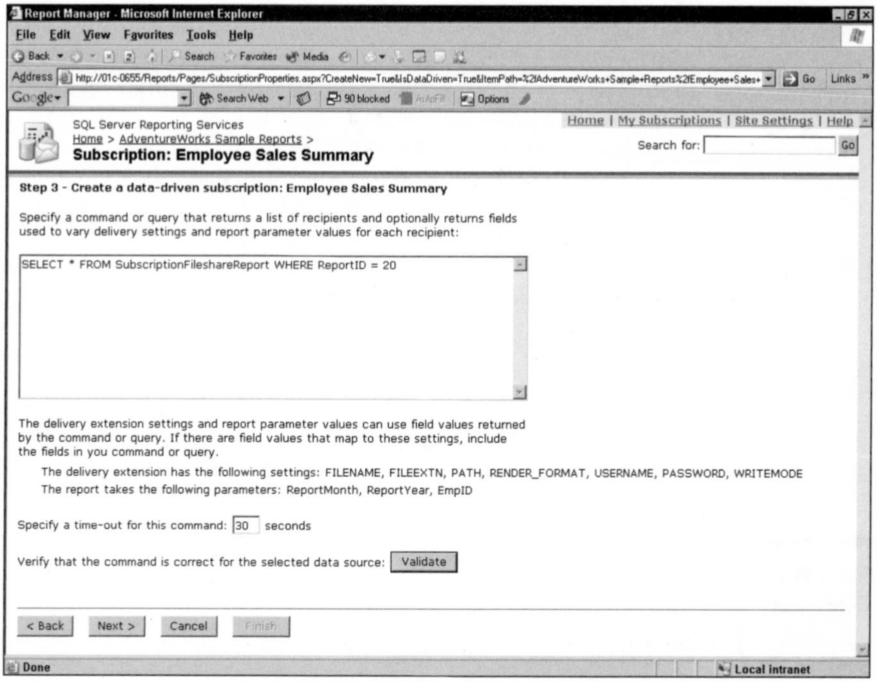

Figure 11-10:
Defining the
query to
return the
required
fields to
complete
the
specifica-
tion for the
fileshare
delivery
data-driven
subscrip-
tion.

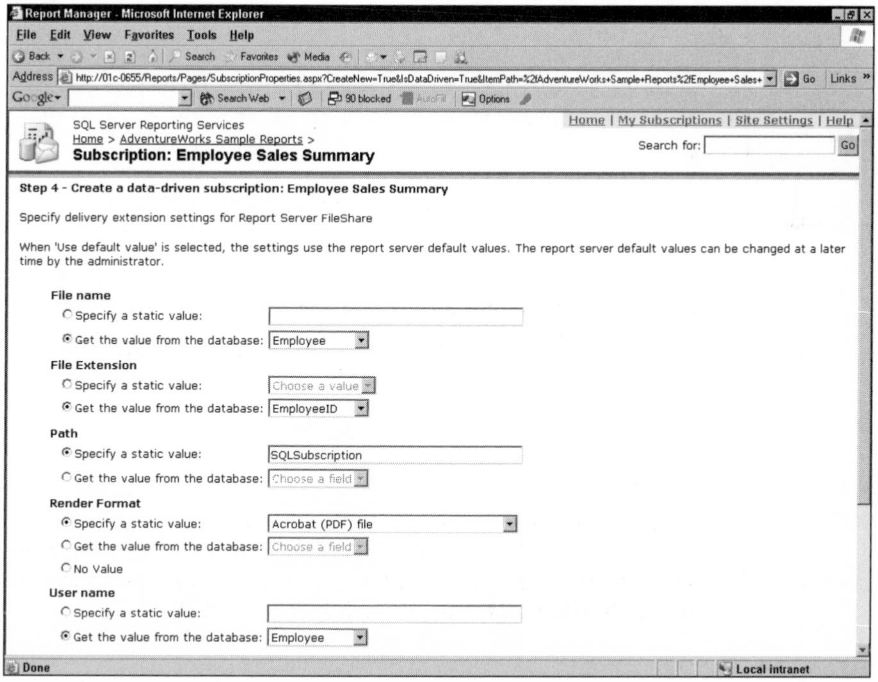

Figure 11-11:
Defining the
delivering
settings to
complete
the speci-
fication for
the fileshare
delivery
data-driven
subscrip-
tion.

3. Specify parameters values.

You can indicate that parameters are determined by either specifying a static value or as values from a database. For either choice, you are presented with a drop-down list of static values as well as a drop-down list to select the default value option for each parameter you would like to use for the data-driven subscription. You can select which method to use and which static value or database value to use. This is shown in Figure 11-12. Then click Next.

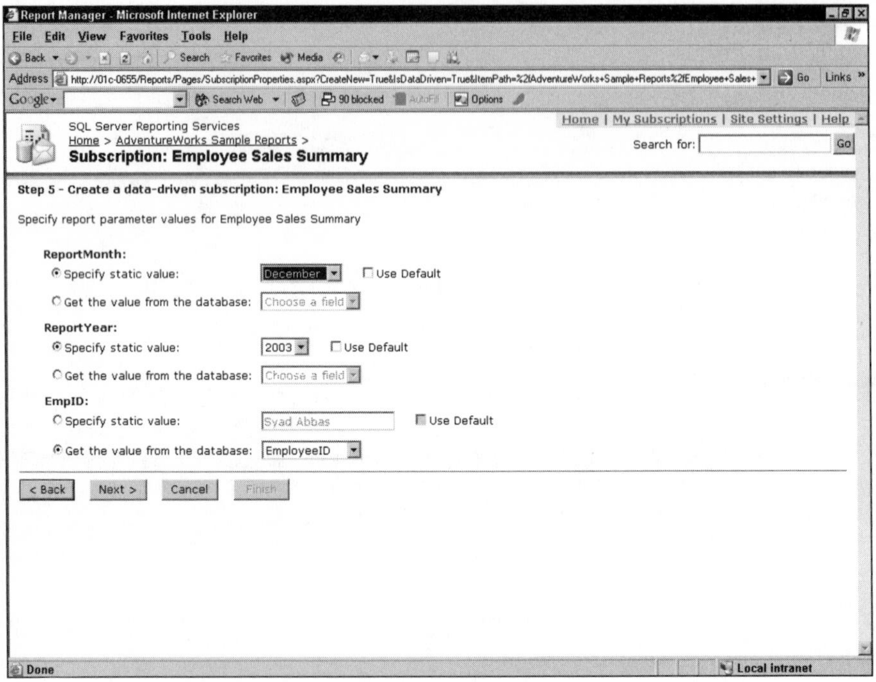

Figure 11-12: Defining the delivery settings to complete the specification for the fileshare delivery data-driven subscription.

4. Define the schedule and select Recipients from the options.

You can select whether you want to notify recipients when the report data is updated on the report server or on a schedule created for this subscription. These options are shown in Figure 11-13.

5. Click Finish.

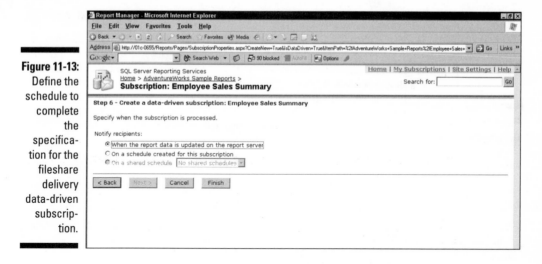

Figure 11-13:
Define the
schedule to
complete
the
specifica-
tion for the
fileshare
delivery
data-driven
subscrip-
tion.

E-mail delivery of data-driven subscriptions

Beginning with Step 5 of the data-driven subscription process, I review the steps to complete an e-mail delivery of a subscription.

1. **Define the query for the e-mail delivery method.**

   You should enter a query that will return all the key fields required for the remaining specification of the subscription. If you use the definitions outlined in an earlier section, you can enter the query

   ```
   SELECT * FROM SubscriptionEMailReport WHERE ReportID =
        10.
   ```

   This is shown in Figure 11-14. Then click Next.

2. **Define delivery settings.**

   Configure the properties required by the fileshare data-driven specifica-tion. All the values you need to provide come from the database and should be available from the drop-down list box for each field you need to specify. Then click Next.

3. **Specify parameter values.**

   Select from the drop-down list of values or select the default value option for each parameter you would like to use for the data-driven subscrip-tion. This is similar to what was shown in Figure 11-12. Then click Next.

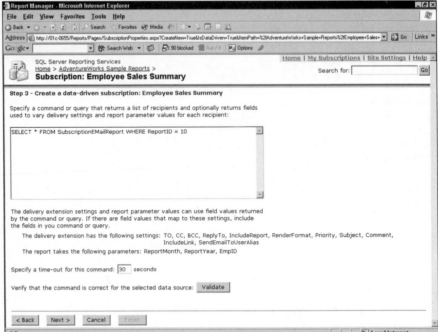

Figure 11-14:
Defining the
query to
return the
required
fields to
complete
the
specifica-
tion for the
e-mail
delivery
data-driven
subscrip-
tion.

4. **Define the schedule and select how you want to create the subscription.**

   You can select when the report is updated on the server or on a scheduled basis. These options are similar to what is shown in Figure 11-13.
   Click the Finish button.

Null delivery of data-driven subscriptions

Beginning with Step 5 of the data-driven subscription process, I review the
steps to deliver reports to the report server database. This option creates
report snapshots. Choose this option when you want to preload the Report
Server with parameterized report snapshots on a specific schedule. Follow
these steps:

1. **Define the query for the null delivery method.**

   You should enter a query that will return all the key fields required for
   the remaining specification of the subscription. If you use the definitions
   outlined in an earlier section, you can enter the following query:

   ```
   SELECT * FROM SubscriptionEMailReport WHERE ReportID =
        10.
   ```

   This is shown in Figure 11-15. Then click Next.

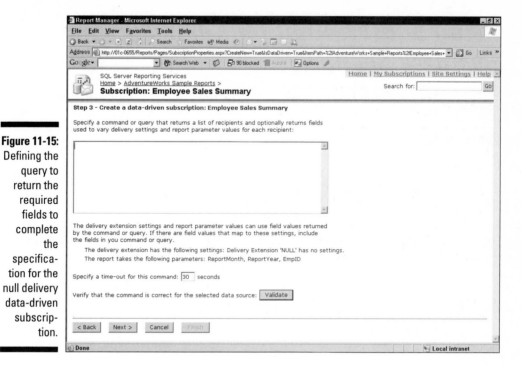

Figure 11-15:
Defining the
query to
return the
required
fields to
complete
the
specifica-
tion for the
null delivery
data-driven
subscrip-
tion.

2. Define Delivery Settings.

Configure the properties required by the fileshare data-driven specification, similar to what appears in Figure 11-11. All the values you need to
provide come from the database and should be available from the drop-
down list box for each field you need to specify. Then click Next.

3. Specify parameter values.

Select from the drop-down list of values or select the default value
option for each parameter you would like to use for the data-driven subscription. This is similar to what was shown in Figure 11-12. Then click
Next.

4. Define the schedule. Select from the options provided how you would like to create the subscription.

You can select when the report is updated on the server or on a scheduled basis. These options are similar to what is shown in Figure 11-13.

5. Click Finish.

Using Subscription for Common Business Scenarios

You can use subscriptions to automate the delivery of information to your business users. In the following sections, I provide some ideas on how to utilize subscriptions to make the reporting experience better for your business users.

Preloading a snapshot report

If you have multiple instances of a report (which many people want to access) with parameters for filtering your dataset you can preload reports in the cache to reduce processing time used to display the report. You can do this as a standard subscription with a null file delivery extension on a snapshot report. This will increase the overall performance for the system and make business consumers of this information happier. You can even use a regular schedule that runs with the update frequency you require of the information, reloading the cache so that the business team sees the latest information available with the fastest performance possible.

Providing access to latest reports in a file directory

If your users prefer to access a directory or if your portal repository requires a single directory to access the latest report information, you can create subscriptions that deposit reports as files in specified directories for this. You can do this in a standard subscription using the fileshare delivery method. You can render the reports in the format that best meets your business requirements.

Broadcasting exception reports

You can define reports as exception reports and use any type of subscription to e-mail the exceptions to key users on a regular basis. You can build a report to filter out everything but exceptions that need to be addressed and process the subscription to e-mail these exception reports to key business users as frequently as the business process being monitored requires. This is a common strategy to create alerts to business situations that require immediate attention.

Bursting reports

Bursting a report refers to creating a parameter-based report that serves a variety of users, each requiring a different view of the information that the parameter helps provide. The data-driven subscription is the best subscription to use for this, as you can send different views of the same report to a large group of users. A common way to provide the information to the user is to e-mail it on a scheduled basis.

Maintaining Your Subscriptions

Administrators of good reporting environments need to attend to the care and feeding of the subscriptions that are being utilized. In the following sections, I highlight some situations where subscription specifications need to be reviewed and maintained.

Working with inactive subscriptions

If a subscription becomes inactive, you should either delete it or reactivate it by resolving the underlying conditions that prevent it from being processed. An inactive subscription is indicated by a message in the subscription itself. The message includes information about the cause and what steps you should take to reactivate the subscription.

Subscriptions can become inactive if conditions occur that prevent processing. These conditions include

✔ Removing or uninstalling the delivery extension specified in the subscription.

✔ Changing credential settings from stored to integrated or prompted values.

✔ Changing a parameter name or data type in the report definition and then republishing a report. If a subscription includes a parameter that is no longer valid, the subscription becomes inactive.

✔ Changing the execution mode of a report (for example, modifying an on-demand report so that it runs as a report execution snapshot).

When conditions cause the subscription to become inactive, the subscription reflects this fact when the report server runs the subscription. If a subscription is scheduled to deliver a report every Friday at midnight, and the delivery extension it uses was uninstalled on Monday at 9 a.m., the subscription will not reflect its inactive state until Friday at midnight.

Execution mode modifications and subscription processing

If you change the execution properties of a report for which there is a subscription, the report server deactivates the subscription to indicate that the parameters in your subscription will no longer be used. For example, if you modify execution properties to change a report snapshot so that it runs as an on-demand report, your subscription will be deactivated.

To activate the subscription, open and then save the subscription. When you open the subscription, the report server updates the subscription parameter values to those specified for the snapshot.

Managing subscriptions with My Subscriptions

Report Manager includes a My Subscriptions page that organizes all of your subscriptions into one place. You can use My Subscriptions to view, modify, and delete existing subscriptions. However, you cannot use it to create subscriptions. My Subscriptions is a link on the menu at the top right of each Report Manager page.

Within My Subscriptions, you can sort subscriptions by folder, report, description, trigger, last run, or status. All values are sorted alphabetically except for Last Run, which is in chronological order.

My Subscriptions shows only the subscriptions that you create. It does not list subscriptions that are owned by other users, even if you are added as a subscriber to those subscriptions. Data-driven subscriptions that a report administrator defines for you are also not represented here.

To manage subscriptions on a server-wide basis, you must be a member of the Content Manager role or be assigned to a role that supports the Manage All Subscriptions task.

Configuring Subscription Processing

The e-mail message used to deliver the report must be sent from an e-mail account that is defined on the e-mail server. The e-mail account is used for all reports delivered by the e-mail delivery extension; you cannot specify multiple accounts or vary the account for individual reports. A configuration setting specifies the e-mail account.

You can configure a report server to limit e-mail distribution to specific host domains. For example, you can prevent a report server from delivering a report to all domains except those listed in the configuration file.

You can also set configuration settings to hide the To field in a subscription. In this case, reports are delivered only to the user defining the subscription. However, after a report is sent to a user, you cannot explicitly prevent it from being forwarded.

Part IV
Maintaining Your Reports

The 5th Wave   By Rich Tennant

WELL, OBVIOUSLY ONE OF THE CELLS IN THE NAVIGATIONAL SPREADSHEET IS CORRUPT!

In this part . . .

You can manage your reports in so many ways after you create and save them. *Microsoft Reporting Services 2005* provides a nice tool called the Report Manager, which enables you to manage reports by using folders. In addition, you can schedule an automated run reports by using the built-in scheduler. You can even broadcast reports to a group of people by e-mail or refresh a set of reports provided on a Web site that you have access to.

You say you want information secured? Of course you do, and you have many options to provide secure access. You want information quickly? Is that possible if you're reporting from a very large database? In this part, I give you some pointers for optimizing the report processing performance.

Chapter 12

Managing and Administering Your Reports

*J*ust as your desk needs cleaning, your car needs an occasional wash, and those nasty spills need a quick hand with a paper towel, your reporting environment needs attention to ensure that it runs like a well-oiled machine. Your report administrator, fortunately, has a handy set of tools for this task. I devote this chapter to how to use these tools.

The two tools available for managing reports with Reporting Services are the SQL Server Management Studio — new in SQL Server 2005 — and the Report Manager. You can use Report Manager or SQL Server Management Studio to perform many key tasks such as viewing, searching, and subscribing to reports, and creating as well as managing report folders, linked reports, report history, schedules, data source connections, and subscriptions. In Chapter 11, I describe how to set properties and report parameters. In Chapter 13, I cover managing role definitions and assignments that control user access to reports and folders.

This chapter is concerned with how to manage reports, how to administer the objects in Reporting Services, and special considerations about managing the disk space requirements of the Report Server.

Managing Your Reports

You can manage reports in SQL Server 2005 in two ways: The Report Manager, which I introduce in Chapter 9, is a Web-based application that runs on the server and provides some great report management capabilities. The other, called the SQL Server Management Studio, is a new tool and contains a superset of Report Manager functionality.

Using Management Studio

SQL Server Management Studio is an integrated environment for accessing, configuring, managing, administering, and developing all components of SQL Server. All of the Reporting Services management functions are available after you connect to the Report Server. To connect to the Report Server from the Management Studio, follow these steps.

1. **Start the SQL Server Management Studio by choosing Start⇨All Programs and then selecting the SQL Server 2005 program group.**

   You see an option for starting SQL Server Management Studio.

2. **Connect to the Report Server by clicking the Connect button in the Object Explorer and selecting Report Server from the drop-down list that appears (see Figure 12-1).**

Figure 12-1:
Connecting to the Report Server in the SQL Server Management Studio.

SQL Server Management Studio combines many graphical tools with some very capable script editors to provide access to SQL Server to developers and administrators of all skill levels. One of the key advantages of using the

Management Studio is that it can generate a script for most activities on the database that can be leveraged in future database administration and maintenance functions.

Within the SQL Server Management Studio, you can work with the underlying subject matter databases, compose queries to review data, work with Analysis Manager cubes, compose data transformation processing, and interface with notification services, in addition to managing reports. This is an ideal interface for a developer, and database administrators get a single comprehensive utility that combines easy-to-use graphical tools with rich scripting capabilities.

If you right-click the Home folder, you see several options in the menu bar. You can delete a folder, create new folders, add new data sources, or import new files. You can also open a folder to see its contents by clicking the link to that folder (see Figure 12-2). You can also move folders other than the home page and rename folders under the Home folder.

Figure 12-2:
The menu
on the
Home folder
in the SQL
Server
Manage-
ment Studio
showing
all the
mainten-
ance
options.

You can maintain the site settings for Reporting Services by right-clicking the Report Server name in the Object Explorer and selecting the Properties menu item from the list that appears. This will show the General tab of the Server Properties window. If you would like to enable a nice feature of allowing a My Reports folder for each user, simply select the check box for this option and select a role to apply to each user folder. (My Reports role will suffice. This is covered in more detail in Chapter 13.) The dialog box appears similar to that shown in Figure 12-3.

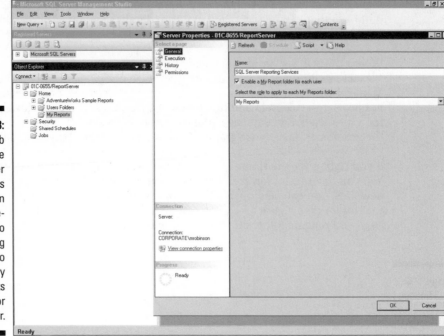

Figure 12-3:
General tab
of the
Server
Properties
dialog box in
Manage-
ment Studio
showing
how to
enable a My
Reports
folder for
each user.

Using Report Manager

Report Manager provides another type of user interface to Report Server. The user interface consists of Web pages and controls. There are pages for viewing items, setting properties, and creating and modifying subscriptions, schedules, shared data sources, and roles. You can access items that are stored in a report server by navigating the folder hierarchy and clicking on items that you want to view or update.

Performing a task in Report Manager depends on user role assignment. A user with full permissions who is assigned to a role such as a report server administrator has access to the complete set of application menus and pages. A user with permission to view and run reports sees only the menus and pages that support those activities. I cover user roles and other security considerations in detail in Chapter 13.

If Reporting Services is installed on your local computer, you can also select Report Manager from the Start menu, from the SQL Server program group. Report Manager is installed during Reporting Services setup on the same computer as the report server.

To run Report Manager, type the Report Server URL in the Address bar of a Web browser. By default, the URL is:

```
http://<Webservername>/reports
```

The home page for Report Manager is shown in Figure 12-4.

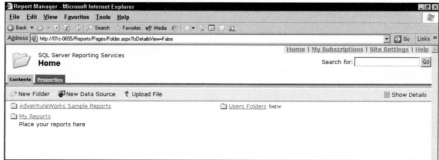

Figure 12-4:
The home page for Report Manager, with the My Reports folder enabled.

In Report Manager, the root node is named Home. If you are using a browser to connect directly to a report server, the root node is the name of the report server virtual directory. From the root node, you can create additional folders to organize the reports and items you want to store. Folders provide the navigation structure and addresses of all items stored in a report server.

If you click the Show Details button on the far-right side of the Report Manager home page toolbar, you can see the complete list of folders and reports with all their properties, including description, modification date, who modified it, and when it was last run. See Figure 12-5.

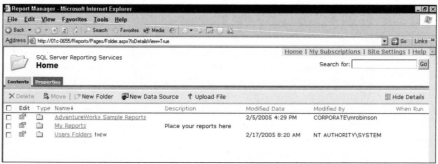

Figure 12-5:
The home page for Report Manager after clicking the Show Details button.

Notice the variety of tools available from the Report Manager home page. You can delete or move folders, create new folders, add new data sources, or upload new files. You can also open folders to see their contents by clicking the links to those folders.

Click the Edit button and you can rename a folder or hide it in a list. Figure 12-6 shows the Report Manager home page.

Figure 12-6:
The General
Folder
Properties
pages
within
Report
Manager
available
when you
edit a folder
on the
Report
Manager
home page.

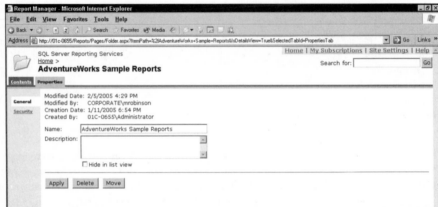

You can also manage all the site settings for Report Manager by clicking the Site Settings link on the top right of the Report Manager page. This will bring you to the Site Settings page shown in Figure 12-7.

Uploading files

Use the Upload File page to copy a file from the file system into the report server database. Uploaded files are represented as items in the report server folder hierarchy. Uploaded .rdl files are published to a report server as reports. All other file types are stored as resources. The folder from which you initiate the upload operation is the folder that will contain the uploaded file. After the upload is complete, you can move the item to a different location.

To open this page, click Upload File on the Contents page. You can only add files to a folder for which you have permission to add content. Enter the file-name or click the Browse button to navigate to the file to upload. You also provide a name to use for the file within the Report Manager. Finally, you can specify that you want to overwrite the file already in Report Manager completely. These options are shown on the Upload File page shown in Figure 12-8.

Figure 12-7:
The Site
Settings
page in
Report
Manager
showing
options
similar to
the options
available in
the SQL
Server
Manage-
ment Studio
Properties
dialog box.

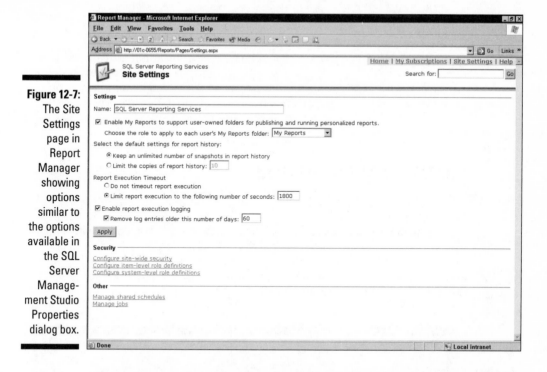

Figure 12-8:
The Upload
File page
showing all
options for
selecting a
file from
your file
system.

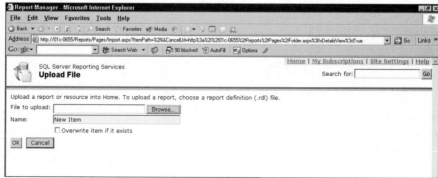

An analogous option also exists within the Management Studio that you can
access with a right-click on any folder.

Moving files

Not all items that you work with can be moved. You cannot move items that are extensions of a report, such as subscriptions or report history. Those items move with their associated reports. Similarly, you cannot move items, such as shared schedules, that exist outside of the folder hierarchy. Finally, you cannot move items if you lack permission to do so.

Using linked reports

Repurpose an existing report by attaching a different set of properties, parameter values, or security settings to a named instance of a report. To the user, each linked report appears to be a stand-alone report. You can create a linked report by clicking the Create Linked Report button on the General tab of the Properties page for any report, as shown in Figure 12-9. The text below the button indicates that you can create a linked report when you want to use different security or parameters with the report.

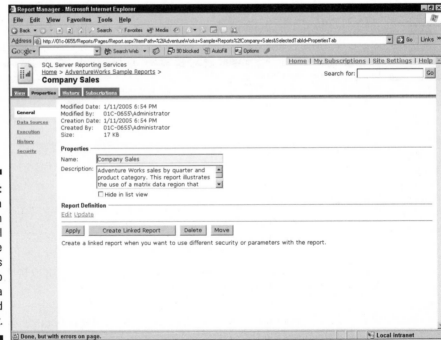

Figure 12-9:
Click a
button on
the General
tab of the
Properties
page to
create a
linked
report.

When you click the Create Linked Report button, you see the page shown in Figure 12-10. As you can see, you can name this linked report, change its location, and maintain anything about this report in the other tabs including parameters, data source security, execution, and history.

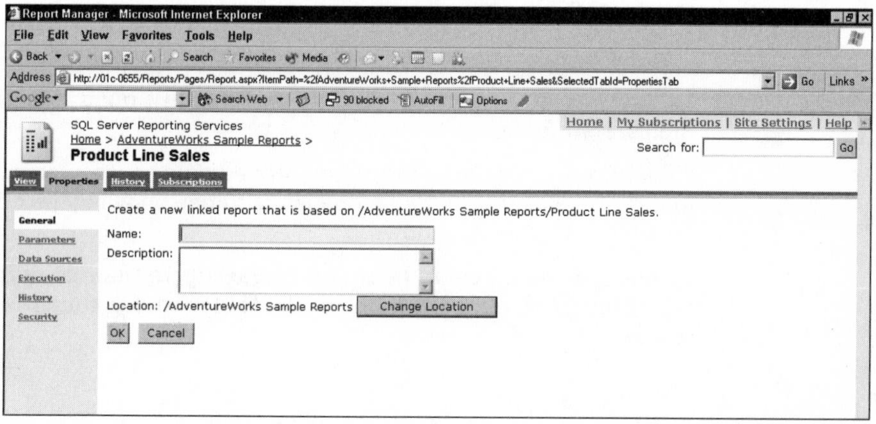

Figure 12-10: The page allowing you to completely specify all aspects of a linked report.

Consider a scenario where you have a single company sales report that shows sales data for all channels in your sales organization. To use this report for different groups in your organization, you define one linked report for Retail Sales and another linked report for Distributor Sales, both of which are based on the Company Sales report, but use different parameters to select only the data that each group is interested in.

A linked report uses the report definition of the original report. This means that it always inherits report layout and data source properties of the original report. All other properties and settings can be different from those of the original report, including security, parameters, location, subscriptions, and schedules.

Although linked reports are typically based on parameterized reports, a parameterized report is not required. You can create linked reports whenever you want to deploy an existing report with different settings.

Searching for reports

When you search a report server database, the contents of your My Reports folder are included in the search, while the contents of other user's My Reports folders are excluded. Search results list only the reports to which you have access.

Navigating hierarchies in Report Manager

To navigate a folder hierarchy, follow these steps:

1. **To view the contents of a folder, click the folder name on the Contents page.**

   A folder page opens, displaying the contents of the folder.

2. **To navigate down through the folder hierarchy, open a subfolder of the current folder.**

   Folders contain reports, resources, shared data source items, and other folders. Clicking a folder icon opens the folder, showing the contents of the hierarchy one level down.

3. **To navigate up through the folder hierarchy, in the row of links at the top of the page, click the name of the folder whose contents you want to see.**

Working with the My Reports folder

The My Reports feature is disabled by default. You can either enable or disable the feature for all users, but you cannot enable it for a subset of users. Most users and organizations find this feature valuable; study the advantages and disadvantages presented later in this topic to determine whether it is a good fit for your organization.

Deciding whether to use My Reports depends on whether you want to dedicate server resources to support user workspace. My Reports is a powerful feature that enables you to have control over information resources that help you do your job. It also provides a way for you to work with reports that are not intended for general use. One of the most compelling reasons to use My Reports is that it provides secure, manageable support for the segment of users who need to author and review reports. Without this feature, you may find yourself creating folders and security policies for various users on an ad hoc basis. As users and user needs change, this approach results in ever-increasing numbers of folders and policies that are difficult to maintain over time.

Note: If you do activate My Reports, the Report Server creates a My Reports folder for every user who has a domain account who clicks the My Reports link, even if the user doesn't want or need a My Reports folder. No systematic way exists to determine which folders are being used. You must review the folders manually to see whether they contain anything.

To enable My Reports using Report Manager, use the Site Settings page to set the Enable Each User to Have a My Reports Folder option. The role definition used for My Reports determines what actions are supported in the My Reports workspace. For example, if the My Reports role excludes Create Linked Reports, users cannot create linked reports in the My Reports folders.

When My Reports is activated, you see a My Reports folder located under the root folder, Home. In addition to a My Reports folder, report server administrators also see a Users Folders folder that contains the subfolder for each user.

While the feature is activated, Users Folders and its subfolders cannot be deleted. Furthermore, the name My Reports becomes a reserved name for folders created under the root node (Home).

If you activate My Reports after it has been deactivated, the report server creates a new Users Folders folder if one does not already exist. If a Users Folders folder exists, the report server adds new subfolders as users log on to their My Reports folders.

To deactivate My Reports, clear Enable Each User to Have a My Reports Folder. Deactivating My Reports removes all visible indications of the My Reports folder. The folders that provide actual storage (that is, the subfolders in Users Folders) must be deleted manually once the feature is disabled. Only users who have permission to delete folders can do so.

When My Reports is deactivated, the name My Reports is no longer reserved; users can create a personal folder named My Reports under the Home folder. In addition, redirection from My Reports to user-specific My Reports subfolders is no longer performed. Lastly, any report links that include a user-specific My Reports folder in the URL address will no longer work.

Administering Reporting Services

Administration of a Reporting Services implementation is concerned with controlling the server settings and properties, working with trace files and execution logs to understand the operation of the Report Server, and understanding the database storage requirements of the Report Server. This section provides some interesting aspects of this topic.

Applying timeouts

The Report Server provides an option that I affectionately refer to as the governator. This is an option to time out the execution of a report and cancel it with a message to the end user. This governor specifies a timeout value for the limit of how system resources are used. Report Server supports two timeout values:

✔ A query timeout value is the number of seconds that the Report Server waits for a response from the database. This value is defined in a report.

✔ A report execution timeout value is the maximum number of seconds that report processing can continue before it is stopped. This value is defined at the system level. You can vary this setting for individual reports.

Most timeout errors occur during query processing. If you are encountering timeout errors, try increasing the query timeout value. If necessary, adjust the report execution timeout value so that it is larger than the query timeout. The time period should be sufficient to complete both query and report processing.

Query timeout values are specified during report authoring when you define a dataset. You can also specify a query timeout value for data-driven subscriptions. The timeout value is stored with the report in the Timeout element of the report definition. This feature helps you prevent unpredictable source queries from running an undesirable amount of time. When the timeout is exceeded, a failure is returned. Users who have permission to modify the properties of a published report can reset this value by editing the report definition file.

You can set the report execution timeout value to limit the amount of time that a report server uses to process a report. Report execution timeout values can be specified in Report Manager in the Site Settings page (refer to Figure 12-7). You can set a default value for all reports in the Site Settings page and then override that value in the Execution Properties page for a specific report, so the site timeout value can be overridden on a report-by-report basis. This feature helps you prevent any long-running report executions that go beyond your acceptable threshold. By default, the value is set to 1,800 seconds.

The Report Server evaluates running jobs at 60-second intervals. At each 60-second interval, the Report Server compares actual process time against the report execution timeout value. If the processing time for a report exceeds the report execution timeout value, report processing stops.

If you specify a timeout value that is less than 60 seconds, the report may execute in full if processing starts and completes before the report server evaluates the report execution timeout.

Using trace files

Reporting Services trace logs contain very detailed information that's useful if you're debugging an application or investigating an issue or event. Trace logs contain information about the various Report Server operations like system information, events in the application log, and exceptions and warnings generated by the Report Server.

Trace logs are text files, so you can use any text editor to view a log file. The trace log file contains the following types of event information:

- ✔ Events logged by the application log
- ✔ Exceptions generated by the report server
- ✔ Low resource warnings logged by the report server

The trace files are written to log files in the directory:

```
C:\Program Files\Microsoft SQL Server\<SQL server
          instance>\Reporting Services\LogFiles
```

The trace files use the local time of the Report Server to generate a single log file per day with the following names:

```
ReportServerService_<timestamp>.log - Trace server log for
          the Report Server windows and Web services
ReportServerWebApp_<timestamp>.log - Trace server log for
          Report Manager
ReportServer_<timestamp>.log - Trace server log for the
          Report Server engine
```

You can control the level of information recorded to the trace logs by modifying the DefaultTraceSwitch configuration setting in the `ReportingServices Service.config` file. The settings you can select from are 0= Disables tracing, 1= Exceptions and restarts only, 2= Exceptions, restarts, warnings, 3= Exceptions, restarts, warnings, status messages (default), and 4= Verbose mode.

Using the execution log

You can log information about job executions to the Report Server database. This can help you to monitor execution performance, troubleshoot report executions, and optimize report executions.

For each execution, there is a variety of captured information. The following types of information can be captured in the execution log:

- ✔ Name of the report server instance that handled the request
- ✔ Report identifier
- ✔ User identifier
- ✔ Request type (either user or system)
- ✔ Rendering format

✔ Parameter values used for a report execution

✔ Start and stop times that indicate the duration of a report process

✔ Percentage of time spent retrieving the data, processing the report, and rendering the report

✔ Source of the report execution (1=Live, 2=Cache, 3=Snapshot, 4=History)

✔ Status (either Success or an error code; if multiple errors occur, only the first error is recorded)

✔ Size of rendered reports in bytes

✔ Number of rows returned from queries

You can, for example, use the report execution log to find out how often a report is requested, what formats are used the most, and what percentage of processing time is spent on each processing phase.

Logging is enabled by default in Report Manager, with removal frequency of log entries whose default is 60 days.

Reporting Services provides an ETL package that you can use to export logged records to another database for viewing and analysis. The report server logs data about report execution into an internal database table. This table does not provide complete information by itself, nor does it present data in a format that is understandable to users.

To view report execution data, you must run a DTS package that Reporting Services provides to extract the data from the execution log and put it into a table structure that you can query.

Querying the Report Execution Log

You can turn report execution logging on or off by selecting options in Report Manager on the Site Settings page. On this page, you can also specify how long you want to keep log entries. By default, this value is 60 days. Entries that exceed this date are removed at 2 a.m. every day.

You can extract the execution log data and store it in a separate local report execution log database. SQL Server ships with a Data Transformation Services (DTS) package called RSExecution_LogUpdate.dts to enable this process. This DTS package extracts the data from the report execution log and puts it into a table structure that you can query.

To set up your computer for querying report execution log data, follow these steps:

1. **Verify that Data Transformation Services 2000 Runtime is installed on the computer running SQL Server 2005. Look for the following file:**

```
C:\Program Files\Microsoft SQL
        Server\90\Tools\Binn\dtsrun.exe
```

If the file is missing, choose Add or Remove Programs in the Control Panel to install Microsoft SQL Server 2005 Tools. This installs the Data Transformation Services 2000 Runtime.

2. **Create a database for the Report Execution data.**

In SQL Server Management Studio, in Object Explorer, create a new database that the DTS package can use as its destination database.

For the database name, use the name `RSExecutionLog`.

3. **Add tables to the database.**

To add tables to the database, select `RSExecutionLog` from the Available Databases list box on the toolbar in SQL Server Management Studio (see Figure 12-11). Choose File⇔Open and then click File. Browse to the following file:

```
C:\Program Files\Microsoft SQL
        Server\90\Tools\\90\Tools\Reporting
        Services\Execution Log\Createtables.sql
```

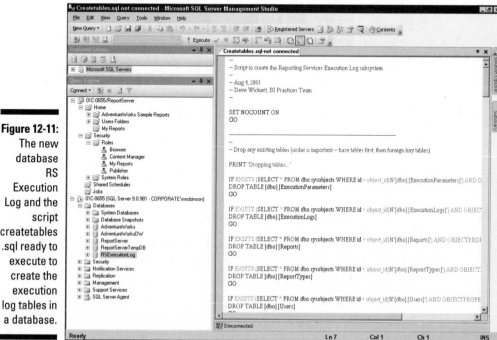

Figure 12-11:
The new database RS Execution Log and the script createtables .sql ready to execute to create the execution log tables in a database.

4. **Click OK.**

5. **Run the query by clicking Execute on the toolbar.**

   This creates the tables you need in your RSExecutionLog table.

6. **If the Report Server database that you're using as the source of your execution log data isn't named Report Server, specify the correct report server database name in the Source section of this file.**

   If the report execution log database that you are using as the destination is not named RSExecutionLog, specify the correct report execution log database name in the Database section of this file. Save changes and close the file.

7. **Extract the Report Execution Log data. Run a command prompt on the computer running SQL Server, and change directories to the directory containing the Dtsrun.exe utility by issuing this command:**

   ```
   cd \Program Files\Microsoft SQL Server\90\Tools\Binn
   ```

8. **Run the package by typing the following at the command prompt:**

   ```
   Dtsrun /f "C:\Program Files\Microsoft SQL
           Server\90\Tools\Reporting Services\Execution
           Log\RSExecutionLog_Update.dts"
   ```

   When this has completed running, you will see the message "Package execution complete."

9. **Refresh the Execution Log data.**

   To update RSExecutionLog with information from the report execution log, run the RSExecutionLog_Update.dts package periodically. The DTS package appends new log entries to the existing entries. It does not remove old entries or historical data.

If you don't want to save historical execution log data, you can periodically run the Cleanup.sql query on RSExecutionLog. To do this, select RSExecutionLog from the Available Databases list box on the toolbar in SQL Server Management Studio. Click File, select Open, and then click File. By default, this folder is:

```
C:\Program Files\Microsoft SQL Server\\90\Tools\Reporting
           Services\Execution Log
```

Browse to the folder containing Cleanup.sql, select that file, and then click OK. Click Execute on the toolbar to run the query.

Understanding database storage

A Reporting Services installation uses two databases to separate persistent data storage from temporary storage requirements. The databases are created together and bound by name. By default, the database names are `ReportServer` and `ReportsServerTempDB`, respectively.

The Report Server database stores reports, folders, shared data sources and metadata, resources, snapshots, and report history. The `ReportServerTempDB` database stores session cache and cached instances. It is the snapshots, report history, session cache, and cached instances that require the most consideration from a storage perspective. The ChunkData table in the Report Server database contains the snapshots and report history. This same table in the `ReportServerTempDB` contains the session cache and the cached instances.

To determine the disk space requirements for your databases, you need to estimate the number of reports and look at the size of the intermediate reports. For the Report Server database, you need to factor in the persistence of the intermediate report, whether it's a snapshot (only one allowed per report at any point in time) or report history (how long it is maintained). For the `ReportServer TempDB`, you need to factor in the session cache size. Cached instances exist for each combination of report parameters and persist until they expire; the number of users affects the size of the session cache.

Chapter 13

Securing Report Server

· ·

· ·

*W*hen you're safeguarding corporate assets through the secure distribution of information to people on a need-to-know basis (which business intelligence can get into), it becomes a federal case when secure information gets into the wrong hands. Security considerations alone are enough to eliminate a reporting tool from the list of permitted tools in any organization. Secure information access and delivery are key to safeguarding the assets of your company. Without secure information management capabilities, we would still be in the Dark Ages of paper reports distributed on a need-to-know basis within the bowels of the company. Therefore, knowing how to secure a reporting platform to ensure that information is made available based on a permission system is key to the successful deployment of reporting and analysis capabilities. This chapter covers the security considerations you need to know.

Understanding Security Fundamentals

Reporting Services uses a role-based security model to control access to reports, folders, and other items that are managed by a Report Server. The role-based security model is similar to role-based security models offered by other applications. Reporting Services enables you to categorize users into groups or roles base on how they interact with the system and its resources. You can map specific user groups to specific roles that can perform specific tasks. I talk about the Security role model in the sections that follow.

Introducing the Authorization Model

Reporting Services provides an authorization model, but it doesn't include an authentication component. In order for authorization to work, the underlying network security must be able to authenticate the users and groups who access the report server. Authentication is performed by the Windows operating system.

Note: You can also use custom authentication if you create a security extension to support it.

The security model consists of the following components:

- One user account or group that can be authenticated by Windows security or another authentication mechanism.
- Securable object such as an item object, like a report, or a system object, like a shared schedule.
- Role definitions that specify the set of permissible item or system tasks. Examples of role definitions include System Administrator, Content Manager, and Publisher.

The combination of all these elements is characterized as a role assignment. In Reporting Services, role assignments provide the security context for items and the report server itself. The *role assignment* is a security policy that defines the tasks that users or groups can perform on specific items or branches of the Report Server folder hierarchy.

Creating role assignments

A role-based security model grants end-user access to specific operations through role membership. All users who are members of a role can perform the operations that are defined for the role.

Role-based security is flexible and scalable, particularly when you use it with group accounts. You can map group accounts to role definitions, and then allow the changing membership of those groups to automatically adjust for new report users coming into the organization or moving to different positions in the organization, and other report users exiting the organization.

Use role-based security to control access to folders, reports, and resources. Security settings follow an inheritance pattern through the folder structure. You can vary security at any branch to redefine user access at the item level. Role-based security works with Windows authentication. A default security model provides initial security. Security is in place when the product installs.

Reporting Services includes several predefined roles to accommodate various categories of users. You can see the roles defined in SQL Server Management Studio when you expand the Roles folder within the Security folder in the Report Server (see Figure 13-1). If you right-click one of these roles and choose Properties from the list that appears, you will see the detail task permissions checked for that role. Figure 13-1 shows the four predefined roles in the Object Explorer on the left side and the specific task permissions available for the Browser role on the right side.

You can create additional roles if the predefined roles are insufficient. You can modify or delete either the predefined roles or the custom roles you create, as long as you don't invalidate the last remaining role assignment for your report server. You can define a new role or edit an existing role within Report Manager of the SQL Server Management Studio.

To create a role assignment in Report Manager, proceed as follows:

1. **Navigate to the Contents page, and open the folder that contains the item for which you want to apply a role assignment.**

2. **Click the Properties tab, then click the Security tab, and perform one of the following:**

   a. If the item uses the security settings of a parent item, click Edit Item Security, click OK, and then click New Role Assignment.

Figure 13-1:
The User role properties in the SQL Server Management Studio showing the Security roles in the Object Explorer and the task permissions for the Browser role.

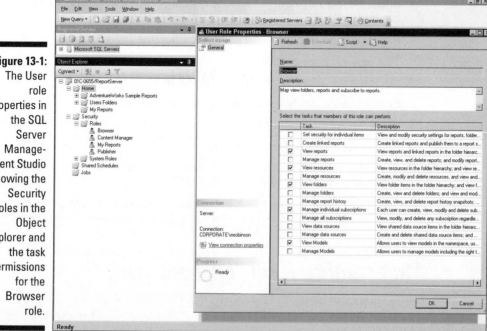

> b. If the item already has item-specific security defined for it, click New Role Assignment.

3. **Type the name of a group or user account.**

   You can specify only one account name for each role assignment.

4. **Select one or more role definitions that describe how the user or group should access the item, and then click OK.**

5. **To determine which tasks a role definition supports, click the name of the role definition.**

6. **If existing role definitions are insufficient, click New Role to create a new one.**

Role definitions can contain either item-level or system-level tasks. You cannot combine tasks from both levels into a single role definition. Because the number of tasks that you can work with is relatively small, you typically don't need a large number of role definitions. Creating or modifying a role definition requires careful consideration. If you create too many roles, the roles become difficult to maintain and manage. If you modify an existing role, you may not know the various places in which it is used or how users will be affected by the modification. Role-based security is central to the security model of Reporting Services, and understanding its implications is important.

To create a role assignment in SQL Server Management Studio, follow these steps:

1. **In the Object Explorer, expand a report server node, then navigate to the item for which you want to set item-level security.**

2. **Right-click an item, and then click Properties.**

   The General page of the item's Properties dialog box appears.

3. **Click Permissions in the Select a Page area.**

4. **Select Use These Roles for each group or user account.**

5. **Click the Add Group or User button.**

   The Select Users or Groups dialog box appears.

6. **Type the account name of the group or user that you are creating a role assignment for, and then click OK.**

7. **Select one or more roles that best describe the actions that you want the user or group to be able to perform on the current item. Then click OK.**

Maintaining item-level security

Folders in Report Manager provide the foundation for item-level security. Role assignments that you define for specific folders extend to the items in that folder and to additional folders that branch from that folder.

You can view the item-level roles in Report Manager by navigating to the Site Settings page and then clicking the link <u>Configure item-level role definitions</u>. This will bring up the predefined item-level roles, as shown in Figure 13-2.

Figure 13-2: Predefined item-level security roles in the Report Manager.

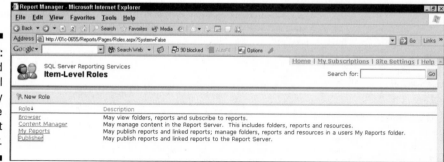

The Browser role permits only navigating the folder hierarchy, viewing reports and resources, and managing their own subscriptions. The Publisher role permits report definitions to be uploaded and deployed, creating linked reports and some other report management tasks. A user assigned to the Publisher role cannot execute a report unless he or she is also assigned to the Browser role. The Content Manager role sits at the top of the trust scale. This role provides full administrative ability for managed report components such as folders, reports, resources, and shared data sources. The My Reports role is almost as powerful as the Content Manager role, but it is used only on each user's own special My Reports folder.

If you select the Publisher role, you will see a detailed task-level permissions list with the privileges available reflected in the checked boxes next to the tasks (see Figure 13-3). These tasks are relevant only to the item-level security for folders and their contents.

You can view the equivalent information using the SQL Server Management Studio by right-clicking on the security roles and selecting Properties from the pop-up menu.

To modify the folder-level security permissions, edit the folder and navigate to the security properties page to view or modify the security settings for that folder. This page is available for items that you create or have permission to modify. You can also access this through SQL Server Management Studio by right-clicking on the folder and selecting Properties from the list that appears. You then will see the item-level security role assigned to specific user groups, as shown in Figure 13-4.

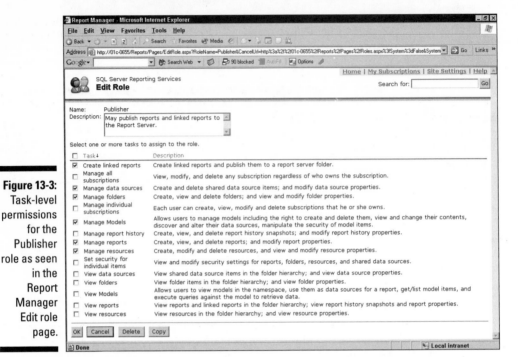

Figure 13-3: Task-level permissions for the Publisher role as seen in the Report Manager Edit role page.

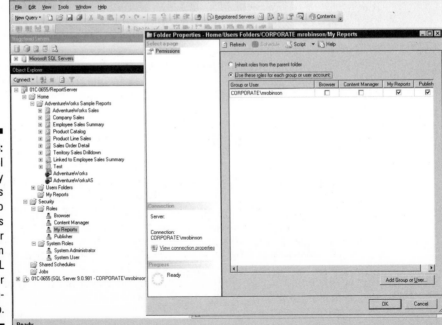

Figure 13-4: Item-level security roles assigned to user groups for a folder as shown within SQL Server Management Studio.

The corresponding view of this same information as shown in Report Manager is shown in Figure 13-5. You would navigate to this page by navigating to the folder in question and editing this in the Report Manager.

Figure 13-5:
Item-level
security
roles
assigned to
user groups
for a folder
as shown
within
Report
Manager.

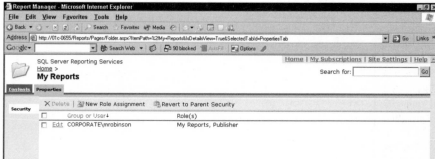

You can access items based on your task-level permissions in your role assignment. A role assignment consists of one user or group name and one or more role definitions that specify a collection of tasks.

Security settings are inherited from the root folder down to subfolders and items within those folders. Unless you explicitly override inherited security, subfolders and items inherit the security context of the parent item. If you redefine a security policy for a folder in the middle of the hierarchy, all its subfolders and items contained within the folder assume the new security settings. You can view the folder properties Permission tab in SQL Server Management Studio by right-clicking on a folder under the Home folder and selecting Properties from the list that appears. This will show the Folder Properties page as shown in Figure 13-6.

Each object within the Report Server has a Permissions tab on the Properties page showing the roles available for each group or user account. You cannot delete a role assignment if it is the only one remaining, or if it is a built-in role assignment (for example, Built-in\Administrators) that defines the security baseline for the report server. Deleting a role assignment does not delete a group or user account or role definitions. You can add new role assignments for the current item (folder, report, and so on). Existing role assignments for the current item are defined for the groups and users that appear in this column. You can click a group or user name to view or edit role assignment details. If multiple roles are assigned to a group or user account, that group or user can perform all tasks that belong to those roles. To view the tasks that are associated with a role, click the group or user name to view the role assignment, and then click the role definition.

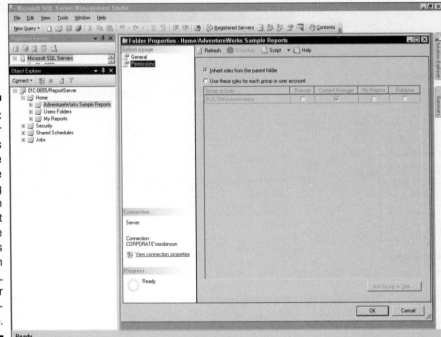

Figure 13-6:
Folder
Properties
page
showing the
inheriting
roles from
the parent
folder as the
default as
shown
within SQL
Server
Manage-
ment Studio.

Using system-level security

The Report Server site can be secured through system role assignments. You set security at the system level by creating role assignments that give selected users the capability to perform tasks that affect the Report Server site as a whole. These tasks include creating shared schedules, managing jobs, and setting properties. System-level security does not determine access to items in the report server folder hierarchy.

Reporting Services provides two predefined system role definitions. The System User role can view the schedule information in a shared schedule, or view the other basic information about the Report Server. The System Administrator role can enable features and set defaults, set systemwide security, create role definitions, and manage jobs. The task-level permissions for the System Administrator role can be viewed in Report Manager by navigating to the Site Settings page and clicking the link to configure system-level role definitions. The privileges for the System Administrator are shown in Figure 13-7. These tasks relate to system-level operations that can be performed for the site and do not apply to the items within the folder hierarchy.

You can manage this through SQL Server Management Studio by right-clicking the system role in the Security System Roles folder and selecting Properties from the list that appears.

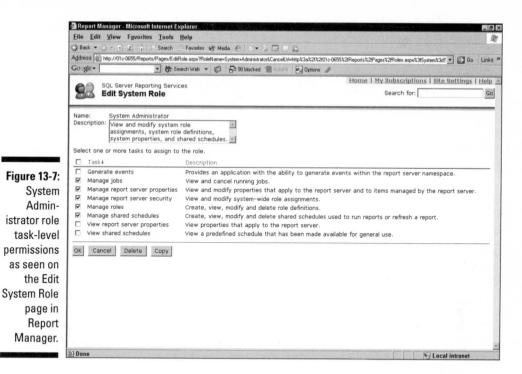

Figure 13-7:
System
Admin-
istrator role
task-level
permissions
as seen on
the Edit
System Role
page in
Report
Manager.

Reporting Services doesn't create its own user account for system security and instead references existing local or domain accounts and groups defined in the server operating system. Also, members of the local administrators group can always access a Report Server to change site settings no matter what role assignments are set. To ensure that a local administrator does not have rights to highly secure reports, you must secure the reports at the data-access level, requiring users to provide credentials to view the report.

Best Practices for Protecting Against an Attack

Running a report under an account that has very secure permissions exposes your SQL Server to a security threat if the report query contains malicious Transact-SQL statements (for example, statements that create unauthorized logons, modify or delete data, or introduce erroneous data), and the report is run by a user who has very secure permissions on the server that hosts the data source. For example, if an attacker publishes a report that contains a malicious query, the query will be processed under administrator credentials if either of these conditions is present:

✔ The report data source is configured to use integrated security and the user running the report is logged on as an administrator.

✔ The report data source is configured to prompt for credentials and the user types his or her administrator credentials to run the report.

To mitigate the threat of an elevation of privileges attack, follow one or more of these recommended security practices:

✔ Use least-privilege accounts to access the external data sources that provide data to a report. You can configure report data sources to always use the stored credentials of a least-privilege account.

✔ Use shared data sources in your reports to specify dataset connection information. You can use role assignments on the shared data source to control access to the connection string and settings that define how credentials are obtained at run time.

✔ Use role assignments to ensure that only trustworthy reports are published to a report server. Through role assignments, you can restrict report publication to specific folders, and then require administrators to inspect the RDL file (and the query) of a newly published report before moving it to a final location. There is no functionality in Reporting Services to enforce an inspection requirement prior to publication. This must become a standard operating procedure.

✔ Disable integrated security as a report data source credential option.

The use of integrated security to access external data sources poses a special concern for report users who may not know that their security token is being passed to an external data source (users are not warned in advance of running a report that the report is configured to use integrated security). In addition, users may not have the same concerns about opening a report as they would if they were opening an e-mail attachment from an unknown source. However, the security risks are the same in both scenarios. A malicious query can damage or compromise a server in the same way a malicious script that is exposed through a hyperlink or hidden in an e-mail attachment can damage or compromise a workstation.

Note that if you disable integrated security, any report data source that is currently configured to use integrated security (or configured to use integrated security after the feature is disabled) will no longer run. The error returned when running such a report is: This data source is configured to use Microsoft Windows NT integrated security but Windows NT integrated security is disabled for this server. To disable integrated security, you must use script or code to modify the `EnableIntegratedSecurity` system property.

Secure support for external users

If you want to support external users but don't want to code a custom security extension, you can use Windows authentication or Microsoft Active Directory. The following guidelines describe how to support this scenario:

1. Create a low-privileged domain user account with read-only permissions. The account must have access to the computer hosting the report server. Provide a custom Web form so that users can log on using the low-privileged domain account.

2. Create role assignments that map the user account to specific items in the report server folder hierarchy. You can limit access to read-only operations by choosing as the role assignment the predefined Browser role.

3. Configure reports to use stored credentials to get data for the report. This approach is useful if you want to query the external data source using an account that is different from the account that allows access to the report server.

Understanding data security

You can restrict which users see specific data within a report, which is a finer grain of security than the role assignments. Role assignments will determine if the report can be run at all by a particular user assigned to a specific role with specific permissions.

Consider the expression =User!UserID. This expression returns the user ID of the person running the report. You can utilize this parameter value with a custom permissions table of your design that associates which users can see specific groups of data within the system. For example, if you have an office sales results report that filters on the salesman ID requesting the report, you can define in a permissions table in your database which user IDs have access to which office sales information. In this Permissions table, you need to associate the Windows username with the permission level relevant to your application database.

For example, assume that you want to control which users are able to see sales data for specific offices within your application. When you define the dataset used to prompt the user for which office to select, you can add a permissions table with at least two columns: user and office. The table is populated with the combination of users that have access to specific office sales data. Therefore the dataset based on your permissions table would filter the parameter options presented to the current user. This filtered set of offices can be derived from the permissions table with the following query:

```
Select office
From permissions
where userid = User!UserID
```

This filters down all the offices, which only the accessing user can see. You can use this strategy either in the source query or with a filter that restricts the report based on the current Windows user.

Chapter 14

Optimizing Report Performance

. . . .

In This Chapter

▶ Monitoring report server performance

▶ Implementing a strategy for performance tuning

▶ Understanding report server database requirements

▶ Configuring Reporting Services components

. . . .

*H*ow many times do you have to stand in line on a given day? And how patient are you in that line? I would go as far as paying someone else to stand in a long line for me so that I can do something more productive (such as reprogramming my Gameboy to do my taxes) until it's my turn. This same logic applies to waiting for information in a report. This highlights the importance of optimizing your reporting system's performance. This chapter is about the performance considerations for your reporting environment.

Monitoring Report Server Performance

You can use performance monitoring tools to monitor report server performance to evaluate server activity, observe trends, diagnose system bottlenecks, and gather data that can help you determine whether the current system configuration is adequate.

A combination of technologies and tools enables you to get comprehensive information about how the system is performing. Microsoft Windows Server operating systems provide performance information through the following tools: Task Manager, Event Viewer, and Performance console.

Using Task Manager

Task Manager provides information about programs and processes running on your computer. You can use Task Manager to monitor key indicators of your report server's performance. You can also assess the activity of running processes and view graphs and data on CPU and memory usage.

Using Event Viewer

Using Event Viewer, you can view and set logging options for event logs in order to gather information about hardware, software, and system problems.

A server records events in three kinds of logs: ·

✔ **Application log:** Contains events logged by applications or programs. For example, a database program might record a file error in the application log. Application developers decide which events to log.

✔ **Security log:** Records events such as valid and invalid login attempts, as well as events related to resource use such as creating, opening, or deleting files or other objects. For example, if login auditing is enabled, attempts to log in to the system are recorded in the security log.

✔ **System log:** Contains events logged by Windows system components. For example, the failure of a driver or other system component to load during startup is recorded in the system log.

The event types logged by system components are predetermined by the server. Event Viewer displays five types of events:

✔ **Error:** A significant problem, such as loss of data or loss of functionality. For example, if a service fails to load during startup, an Error is logged.

✔ **Warning:** An event that is not necessarily significant, but might indicate a possible future problem. For example, when disk space is low, a Warning might be logged.

✔ **Information:** An event that describes the successful operation of an application, driver, or service. For example, when a network driver loads successfully, an Information event is logged.

✔ **Success Audit:** Any audited security event that succeeds. For example, a user's successful attempt to log on to the system is logged as a Success Audit event.

✔ **Failure Audit:** Any audited security event that fails. For example, if a user tries to access a network drive and fails, the attempt is logged as a Failure Audit event.

Using Event Viewer, you can define logging parameters for each kind of event log. To define parameters, right-click a log in the console tree and click Properties. On the General tab, you can set the maximum size of the log and specify whether the events are overwritten or stored for a certain period of time.

Using Performance console

You can use the Performance console to monitor specific performance counters. These counters enable you to

- Estimate system requirements needed to support an anticipated workload

- Create a performance baseline to measure the impact of configuration changes or application upgrades

- Monitor application performance under certain loads, whether real or artificially generated

- Verify that hardware upgrades have the desired impact on performance

- Validate that changes made to your system configuration have the desired impact on performance

Reporting Services includes two performance objects: RS Web Service, which monitors report server performance, and RS Windows Service, which monitors scheduled operations and report delivery.

The RS Web Service performance object includes a collection of counters used to track report server processing typically initiated through interactive report viewing operations. These counters are reset whenever ASP.NET stops the Reporting Services Web service.

The RS Windows Service performance object includes a collection of counters used to track report processing that is initiated through scheduled operations. Scheduled operations include subscription and delivery, report execution snapshots, and report history.

If you have multiple report server instances on a single computer, you can monitor the instances together or separately. Choose which instances to include when adding a counter. For more information about using Performance console and adding counters, see the Microsoft Windows product documentation.

Use performance monitoring tools to monitor report server performance by evaluating server activity, observing trends, diagnosing system bottlenecks, and gathering data that can help you determine whether the current system configuration is adequate. To access Performance console, follow these steps:

1. **Choose Start➪Performance from the Administrative Tools menu to open the System Monitor.**

   The System Monitor appears.

2. **Add Counters to the list by right-clicking in the grid showing various counters in the view and selecting Add Counters from the menu that appears (see Figure 14-1).**

3. **Select the RSWeb service counters.**

   In the Add Counters dialog, select RSWeb Service from the drop-down box for the Performance object. Then click the All Counters radio button. Finally, click OK.

4. **View the System Monitor.**

   You see all RD Web counters below the chart displayed on the performance monitor, each corresponding to a unique color on the display.

I describe the counters available for monitoring in Table 14-1.

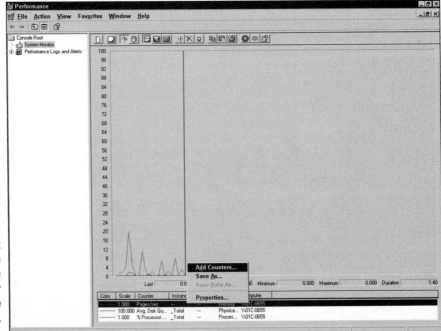

Figure 14-1:
Security roles in the Object Explorer with the task permission for the Browser role on the right side.

Table 14-1	Report Services Performance Counters
Counter Name	*Description*
Active Sessions	Count of all browser sessions generated from report subscriptions (active or not).
Cache Hits/Sec	Number of requests per second for re-rendered cached reports.
Cache Misses/Sec	Number of requests per second that failed to return a report from cache to determine whether the resources used for caching (disk or memory) are sufficient.
First Session Requests/Sec	Number of new user sessions started from the report server cache each second.
Memory Cache Hits/Sec	Number of times per second that reports are retrieved from the in-memory cache (no query of SQL Server for cached content).
Memory Cache Misses/Sec	Number of times per second reports could not be retrieved from the in-memory cache.
Next Session Requests/Sec	Number of reports rendered from a session snapshot.
Report Requests	Number of reports currently active and being handled by the report server.
Reports Executed/Sec	Number of successful report executions per second.
Requests/Sec	Number of requests (all types) per second made to the report server.
Total Cache Hits	Total number of requests for reports from the cache after the service started.
Total Cache Misses	Total number of times a report could not be returned from the cache after the service started.
Total Memory Cache Hits	Total number of cached reports returned from the in-memory cache after the service started.
Total Memory Cache Misses	Total number of cache misses against the in-memory cache after the service started.
Total Processing Failures	Total number of report processing failures that have occurred after the service started.
Total Rejected Threads	Total number of data processing threads (one data source per thread) in excess of capacity, requiring serial processing.

(continued)

Table 14-1 *(continued)*

Counter Name	Description
Total Reports Executed	Total number of reports that ran successfully after the service started.
Total Requests	Total number of all requests made to the report server after the service started.

You can use Performance console and Event Viewer to create logs and alerts about report processing and resource consumption. To create a performance log, proceed as follows:

1. **In Control Panel, open Administrative Tools and open Performance.**

2. **In the Windows Performance tool, expand Performance Logs and Alerts, right-click Counter Logs, and then click New Log Settings.**

3. **Type a name for the counter log and click OK.**

4. **Click Add to add as many counters as necessary for your Notification Services instance and other important values, such as processor time, disk time, and database counters.**

   The number of counters you add doesn't significantly affect system performance.

5. **Click Close.**

6. **Click the General tab and, under the section Sample Data Every, configure a sampling interval.**

   Start with a moderate sampling interval, such as five minutes, and then adjust the interval if necessary. The shorter the interval, the more system resources and disk space will be used. Additionally, intervals shorter than the quantum period can cause a performance report to show sporadic performance numbers because you will have processing spikes mixed with no activity.

7. **On the Log Files tab, configure the properties of the log file. You can view comma-delimited files later in a reporting tool such as Microsoft Excel.**

8. **On the Schedule tab, configure a monitoring schedule.**

Strategy for Performance Tuning

Having a finely-tuned engine is the key to achieving the best gas mileage. Better gas mileage means fewer trips for fill-ups. Having a finely-tuned reporting solution is the key to great performance in terms of the speed of information retrieval. This means avoiding embarrassing conversations with your end users about how slow reports are running. Many aspects of a reporting solution can influence the performance of the entire solution. I cover some of these areas in the following sections.

Benchmarking system performance

Before system performance can be monitored, you must know what level of performance is reasonable given normal working conditions. To do this, establish a server performance baseline by monitoring the report server performance at regular intervals, even when no problems occur.

Searching for performance bottlenecks

Demand on system resources may become extreme enough to cause bottlenecks for the following reasons:

- Resources are insufficient and additional or upgraded components are required.

- Resources are not sharing workloads evenly and need to be balanced.

- A resource is malfunctioning and needs to be replaced.

- A program is monopolizing a particular resource; this might require substituting another program, having a developer rewrite the program, adding or upgrading resources, or running the program during periods of low demand.

- A resource is incorrectly configured and configuration settings need to be changed.

Tuning system performance

Insufficient memory is the most common cause of serious performance problems in computer systems. If you suspect other problems, check memory counters to rule out a memory shortage. Poor response time on a workstation is most likely the result of memory and processor problems; servers are more susceptible to disk and network problems.

Before you start tuning, consider the following recommendations:

- ✔ **Make one change at a time.** In some cases, a problem that appears to relate to a single component might be the result of bottlenecks involving multiple components. For this reason, it is important to address problems individually. Making multiple changes simultaneously may make it impossible to assess the impact of each individual change.

- ✔ **Repeat monitoring after every change.** This is important for understanding the effect of the change and to determine whether additional changes are required. Proceed methodically, making only one change at a time to the identified resource and then testing the effects of the changes on performance. Because tuning changes can affect other resources, it is important to keep a record of the changes you make and review the record after you make each change.

- ✔ **Review event logs.** In addition to monitoring, review these logs because some performance problems generate output you can display in Event Viewer. For more information about using Event Viewer, see the earlier section, "Using Event Viewer."

- ✔ **Compare the performance of network programs to locally run programs.** This can help you determine whether network components are playing a part in performance problems.

Understanding Database Requirements for Report Server

A report server database provides internal storage to one or more report servers. Disk space requirements can vary widely and are difficult to predict. Variables include the number of servers and users serviced by a single database and whether you persist full reports that include data (cached reports or report histories, for example).

To understand your disk space requirements, you must monitor the database size over time and during high-use periods. The topics I mention in the following sections affect the overall space requirements in a report server database.

Reports, folders, shared data source items, and metadata

Report definitions, folders, shared data source items, and other metadata such as schedules, subscriptions, and properties are stored in a report server database. The storage space for these items is small in comparison to the overall storage.

Resources

Resources are stored as binary large objects (BLOBs). If you store image files and collateral documents with your reports, the amount of space you allocate to resources can be small. However, if you use resources as part of an archiving strategy (for example, uploading a generated report as a PDF file), your storage requirements for resources could be very large.

Session state information

Session state information is stored in temporary tables that grow in response to the number of open sessions. Space requirements vary based on the number of users. One row is created for each new session. Unless you have a very large number of users, session state data is not a significant consideration in estimating database size requirements.

Cached reports

Cached reports are stored in temporary tables for a period of time (a cached copy may expire after a number of minutes or at a scheduled time). A cached report includes query results. It can be far larger than the report definition upon which it is based. If caching reports is part of your performance plan, you should allocate a sizeable amount of space for these reports.

For parameterized reports, a separate cached report can be created for every combination of parameter values. For example, if a report has a Region parameter that accepts North, South, East, and West as values, a cached copy for each region may be created.

Report history snapshots and report execution snapshots

Snapshots, whether saved as report history or used only for performance gains, are stored in the report server database (not in temporary tables). As with cached reports, these items may include a large row set. If you use report history to archive reports, you must plan on allocating more space over time to accommodate additional snapshots.

All the items I describe in the preceding sections are allocated space in a report server database. Although I describe each item separately, you cannot allocate or control space for individual item categories. For example, you cannot specify maximum limits for resources, caching, or report history. When estimating database size requirements, you must consider all these items as a whole.

Providing adequate space for caching

If caching reports is part of your performance plan, you should allocate a sizeable amount of space for these reports.

Optimal performance comes from minimizing response times and maximizing throughput; these, in turn, depend on efficient network traffic, disk I/O, and CPU time. This goal is achieved by thoroughly analyzing the application requirements, understanding the logical and physical structure of the data, and assessing and negotiating tradeoffs between database usage.

Response time is the length of time required for the first row of the result set to be returned to the user in the form of visual confirmation that a query is being processed. *Throughput* is the total number of queries handled by the server during a given time. As the number of users increases, so does the competition for a server's resources, which in turn increases response time and decreases overall throughput.

Factors that affect overall system performance include system resources, network architecture, the operating system, and the other database and client applications running on the server.

Configuring Reporting Services Components

Behind-the-scenes components of Reporting Services affect overall system performance. A basic knowledge of how to use these components, how to set their properties, and what to turn off are important in optimizing system performance. I discuss how to deal with these components in the following sections.

Configuring and running large reports

If you're working with a large report, you must choose report generation, rendering, and delivery options that can accommodate large documents. Report size is determined by the row set that comes back from the query. To estimate the size of a report after it is processed, review the row count returned from the query. If it is many thousands or hundreds of thousands of rows, I provide you with some recommendations in the list that follows.

For reports that contain volatile data, report size can change dramatically from one report run to the next. Be sure to monitor the data source to determine how data volatility affects your report and whether you need to follow the steps I prescribe for large reports.

Here are some general recommendations when you're considering how to configure and run large reports:

- ✔ Design the report to support pagination. The report server sends a report one page at a time. If the report includes pagination, you can control how much data is streamed to the browser.

- ✔ Configure the report to run as a report execution snapshot. Use this option if you can't add page breaks. Do not set a time-out value for report execution. Use a schedule to determine when the report data is refreshed.

- ✔ Never run a large report on demand because it almost never succeeds. Configuring a report to run as a report execution snapshot prevents it from running on demand. The HTML rendering format used to initially render a report opens the report in a browser, and most browsers cannot accommodate very large documents. For example, a report that contains 5,000 rows of data almost certainly cannot be viewed in a browser in a single page.

- ✔ Consider distributing a report as a file share on a file directory. If the report is very large, it will hang the browser when a user opens the report in Report Manager.

- ✔ Configure the report to use a shared data source if you want flexibility in determining whether the report is processed. One advantage to using a shared data source is that you can disable it so that it cannot be used to get data for the report. Disabling the data source prevents report processing.

- ✔ Use stored credentials for the data source connection for security and to enable data-driven subscriptions for the report.

- ✔ Disable report history (optional) if you want to conserve disk space. The recommendations for report distribution offered later in this chapter (see the "Distributing reports" section) provide an alternative to storing a large report in report history. To disable report history, clear all the check boxes on the History properties page.

- ✔ Configure the report to use item-level security. Limit access to users who define the subscription and manage the report.

✔ Specify item-level security to allow you to control access to the report. By default, users can open any report that they can view in the folder hierarchy. Even if you configure a report to run as a snapshot, users who can view the report item in a folder can open the report.

✔ To restrict access to the report, edit item security by replacing the default role assignments with new ones that allow access to just those users who need to create the subscription or manage the report.

✔ Leverage the query and execution timeout settings for long-running reports that process during the business day. You want to ensure that the report does not unduly hamper overall system performance during a normal business day of report processing.

Rendering reports

Before you configure report distribution, you need to know which rendering clients can accommodate large documents. The recommended format is Adobe Acrobat Reader (PDF), but you can choose from any format that supports pagination. You can specify the format when you define how the report is distributed.

Distributing reports

You can distribute reports via subscription — an important consideration for working with large reports. Through a subscription definition, you control how the report is distributed and rendered. You can use either a standard subscription or a data-driven subscription to deliver the report. You can also configure your subscriptions to be rendered as a PDF in a file share delivery. Use a desktop application to work with the report after it is generated. Set permissions on the file share to determine who can view the report. Note that after the report is on the file share, it is no longer controlled or secured by Reporting Services.

Using parameters and filters

Because the full set of data is retrieved and then filtered on the report server, the report may not perform as well as a report that filters data at the source using query parameters.

I note in Chapter 7 that for any report a query must be executed and the dataset regenerated each time you change a parameter that modifies the SQL query. It is possible to get better reporting performance by pulling a larger set of data into the dataset and then filtering the rows that will appear in the report.

Using snapshots

When you request a report, Reporting Services merely retrieves and renders the snapshot. You then see the data and layout that were current for the report at the time the snapshot was created. As I mention in Chapter 10, using a snapshot approach helps to improve the overall performance of your reporting environment in a number of situations:

- ✔ **Providing multiple people with access to the same data at the same time.** For example, finance, marketing, and sales want the monthly financial reports when they are produced. You can specify that financial reports be set up as snapshots that execute each month.

- ✔ **Preventing arbitrary report execution.** For example, an invoice report requested during business hours slows overall system performance. In order to alleviate the system load and avoid inconsistent results, you can execute the invoice report as a snapshot every evening.

- ✔ **Controlling long-running reports with queries that take a long time.** For example, the weekly sales report runs a long time and each salesman wants to know results the first thing Monday morning. You can specify that the weekly sales report run every Sunday evening so that it's ready to go on Monday morning.

- ✔ **Using filters for greater flexibility.** Changing the filter values filters only the current snapshot of a particular report.

Caching in on performance

Caching is a performance-enhancement technique. To enhance report server performance, you can preload the cache. To preload the cache with a collection of parameterized report instances, you create a data-driven subscription that uses the Null Delivery Provider. Preloading the cache is achieved through a specialized rendering extension called the *null rendering extension*. When you specify the Null Delivery Provider as the method of delivery in the subscription, the report server targets the report server database as the delivery destination.

This feature is especially useful if you want to cache multiple instances of a parameterized report in which different parameter values are used to produce different report instances. Note that you can only specify query-based parameters on the report. In contrast with other delivery extensions, the Null Delivery Provider does not have delivery settings that you can configure or drive through a subscription definition.

Part V
Developing Advanced Reports

The 5th Wave   By Rich Tennant

"I did this report with the help of a satellite view atmospheric map from the National Weather Service, research text from the Jet Propulsion Laboratory, and a sound file from 'The Barfing Lungworms' new CD."

In this part . . .

In this part, I suggest techniques for you to arrange data in a report to ensure that your report consumer gets the point! You start to master the use of interactive components that the end user can use when the report is presented. Drilling down, navigating seamlessly to other reports, and constructing natural intuitive reports that even executives can understand create some exciting opportunities for reports you can easily build.

To make your choices more plentiful, there are even ways to query OLAP databases that allow extremely fast response time in reporting from potentially huge underlying databases. *Microsoft Reporting Services 2005* has so much capability to advance your reporting capability.

Chapter 15

More About Interactive Reporting

*I*n Chapter 7, I examine some of the capabilities of Reporting Services that enable users to control the report when the report is executed. This means one report can serve many needs. It also provides for interactivity with the user in reporting. By interactive, I'm referring to the fact that the user can click on something in the report as he or she is viewing it and the report responds with an immediate action.

This chapter deals with more interactive features of reports. In this chapter, I review how you can use the visibility to show or hide report items at runtime. I also describe some capabilities of navigating different types of hierarchies and using visibility to provide some interesting interactive effects. I also cover the use of ToolTips to provide cues to the user and document maps to assist in navigating large reports — another interactive aspect of reporting.

Using Visibility Options

If you've read the book *The Invisible Man,* you may have marveled (as I did) at what you could accomplish if you were invisible. You could influence events by being present but invisible. In Reporting Services, you can control the visible properties of almost any control in a report. Specifically, this feature can help you in creating drill-down reports.

A *drill-down report* is an interactive report that allows you to expand and collapse sections of the report to uncover more detail as desired. The technique is useful in delivering information where you want to highlight the general trends but, at the same time, allow investigation into more detail within the same report. In the rest of this chapter, I show you this concept.

Hiding items in a report

Each item in a report has a set of properties that controls the visibility of the item. You can set items to be visible or invisible (but not translucent). These properties are at your disposal for hiding items on a report, conditionally hiding data based on other data in the report. You can conditionally hide data by clicking a control that *toggles* items between visible and hidden. For example, you can create a drill-down report that shows summary data when the report is first loaded and shows detail rows when users click a particular. The secret of this technique is to use the two components of the visible property — namely, Hidden and ToggleItem.

Drilling down on reports

Suppose you want to show a report with the same columns as the Product Profitability report in Chapter 7, but for the rows, you want to show all detail from product category, subcategory, and actual product sold. Furthermore, you want to filter on Reseller (which you can call Customer for our purposes) to see the product sales for a specific customer. Finally, to create a drill thru effect, show detail to the Product SubCategory level initially and provide the user the options to drill down in the same report to see product detail. Follow these steps:

1. **Design the report with all levels of detail desired.**

   Begin with the most detailed level report. This is shown in Figure 15-1. In this example, I added an expression to change the color of the BackgroundColor of the Margin % column based on its values.

2. **Hide the Product Detail and the SubCategory footers by right-clicking to the left of the Detail row and Subcategory footer lines and selecting Properties from the menu that appears. Then expand the Visibility property and set the Hidden property to True.**

3. **Preview the report.**

   Notice that because detail and SubCategory is hidden, they will not show on the report. Instead, the SubCategory headers show as well as the subtotals.=

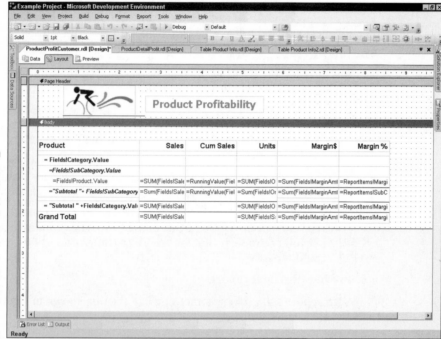

Figure 15-1:
Layout of
the Product
Profitability
report with
`Customer`
parameter
showing all
product
levels of
detail.

4. Toggle the visibility of the hidden rows.

This is the maneuver that makes the drill-down effect really work. The second component of the Visibility property is ToggleItem. This property enables you to interactively toggle the Hidden state of the specified report items. When you designate a report item as a ToggleItem, it gets a small plus sign next to it when the report renders. Clicking that plus sign toggles the visibility of any linked report item. Proceed as follows:

a. Right-click to the left of the Detail row to select the entire row and then click Properties.

b. In the Properties window, expand the Visibility property, and in the ToggleItem property drop-down list, click SubCategory. This enables you to click on the SubCategory and show the detail product rows underneath.

c. Right-click to the left of the SubCategory footer row to select the entire row and then click Properties.

d. In the Properties window, expand the Visibility property and in the ToggleItem property drop-down list, click SubCategory. As a result of clicking on SubCategory, you will see detail rows and the subcategory footer showing subtotals as well.

5. **Show the SubCategory totals when the detail is hidden.**

   Because you still want to be able to see the SubCategory totals when the detail rows are hidden, copy the subcategory totals from the footer row to the header row and then use the same toggle that displays the detail rows to hide the totals in the header row so that the totals are hidden when you drill down. Proceed as follows:

   a. Click on the SalesAmount cell in the SubCategory footer row and hold down the Ctrl key as you click the CumSales, Units, and Margin % cells. With all these columns highlighted, right-click and then select Copy from the list that appears.

   b. Right-click the SalesAmount cell in the Subcategory header row and click Paste. This paste does not copy the Visible property settings, so you need to set these next.

   c. For each of the copied cells, in the Properties window, expand the Visibility property and set the ToggleItem property to SubCategory.

6. **Preview the final report.**

   Your report should look something like the one shown in Figure 15-2.

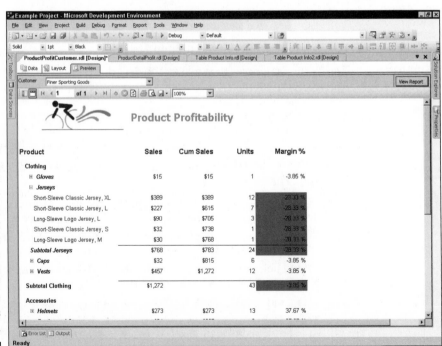

Figure 15-2:
Preview of the Product Profitability report showing a drill-down with Hidden and ToggleItem properties set.

Note: To set the Visible properties for cells in the data region, you can alternatively use the Textbox Properties dialog box, shown in Figure 15-3. To do this, right-click on the cell (such as the SubCategory header SalesAmount cell). This will show the Textbox Properties dialog box (like that shown in Figure 5-3, for example). Click the Visibility tab to select Hidden or Visible and a ToggleItem if appropriate. This is equivalent to setting these Visible property components in the Properties window. You cannot set the Visibility properties for the entire Detail and SubCategory rows in this manner — you must use the Properties window. The Row/Column settings also supersede the individual cell properties within the Row/Column.

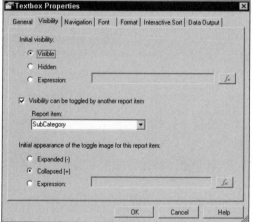

Figure 15-3:
Advanced
Textbox
Properties
dialog box
for the Sub-
Category
header cell
Sales-
Amount.

Drilling down a recursive hierarchy

Consider the example of drilling down on a report of managers and showing all the employees reporting to the manager. This is a little different from the previous example, because this employee hierarchy is usually a *parent-child* relationship in the database. This means that for every employee record in the database, there is an attribute that identifies the manager for that employee. Other types of parent-child relationships that you usually see in databases include departments and business units, cost centers and departments, and territories to regions. How do you tackle this? Follow these steps:

1. **Prepare a query from the DimEmployee table.**

   The Data window for the query is shown in Figure 15-4. You just need the fields EmployeeKey, ParentEmployeeKey, FirstName, LastName, and Title.

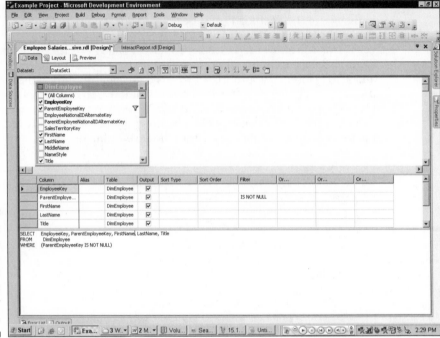

Figure 15-4:
Query
specifica-
tions for the
Employee
Roster
report.

2. Create a simple report layout of employee information.

Define a report with the column headings of Employee Name, Title, Level, and Employee Count. You can drag the Title field from the query into the Title field. You need to define a new calculated field called Employee (or the Employee Name column), which is set to the expression:

=Fields!FirstName.Value + " " + Fields!LastName.Value.

3. Edit the Details Group by clicking inside the table and then clicking the Detail row icon to select the row. Then set the grouping properties as follows:

a. With the details row selected, bring up the Properties window and click on the Grouping property.

b. In the Details Grouping dialog box that appears, enter **RecursiveGroup** as the name.

c. In the Group On section of the General tab, select the =Fields! EmployeeKey.value from the Expression drop-down list. This will group the detail data by employee key.

d. In the Parent Group drop-down list, select the =Fields!Parent EmployeeKey value. This enables you to leverage the parent-child relationships in the data.

4. Display the level number of each employee.

Right-click the cell on the Detail row in Level column and select the Expression menu item. Then in the Edit Expression dialog box, type the following expression:

```
=Level("RecursiveGroup")
```

This Level function returns the current level of depth in a recursive hierarchy. The highest level is 0.

5. **Indent the first column based on level.**

Right-click the first column cell and select Properties menu item to display the Textbox Properties dialog box. Click the Format tab. In the Left spacing textbox, enter the expression:

```
=2 + (Level ("RecursiveGroup") * 20) & "pt"
```

This will left indent by a multiple of 20 points for each level of the employee.

6. **Bold the Highest Level Employee. This will add to the readability of the report. In the Textbox Properties dialog box, click the Font tab. Then for the Weight specification, enter the expression:**

```
=iif (Level ("RecursiveGroup") = 0, "Bold","Normal")
```

Then click OK.

7. **Add the Employee Count field.**

Enter the following expression for this cell in the report:
=Count(Fields!EmployeeKey.Value,"RecursiveGroup",Recursive)

8. **Hide lower levels and toggle the visibility of the lower levels.**

To do this, right-click the detail row and select Edit Group in the list that appears. In the Details Grouping dialog box that appears, click the Visibility tab. Under initial visibility, click expression and enter the following expression:

```
=iif(Level() = 0, False, True)
```

Then check the Visibility Can Be Toggled By Another Report item check box and select Employee as the toggle field.

9. **Preview the report.**

Your final report should look something like the one shown in Figure 15-5.

Dynamically visible data regions

Another way to utilize the visibility options in Reporting Services is to have a textbox toggle the visibility of an entire data region. You can do this by using SubReports within a report while having the textbox be the toggle to showing or hiding the information. Follow these steps:

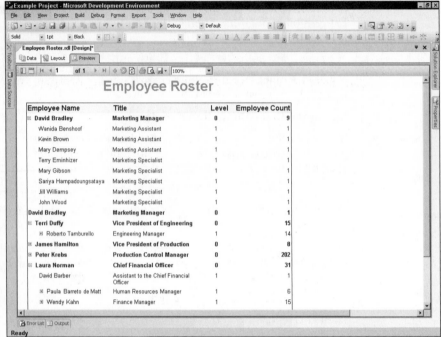

Figure 15-5:
Preview
of the
Employee
Roster with
dynamic
visibility on
parent in a
parent-child
relationship.

1. Build a report with two textboxes and two subreports.

The report I created is shown in Figure 15-6. I have two textboxes labeled Category Sales Analysis and Show Sales Trend. The subreports are actually the reports described in the textbox — the SalesTrend report is a chart showing a sales trend and the Matrix Product Report shows the subcategory sales detail.

2. Set up the SubReports to display when the respective textboxes are toggled.

To do this, right-click on each subreport and select the Properties menu item. This displays the Subreport Properties dialog box. Click the Visibility tab and indicate that this subreport is initially Hidden and then visibility can be toggled by the respective textbox. Do this for each subreport.

3. Preview your report.

Initially you should see a report where the textboxes are visible with a toggle to indicate that they can be expanded. Then click on each textbox. If set up properly, each textbox toggle should show one of the subreports. When both have been toggled on, the report should look like that shown in Figure 15-7.

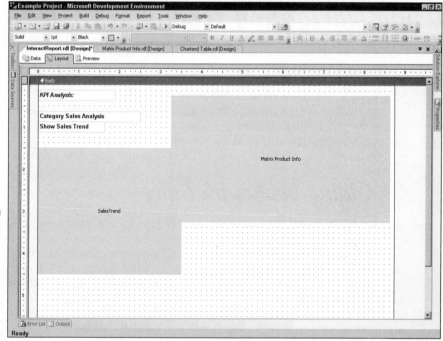

Figure 15-6:
Layout for a report with two textboxes and two subreports.

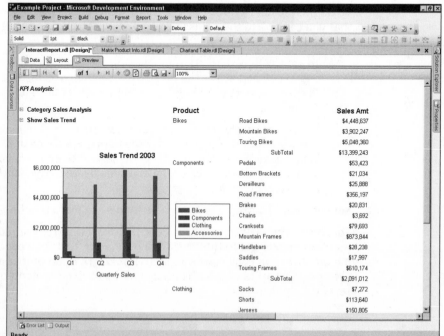

Figure 15-7:
Preview of the report when each textbox has been toggled, showing both subreports.

Using Navigation Techniques

You can also add links to a report to assist in navigating to specific sections of a report quickly. When you add a link to a textbox, image, or chart element, you can specify that the link is a bookmark or a URL. The *bookmark* link provides a link to a bookmark that is set within the current report. The *URL* link provides a way to link to a Web page on the Internet from within a report. I show you some examples and how to use this capability. You can set these up in the Navigation tab of the Advanced Textbox Properties dialog box.

Adding bookmark links

A *bookmark link* is a link that a user clicks to move to another area or page in a report. You set up bookmarks by setting a bookmark on a report item to which users can jump, and by adding a bookmark link on the item you want the users to click to jump to the item with the bookmark. You can set bookmarks on any report item, but you can add bookmark links only to textboxes and images.

The process to define a bookmark and a link to the bookmark is as follows:

1. **Set the bookmark ID for the target to which users can jump.**

   To do this, select a control on the report that requires a bookmark ID so that you can link to this. This will usually be a textbox or a cell within a report.

   a. To set the Bookmark ID, right-click on the target textbox or data region cell and select the Properties menu item. This will show the Textbox Properties dialog box (like that shown in Figure 15-8, for example).

   b. Go to the Navigation tab to set the bookmark. In the bookmark ID textbox, enter the string that is the bookmark ID for that target. In this example, I have set the bookmark ID to an expression: =Fields!Categoryvalue. I want to navigate to the page of the appropriate Category value.

2. **Set the Jump To property from which you can jump to a bookmark.**

   For the source textbox or image control, follow the steps noted in the previous step to get to the Navigation tab in the Textbox Properties dialog box. Then click on the Jump to Bookmark radio button and enter the bookmark ID to which this bookmark link will navigate to on the report. This is shown in Figure 15-8.

Figure 15-8:
Navigation
tab on the
Textbox
Properties
dialog box
showing
how to set a
Jump to
Bookmark
expression.

3. **Preview the report and test the link.**

When you click on the source textbox, you should be able to jump to the report at the bookmark ID indicated in the Jump To command on the bookmark link.

Adding hyperlinks

You can also enable a report to link to a URL that can refer to a file, another report or Web page, or content on the Internet. A hyperlink can be a static URL or an expression that evaluates to a URL. If you have a field in a database that contains URLs, the expression can contain that field, resulting in a dynamic list of hyperlinks in the report. You can add hyperlinks only to textboxes and images.

To set hyperlinks in a report, proceed with Step 2 in the previous section on jumping to bookmarks. In this case, all you need to specify is the Jump to URL for the link when the user clicks on that control in your report. You can hyperlink to the Google Web site by entering the URL http://www.google.com in the combo box under the Jump to URL radio button.

Using Document Maps

Another way a user can interact with a report is through a document map. In the HTML Viewer, a document map appears as a table of contents next to the report. Users can click an item in the table, and the browser jumps to that item in the report.

To add items to a document map, you associate a document map label with each item.

You can use a document map in a report to provide users with a way to navigate to certain areas of the report. When you view an HTML, Excel, or PDF report, a document map appears along the side of the report. Clicking items in the document map refreshes the report and displays the area of the report that corresponds to the item in the document map.

To create a document map, you add document map labels to report items. If any report items have a label, a document map is automatically generated when a user views the report in HTML Viewer.

To add a textbox to a document map, follow these steps:

1. **In the Layout view, right-click the textbox that you want to add to the document map and then click Properties.**

   The Textbox Properties dialog box appears.

2. **Click the Navigation tab.**

3. **In the Document Map Label field, type or select a label or an expression that evaluates to a label.**

   The label or the value of the expression appears in the document map.

A good example of when to use the document maps is when you have multiple page reports where you need to navigate directly to a page selected from a list. To do this, follow these steps:

1. **Define a document map for the report grouping.**

   The report grouping is set in a cell or textbox in a data region. Right-click on the cell or textbox on which the report is grouped (and on which there is a page break set after the group) and select the Properties menu item. The Textbox Properties dialog box appears, as shown in Figure 15-9.

2. **Enter the expression for the items to appear in the document map.**

   In the Document Map Label textbox, enter the expression for the field values you would like to see in the document map that link to specific sections of the report. In this case, for a report with groups defined for Category, I have defined the document map label to be:

```
=Fields!Category.Value
```

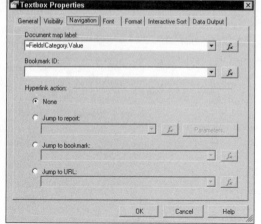

Figure 15-9:
The
Document
Map Label
field to
define a
document
map for a
report.

3. **Preview the Report.**

The completed report is shown in Figure 15-10. This report has a page break after each product category. You can click on one of the product categories listed in the document map to the left of the report and the report will go directly to the page corresponding to the category selected in the document map. You will note that I selected the Components SubCategory from the document map to navigate to that section of the report, which is on the second page of the report.

To add other report items to a document map:

1. **In Layout view, right-click the report item that you want to add to the document map and then select Properties.**

2. **On the Navigation tab, for the Document Map Label field, type or select a label or an expression that evaluates to a label.**

   The label or the value of the expression appears in the document map.

To add a table or matrix group to a document map:

1. **In Layout view, click the table of matrix so that column and row handles appear above and next to the table or matrix.**

2. **Right-click the corner handle of the table or matrix, and then select Properties.**

3. **On the Groups tab, select the group to edit, and then click Edit.**

4. **On the General tab, for Document map label, type or select a label or an expression that evaluates to a label.**

   The label or the value of the expression appears in the document map.

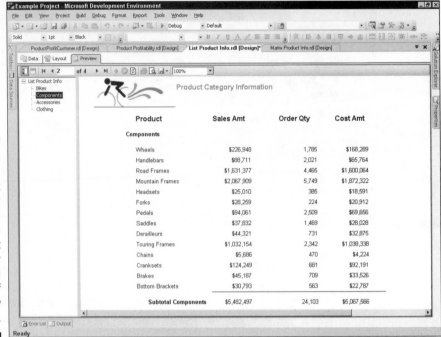

Matrix column groups cannot have document map labels. Only row groups can have a label.

To add a list group to a document map:

1. **In Layout view, right-click the list and then select Properties.**

2. **On the General tab, click Edit Details Group.**

3. **On the General tab, for the Document Map Label field, type or select a label or an expression that evaluates to a label.**

   The label or the value of the expression appears in the document map.

Using ToolTips

A ToolTip appears in a report when the user pauses a mouse pointer over a control on an HTML report. This is helpful in providing users some information about something on a report or help in determining the action the user should take on a report.

To add a ToolTip to a control on a report, proceed as follows:

1. **Go to the advanced properties of the control by right-clicking the control (textbox or data region cell) and selecting Properties from the list that appears.**

   The Textbox Properties dialog box appears.

2. **Enter the ToolTip to be displayed.**

   On the General tab, enter an expression for the ToolTip, such as = `Globals!ExecutionTime`. The expression can also be developed with the Expression Builder by clicking the fx button to the right of the ToolTip textbox. Any expression that evaluates to a ToolTip is valid.

Note: Different rendering formats will use the ToolTip value in different ways.

Interactive Sorting

A final topic on interactive reporting is how end users can change the sort orders on published reports. You would like some tool that enables you to change the direction of a sort on a column, for example, without having to go back into the report and redesign the sort direction. The ability to interact with a report to change the sort order when viewing the report is known as *interactive sorting*.

To add an interactive sort on report, follow these steps:

1. **Right-click on a column heading where you want to change the sort order; then select the Textbox Properties menu item.**

2. **Click on the Interactive Sort tab in the Textbox Properties dialog box.**

   You see an option to add an interactive sort, as shown in Figure 15-11.

3. **Select the check box indicating you want to add an interactive sort item to the report.**

4. **In the Sort Expression combo box, select the field that appears on the detail line in the report for this column.**

5. **Preview the report and notice the icon near the column heading for which you have specified the interactive sort (see Figure 15-12).**

   By clicking this sort icon, you will change the direction of the sort from ascending to descending (and vice versa).

   The new sort order for the specified column in the report will automatically refresh the report to show report detail sorted in the specified direction for the column selected. By clicking on the interactive sort icon again, you again reverse the sort direction.

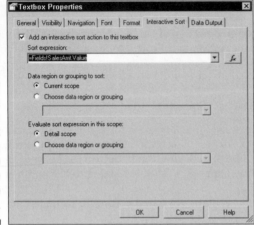

Figure 15-11:
The
Interactive
Sort tab of
the Textbox
Properties
dialog box
showing
how to
specify the
interactive
sort.

You can specify multiple columns in a report to have an interactive sort if needed. This provides flexibility to your end user so he or she has options on how to display a detail report.

Figure 15-12:
Preview of a
report with
interactive
sorting on a
column.
Clicking the
icon at the
column
heading
changes the
sort
direction for
the report
based on
the values in
that column.

Customer Sales for 2004

Store Name	Number of Orders	Total Sales ↓
Roadway Bicycle Supply	2	$265,157.43
Westside Plaza	2	$253,958.70
Field Trip Store	2	$230,230.50
Thorough Parts and Repair Services	2	$225,373.76
Brakes and Gears	2	$223,123.97
Perfect Toys	2	$212,688.04
Rally Master Company Inc	2	$210,548.38
My Stuff, Inc	1	8/27/2005 6:09:02 AM

Chapter 16

Drilling Down to the Details

Remember the good ol' Black and Decker tools? I remember that the Black and Decker drill was an extremely popular market-leading drill allowing you to drill through any type of surface. Every Dad wanted one for Christmas.

In this chapter, I cover the drill-through aspects of reporting. Everyone needs to drill deeper into the details of a report to see what made up its numbers. That's what I mean when I refer to drilling through report information. I survey the techniques available to you for drilling from one report into another from many different perspectives using Microsoft Reporting Services. I also review several scenarios in which you may want to consider drill-through reporting as an innovative way to navigate information that is logically connected but cannot be shown effectively in a single report.

In Chapter 15, I say that you can use dynamic visibility to hide detail until you want to see it in a single report. You also discovered how to use document maps to navigate quickly within a single report to get to more detailed information. This is really an interesting chapter on further interactive reports that you can develop easily. In this chapter, I cover how to drill down to other reports to get more detailed views of more summary information from a starting report. Armed with these valuable techniques, you will be able to amaze friends and impress even the most skeptical in every crowd. These reporting tricks are amazingly easy to set up and enable you to build more complex reporting.

Drilling from Summary to Detail

A *drill-through* report is a report that links itself to another report by passing parameter values to the destination report. You activate the drill-through by clicking a link within your report. Drill-through reports commonly contain details about an item that you see in an initial summary report (sometimes referred to as the *source report* of a drill-through). For example, you may have a sales summary report with a list of orders and sales totals. When a user clicks an order number in the summary list, another report opens containing details about the order. The drill-through report is the detail report containing details about the order.

A destination of a drill-through report is a parameter-based report, the values of which are passed to it by the summary report. To use the same example as the previous paragraph, the drill-through target report contains a parameter that takes an order ID as a value. The summary report includes a drill-through report link for each order number that opens the target detail report when clicked and passes the order ID to it. Any report that you create can be a drill-through report. You can add drill-through links only to textboxes and images.

It doesn't always need to be tabular data from which the drill-through report is linked. It may also be some graphical report. To create a drill-through from a summary report to a detail report, follow these steps:

1. **Create a summary report and a detail report.**

   For this example, I have created a pie chart showing the mix of product category sales for a given year, called ChartCategorySales. This will serve as the summary report. Then I created a detail report which shows the product profitability for all products within a selected ProductCategory. This report is built with a parameter of product category. This detail report is named ProductProfit.

2. **Open the Chart Properties dialog box in the summary report.**

   For this example, I started with the summary report ChartCategorySales. Right-click the chart control and select Properties. The Chart Properties dialog box appears, as shown in Figure 16-1.

3. **Edit the action of the Values of the chart by clicking Edit in the Chart Properties dialog box.**

   The Edit Chart Value dialog box appears.

4. **Click the Action tab.**

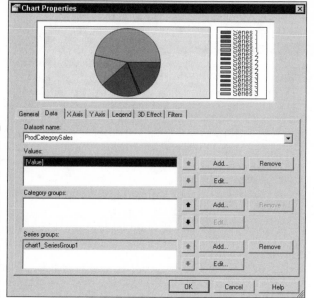

Figure 16-1:
The Chart
Properties
dialog box
showing the
properties
of the Chart-
Category-
Sales
pie chart.

5. **Specify the hyperlink action to be a jump to another report. To do this, select the Jump To radio button on the Action tab and select the detail report ProductProfit from the drop-down list.**

   Note: The list of report names includes all reports in the current report project. If the drill-through report is on the report server but is not in the report project, type the name of the report. The report name can contain a relative or absolute path to the report.

6. **Specify the parameter you will pass to the next report by clicking the Parameter button in the Edit Chart Value dialog box.**

   The Parameters dialog box appears. For each parameter that you need to pass, select it from the drop-down list of parameters defined on the destination report within the Parameter Name column. Then select or enter the expression for the data value from the current report that will be passed when the chart is clicked.

   In this example, you pass the category clicked on the pie chart to the ProductProfit report — so in the Parameter Value column you want to select the expression `=Fields!Category`value that corresponds to the dataset value that is charted in the ChartCategorySales report. This is shown in Figure 16-2.

   Values can contain an expression that evaluates to a value to pass to the report parameter. The expressions in the value list include the field list for the current report.

Figure 16-2:
Parameters
dialog
box for
specifying
the
parameters
passed from
the summary
report
(Chart-
Category-
Sales) to the
detail report
(Product-
Profit).

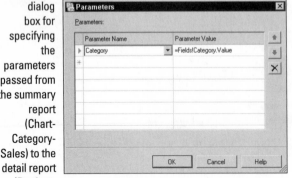

7. Preview your summary report.

The preview of the ChartCategorySales report is shown in Figure 16-3. As you can see, it is a pie chart showing the distribution of Product Category sales for a calendar year.

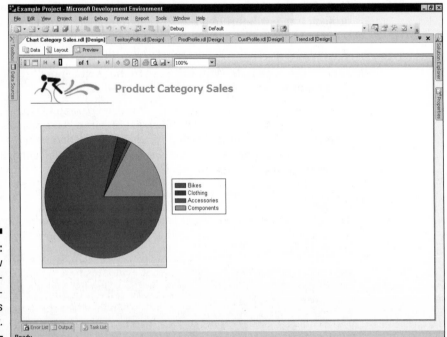

Figure 16-3:
Preview
of the Chart-
Category-
Sales
report.

8. **Test the drill-through capability.**

   Click on the light green area corresponding to Components and, just as designed, the Components value is passed as a parameter to the ProductProfit report. The drill-through report is displayed.

Drilling Down and Pivoting on Detail Lines

Consider pivoting during a drill down. A *pivot* involves drilling down first on one variable and then at that drill-down level, drilling through on another variable. For example, start at the top ten customer list and then drill to a particular customer to see the products purchased by that customer. Then from that view, drill down to see the history of product purchases for that customer over the last two years. In that analysis, which begins with a view of customers, drill down on products and then pivot on time.

Drilling down usually refers to navigating a hierarchy of information. For example, if you begin with Product Category, you can drill down to view the Product Subcategories within the category and drill down further to see the products within the subcategory. All of this can be done on the same report (see Chapter 15 for an example). You would usually use the terms *link* or *drill across* or *pivot* to describe navigating to another report of the information along a different variable. For example, if I drill down the product hierarchy and then want to look at the regions where the product is sold, this would amount to a link or drill across or pivot along the territory variable. This assumes that you have multiple variables along which you can analyze the data. Some people refer to this drilling and pivoting as slicing and dicing the data. Here the Vegematic analogy wins over the Black and Decker drill analogy.

To create a drill and pivot analysis, start from the Top 10 Customers report (TopTenCustomers), then drill through to the Product Profitability report (ProductProfitCustomer) filtered on the selected customer. Finally, from this report, for a selected product line, drill through to the Product Profile report (ProdProfileFilter). This destination report will be filtered on the selected profit product.

Follow these steps:

1. **Modify the top-level report to allow drill-through on the detail line.**

   In this example, I began with the Top Ten Customers report and set up the drill-through. First, right-click on the cell containing the report line description and click the Navigation tab. Then select the Jump to Report option and enter the report to which you want to drill through — the Product Profitability report or ProductProfitCustomer.

2. **Set up the parameter to be passed to the drill-through report. Still at the Navigation tab of the Textbox Properties dialog box, click the Parameters button and specify the parameters required in the dialog box shown in Figure 16-2. For each parameter, specify the data value in the summary report which will be passed to the drill-through report.**

   I specified that the parameter reseller defined in ProductProfitCustomer be supplied with the value

   ```
   =Fields!reseller.value
   ```

   from the current report.

   Note: The number of parameters that display here correspond to the number of parameters on the drill-through report.

3. **Modify the color and text decoration properties of the detail line to make it appear as a hyperlink.**

   To do this, select the cell with the detail line description in the table and bring up the Properties window. Set the Color property to SlateBlue and the TextDecoration property to Underline. You can see this effect behind the dialog box in Figure 16-6.

4. **Modify the drill-through report to enable another drill through to the Product Profile report.**

   To do this, right-click on the cell with the detail line description in the ProductProfitCustomer report and select Properties. The Textbox Properties dialog box appears. Click the Advanced button in the Textbox Properties dialog box, which displays the Advanced Textbox Properties dialog box. Click the Navigation tab, select the Jump to Report option, and enter the name of the report you want to drill through — the Product Profile report or ProdProfileFilter. See Figure 16-4.

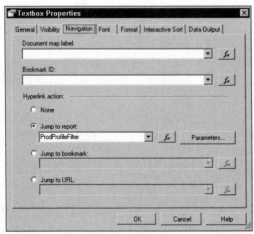

Figure 16-4: The Advanced Textbox Properties dialog box showing the setting to drill through to the ProdProfile-Filter report.

5. Set up the parameter to be passed to the profile report.

In the Advanced Textbox Properties dialog box, click the Parameters button to see the Parameters dialog box, and then select each parameter from the drop-down list in the Parameter Name column. Select the data value in the summary report which will be passed to the drill-through report. I specified that the parameter prod defined in ProdProfileFilter be supplied with the value

```
=Fields!Product.Value
```

from the current report. This is shown in Figure 16-5.

Figure 16-5:
The
Parameters
dialog box
correspond-
ing to the
parameter
for the
Product
Profile
report,
which is the
result of the
drill through
from the
Product
Profitability
report.

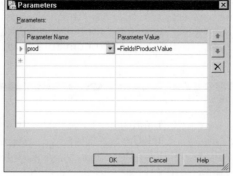

The names in the parameter list must match the expected parameters in the target report exactly. If the names do not match, or if an expected parameter is not listed, the drill-through report fails.

6. Modify the color and text decoration properties of the detail line to make it appear as a hyperlink.

Select the cell with the detail line description in the table and bring up the Properties window. Set the Color property to SlateBlue and the TextDecoration property to Underline. (See Figure 16-6.)

7. Preview your top-level report and test the drill-through capability you have defined.

The starting report in this scenario is the Top Ten Customers report, very similar to Figure 16-8 later in this chapter. Note that each Reseller in the first column of the report appears highlighted as if it is a hyperlink on the Web. Click on any one of these resellers and you will drill down to the Product Profitability report for the clicked customer as shown in Figure 16-6.

You would then expand the product subcategory on this report (featuring the dynamic visibility described in Chapter 15). The product detail lines are then hyperlinked to the Product Profile report. Selecting any product detail line in the report will bring up the Product Profile report for the clicked product, as shown in Figure 16-7.

In the previous example, you can see two types of drill downs featured. The first is the drill-through report for which you change the font to look like a hyperlink to communicate to the user that a drill-down capability is available. The second form of drill-down is the dynamic visibility (described in Chapter 15), where you can expand the subcategory level in the Product Profitability report to see the underlying products purchased by the customer. Alternatively, a document map (see Chapter 15) could be added for yet another drill-down functionality in the Product Profitability report.

Figure 16-6:
Second report in the drill-through scenario — Product Profitability featuring the customer parameter-based filter and hyperlinks for each product detail line.

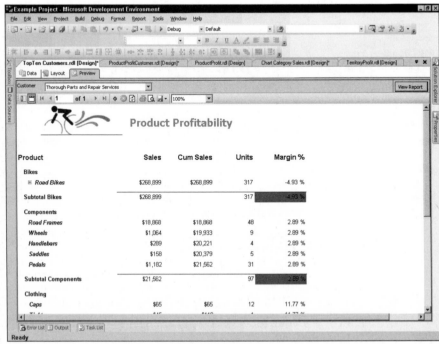

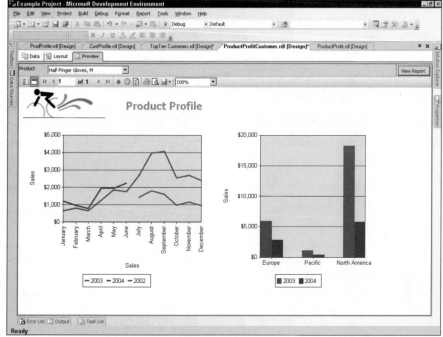

Figure 16-7:
Third report
in the drill-
through
scenario —
Product
Profile
featuring
the product
parameter-
based filter.

Providing Multiple Drill-down Options

Consider the case of the Top Ten Customers report in the previous section. You have allowed the user to drill down from any customer into the product purchase history and then pivot to the product profile. What if you wanted to begin at the Customer list and then go immediately to a Customer Profile report? The Customer Profile report would show a monthly history of product purchases for the last two years as well as the last two years' distribution of product sales across product categories.

In this situation, you need to enable the user to drill down to product detail history as I describe in the previous section. In addition, you need to provide a way to drill or link to the customer profile for any customer selected. One of the ways to enable this is to provide yet another link on each report detail line to allow a jump to the customer profile, passing the customer selected as a parameter.

In order to avoid cluttering the report detail too much, I have elected to put this second link in the last column of the Top Ten Customer report. I used the following steps to create the desired effect:

1. **Add a column to the Report Detail line in the source report.**

   I simply add a column to the right of the last column of the table control in the Top Ten Customers report.

2. **Add an expression that will tell the user what the link will be.**

   In the cell in the detail row in this column, I add the expression:

   ```
   ="Profile"
   ```

   This indicates that the link will navigate to the Customer Profile report.

3. **Format the link to make it appear as a hyperlink.**

   To do this, select the cell with the detail line description in the table and bring up the Properties window. Set the Color property to SlateBlue and the TextDecoration property to Underline. If you preview this report, it should look like Figure 16-8.

4. **Modify the source report to enable another drill-through to the profile report.**

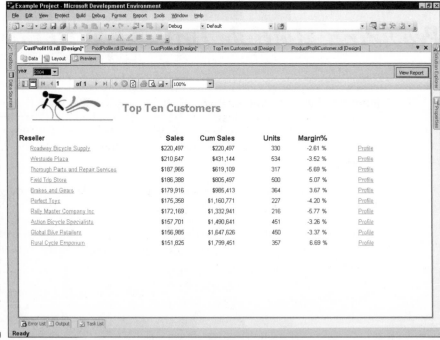

Figure 16-8: Preview of the Top Ten Customers report showing hyperlinks to drill down by customer or pivot to a Customer Profile.

To do this, right-click on the cell with the detail line description in the TopTenCustomer report and select Properties from the list that appears. This will display the Textbox Properties dialog box. Click the Advanced button in the Textbox Properties dialog box, which displays the Advanced Textbox Properties dialog box. Click the Navigation tab and click the Jump to Report option and enter the report to which you want to drill — the Customer Profile report or CustProfile.

5. **Set up the parameter to be passed to the Customer Profile report.**

   Still at the Advanced Textbox Properties dialog box, click the Parameters button to see the Parameters dialog box. Now select each parameter from the drop-down list in the Parameter Name column. Then select the data value in the summary report which will be passed to the drill-through report. I specified that the parameter cust defined in CustProfile be supplied with the value:

   ```
   =Fields!ResellerName.Value
   ```

   from the current report.

6. **Preview your top-level report and test the drill-through capability you have defined.**

   The starting report in this scenario is the Top Ten Customers report shown in Figure 16-8. Note that the <u>Profile</u> hyperlink appears on each report detail line. Click on the <u>Profile</u> link for any customer and you will navigate to the Customer Profile report shown in Figure 16-9 for the selected customer.

You can use other techniques to link to other reports. You can use images and textboxes as well as cells in a table or matrix because all of these controls support a Navigation tab that permits you to use these controls (or their cells) to navigate to other reports. Even a chart control enables you to define an action on each graphic element being rendered. For the chart control, you need to open its Property page and click on the Data tab and edit one of the values. This brings up the Edit Chart Value dialog box where you can select the action tab, which presents the hyperlink actions such as jumping to reports, URLs, or bookmarks.

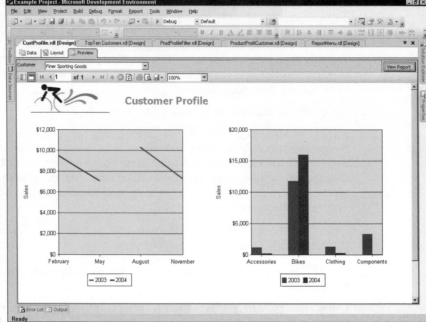

Figure 16-9:
Preview of
the
Customer
Profile
report after
you click the
Profile link.

Providing Navigation Links to Reports

Suppose you want to design reports for instances when you start at one group of reports that represents the top of a pyramid of reports. As an example, you may have a set of top ten reports from which you can start an analysis. From any of these top ten reports, you want to be able to quickly navigate to the other one to determine how you may want to begin your drill-down analysis.

This situation is an example of monitoring information from several standard viewpoints with a need to move quickly between these unique viewpoints. When something in the report provokes further exploration, a drill-down analysis can begin with the drill-through links in each report.

You must accommodate multiple navigation links in each of the top ten reports. You can enable these links by using images to represent links to other reports. If you are not graphically adept (like me), you can use the low-tech approach of making a textbox resemble an image and setting the navigation properties of the textbox to do your work.

I use an example of leveraging Top Ten Customers, Top Ten Products, and Top Ten Salesmen as the high-level reports at the top of the pyramid. Each report will have three buttons (which will be produced with textboxes) to navigate to any of the other reports in this group. So I need three buttons — Customers,

Products, and Salesman. I will show all three buttons when we view each of the reports. To make it interesting, I'll change the BackgroundColor of the textboxes to show one color when the link corresponds to the current report (so clicking it would not navigate anywhere else) and another color when the link will take you to another report.

Follow these steps to make it happen:

1. **Place and format the navigation buttons on each report.**

   Begin with the Top Ten Customers report. Figure 16-10 shows how I placed and formatted the textboxes and where I placed them on the report. I set the BackgroundColor of the textbox to LightCoral if the link is for the current report and to LightSalmon if the link can be taken to the other reports. I personally like pastel colors, but you can be as bold as you want.

   Note: Because you cannot use fields in report headers or footers, buttons used for linking need to be placed in the body of the report.

2. **Set the navigation properties for each of the buttons on each report.**

   To navigate to the Top Ten Products report, set the navigation properties for the Product button. Right-click the textbox and select Properties to bring up the Textbox Properties dialog box. On the Navigation tab, you specify that you want to jump to a report called ProdProfit10 and then select the parameter you need to pass. For all the top ten reports, we are using CalendarYear as a parameter to filter the report for the current year only.

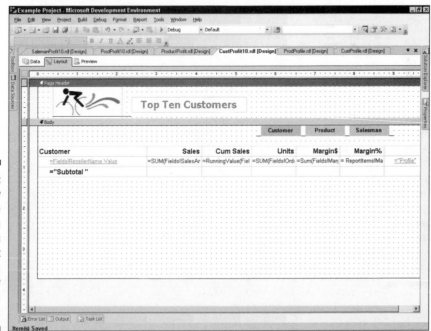

Figure 16-10: Layout view of the Top Ten Customers report showing the new navigation buttons.

TIP

For the sake of review, in order to filter effectively to construct the top ten list style of report, all you need to do beyond constructing the basic report table (or matrix or list) is add the following filter to the detail line group:

```
Operator ‡'Top N'
Value ‡ '=10'
```

For the grand finale, the report flow from this example reporting scenario is illustrated in the following figures. I begin with a logical starting point of the Top Ten Customers (see Figure 16-11).

Click the Products button to navigate to the Top Ten Products report. Note that the Products button has a different background color than the others because this is the current focus of the navigation options.

Then click the Salesman button to navigate to the Top Ten Salesman report.

By clicking the Profile hyperlink on any of the previous reports, you can navigate to the Product Profile report passing the parameter of the current year. This is shown in Figure 16-12. This is merely an illustration of what you can set up for navigating between reports and the parameter passing you would like to implement.

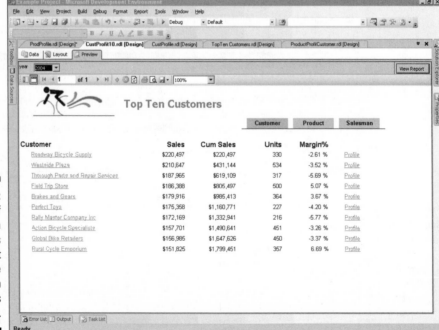

Figure 16-11: Preview of the Top Ten Customers report showing the navigation hyperlinks and buttons.

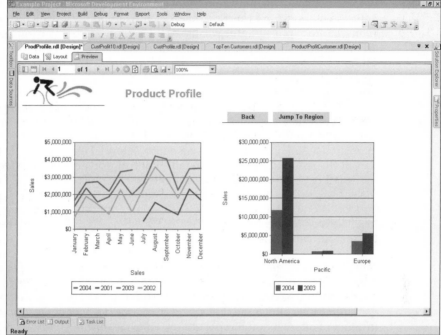

Figure 16-12:
Preview of
the Product
Profile
report with
the year
parameter
passed from
any of the
top ten
reports.

Handling Multiple Drill Paths

Consider another interesting case of drilling through to other reports. Suppose you want to design for the case that you have many different drill paths for investigating information more deeply. For example, starting at the Top Ten Products report, you may want to drill down to see a different report perspective where you see a selected product sales by customer or a selected product sales by region. You would like to make this decision while you are viewing the Top Ten Products report and click a hyperlink to quickly see the desired perspective.

This is where your creativity comes into play. You know how Reporting Services helps you create drill-through reports. You also know how to present navigation links as hyperlinks to the user. You now need to consider how to fit these options into the screen real estate of a report to provide some dynamic analyses at the click of a mouse.

Here's one way to do this. Consider that the image control also permits you to set up navigation to another report while passing the necessary parameters. Images take up less real estate than textboxes (unless the textboxes have a very small font). Pictures speak a thousand words, so you can indicate options with a picture that you teach your users to use. Using images, however, requires some graphics skills — unless you can borrow from some clip art and have common pictures tell your navigation option story to your users.

Now the question of where to place the images. I am going to be so bold to suggest that you place the navigation options to the left of the detail report line descriptions. I want to place them in the detail if I am passing the detail description (in this case, product) to the drill-through report. If I am only interested in doing this analysis at a subtotal level, I can provide these options only at the subtotal line. So in the table control, you need to insert a column to the left of the Product heading column and then place an image control in the corresponding detail cell, as shown in Figure 16-13. Here I have added two options — one for the Drill Down by Customer option represented by the little headlike icon and the other for the Drill Down by Area option represented by the textbox caption Area with an 8-point Arial font.

The preview of this revised Top Ten Products list is shown in Figure 16-14. Note that I have seven different navigation options on this single report. I have the three navigation options at the top ten level represented by the navigation buttons above the report and then four types of navigation from any product of interest in the report body. This has now become an interesting reporting scenario for the user.

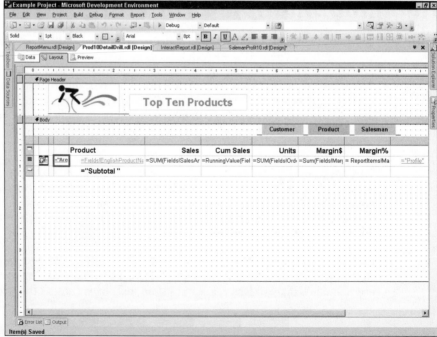

Figure 16-13:
Layout of the Top Ten Products report with two additional drill-by options to the left of the Product column heading.

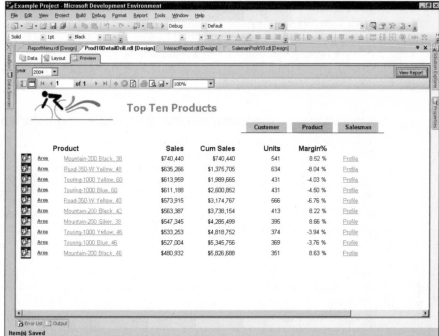

Figure 16-14:
Preview of
the Top Ten
Products
report with
the seven
navigation
options.

Preparing a Report Menu Page

Most business users like to see a set of options to select from in determining where to begin their investigation or what report they would like to see. This main menu approach can also serve as a way to organize the collection of reports available to you.

You have a lot of flexibility through the use of textboxes, images, lines, rectangles, and other controls of the types of reports you can build. You don't even need a dataset to source from if you don't need it. Some designers develop a table of reports available to a given user. You can create a dataset to query that table and present it to the user as a list or table of reports. If you had the URL of the report you would like to render stored in this table, that could be a field in your dataset you can reference in the Jump to URL navigation option. But that requires some planning and perhaps a DBA to set up and maintain the tables.

The low-tech way to set up a report menu as a report is to add textboxes in a report that requires no dataset and set the navigation properties and parameters values (if any) for each textbox. Adding other images and a company logo can spice up the report menu page. I put in a graphic at the base of the report to give it a more polished look.

When I preview this report, I see what is shown in Figure 16-15 — a respectable starting point for my key reports.

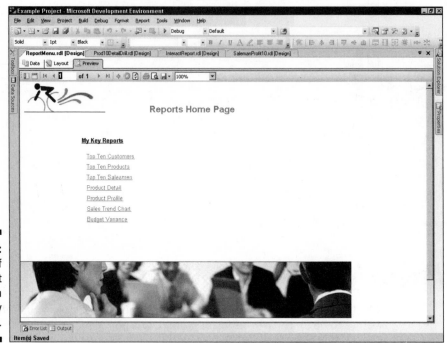

Chapter 17

Reporting from OLAP Data Sources

*A*mong the many abbreviations and acronyms that are common in reporting and analysis is one called OLAP — *online analytical processing*. OLAP is all about gaining easy, speedy access to information representing summaries of vast underlying databases. It's also an analytical framework that shows information rolled up to summary information and provides natural drill-down relationships in the information. This chapter is all about OLAP.

Discovering OLAP Capabilities

OLAP is about delivering meaningful information to users who are sifting through large volumes of data (think retail point-of-sale information from cash registers all over the country for Wal-Mart). The information needs to be well organized and complete, with summary information presented first, and provide an intuitive way of drilling down to more detail. A fundamentally new way of organizing data is required. This new model is called the dimensional model.

OLAP provides these benefits to analytical users:

- ✔ The dimensional model makes navigating and exploring information easy.
- ✔ An analytical query language provides user access to business data relationships.
- ✔ OLAP technology precalculates frequently-queried data to enable fast response to ad hoc queries.

Learning the dimensional model

The relational database provides a scheme to organize information, and SQL provides a language you can use to query the information. The focus of relational database design is to separate redundant data into distinct tables to save on data storage and overhead. This can lead to complex data models where there are bunches of very small tables (few columns) all linked to other small tables. This increases the efficiency of "transaction processing," where you end up having to update only a small number of columns in any given transaction, but bunches of very small tables all linked to bunches of other very small tables can lead to situations where it's darned difficult to maintain some kind of overview.

And when you start to lose the overview, the task of reporting gets more and more difficult. The bewildering spider webs of joins you must perform in SQL to get information out of your databases may have made sense from a transaction processing perspective, but if you want efficient reporting, you need to consider other ways of modeling data.

The dimensional data model is a great way to make any reporting you'd want to do super-efficient. A dimensional model consists of a central table of the facts of the business referred to as a *fact table*. The fact table contains the numerical data or "facts" that are of interest in reporting. The numerical data is referred to as measures. Examples of measures in a fact table of Sales data are sales dollar amount, sales price, product cost, and units sold. Each measure in a fact table references the intersection of business variables describing the context of the data. For example, the day of the sale, the product sold, the store from which it was sold, and information about a coupon if it was used to purchase the product. These business variables are referred to as dimensions of the business. So the fact table consists of keys to each dimension relevant to the fact and its associated measures.

The *dimensional model* refers to how the data model is organized. For each fact table, related dimension tables define the context of the measures. In a data model, this is represented as a central fact table surrounded by the dimension tables that are related to the fact. In the fact table, you find unique primary keys representing distinct rows in the dimension tables. Each dimension table has a primary key of the unique key for the dimension value. The primary key to the fact table is the multipart set of keys of the dimensions. Because there are many facts surrounding a fact that they support, this is usually referred to as a *star schema*. The database `AdventureWorksDW`, which we use to show examples in other chapters and which is installed as part of the Documentation and Samples option in the SQL Server 2005 installation, is an example of a star schema.

Just the facts, Ma'am

When thinking about how facts fit into a dimensional data model, it's important to remember that, with fact tables, the useful facts in the table are additive — meaning they can be added together across multiple dimension values and still remain a fact for a summary level of a dimension. Most queries will span many rows in the fact table as trends are being investigated and reported. Therefore, the fact columns need to be summed in the SQL query. As a result, they must be additive to return meaningful results.

In order to build fact tables from operational data, you need to go through a process called *data transformation*. The transformation process results in a new structure to the underlying data, which is more efficient for reporting and analysis. This transformation requires that you apply some serious logic to the source database. SQL Server 2005 Integration Services provides many features that enable efficient data transformation into dimensional models that are ripe for OLAP.

Understanding dimensions

Dimension tables contain descriptive text information. The dimension attributes are used as the source of the constraints in querying dimensional models and they are most often the source of the row and column headings in the result set. The power of the dimensional database increases with the quality and the number of attributes in the dimension tables. Each dimension value is referred to as a *member* of the dimension. For example, June is a member of the Time dimension and Mountain Bikes is a member of the Product Category dimension.

A dimension is an organized set of categories (levels) that describe data in the fact table. Attributes in a dimension can be organized as levels in hierarchies, which provide navigation paths in a cube. You are used to organization hierarchies since this is how organization charts are laid out. Products are organized into a hierarchy of two levels in the AdventureWorksDW database: Product Subcategories and Product Categories. Multiple products can share the same Product Category, so a hierarchy can be constructed in which the Product Category attribute serves as a higher, parent level to the Product attribute. Dimension members at the highest levels of the hierarchies are referred to as parents of the next level below in the hierarchy (which are referred to as children of the parent). For example, each member in the Product Category attribute can have one or more child members in the Product Subcategory attribute.

These categories typically describe a similar set of members upon which you may want to base an analysis. For example, a geography dimension might include levels for Country, Region, State or Province, and City.

Constructing cubes

A *cube* is a set of data that is organized and summarized into a multidimensional structure defined by a set of dimensions and measures. The multidimensional structure, or cube, is a data storage object that treats data as a dimension and measures information in cells (like cells of a spreadsheet). Each cell is addressed by a set of coordinates that specify a position in the structure's dimensions. For example, the cell at coordinates {SALES, 2005, Chicago, SQL Server} would contain the summary of SQL Server sales in Chicago in 2005. The structure of a cube is determined by business, not data, requirements. In other words, a cube is designed to answer the kinds of questions that users ask instead of questions that applications ask.

Introducing Microsoft Analysis Services

OLAP cubes provide an easy-to-use mechanism for querying data with quick and uniform response times. A new aspect of SQL Server 2005 called Analysis Services allows you to construct OLAP cubes based on information in your relational database. You can build Analysis Services projects within Business Intelligence Development Studio just as you would for Reporting Services projects. The cube structure is illustrated in the Analysis Services project shown in Figure 17-1.

You can see from Figure 17-1 that there are rich capabilities for interacting with measures and dimensions defined for a relational data model and for creating a cube representation using Analysis Services. This is really a subject for another book, so I won't attempt to go into any great detail here. However, it is important to note that SQL Server 2005 does provide rich functionality to create OLAP cubes as data sources for excellent analytical reporting and analysis.

Gaining perspective

The Adventure Works cube shown in Figure 17-1 comes from the AdventureWorks AS sample Analysis Services database that comes with SQL Server 2005. This cube contains 6 measure groups (related measures) and 18 different dimensions, representing sales, sales forecasting, and financial data.

You can utilize Analysis Services to create a perspective that reduces the complexity of a cube by allowing you to define a viewable subset of the cube. The perspective controls the visibility of objects contained by a cube. You can build perspectives that contain only those objects relevant to a specific purpose such as sales forecasting or monthly financial reporting.

Figure 17-1:
Analysis
Services
project
showing the
Cube
Structure
window
highlighting
a star
schema for
financial
reporting.

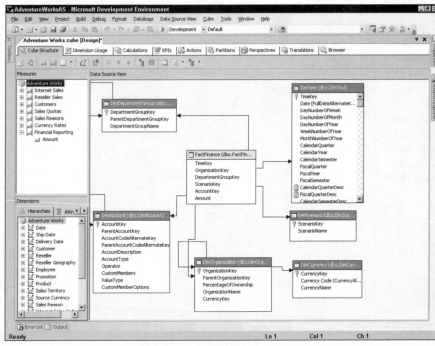

You can utilize Analysis Services to define precalculated summary data called aggregations to allow for even faster response to queries from a cube. Aggregations are created for a cube before business users access it, by running a series of queries against the underlying fact and dimension tables to precalculate the summary data. When you process the cube, Analysis Services uses a combination of proactive caching, multidimensional data storage, relational data storage, and optimized queries to retrieve and calculate summary data for the cube. This is precalculated and available quickly when you query a cube.

After you design a cube using Microsoft Analysis Services, you can process it to create an Analysis Services database. Then you can connect to Analysis Services using the SQL Server Management Studio and browse the data in the cube to begin an analysis. To connect to the AdventureWorksDW Analysis Services database, expand the folders until you see the cube folder and right-click on the cube of interest. If you select Browse from the pop-up menu, you will see a browser window to the right, as shown in Figure 17-2. You can then drag dimensions into the rows, columns, and filters, and you can drag measures into the table of data values. Figure 17-2 shows the result of filtering on calendar year 2003 and Reseller Sales Amount by products and organizational units.

Figure 17-2:
Analysis
Services
cube being
browsed in
SQL Server
Manage-
ment Studio
to show
how
views of
information
can be
created
quickly with
a drag-and-
drop
approach
from a cube.

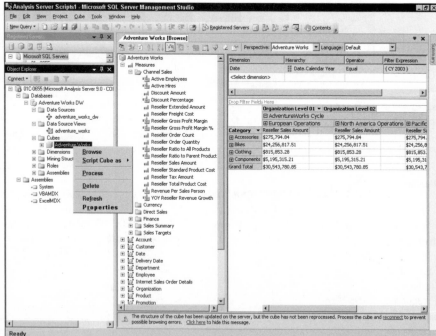

Speaking the Language of OLAP

OLAP products typically use a query language more suited for accessing multi-dimensional information. Microsoft Analysis Services uses the language called MDX, which stands for Multidimensional eXpressions, to access and manipulate multidimensional data. MDX is a unique language that can reference multiple dimensions in a dimensional model within an Analysis Services cube.

Building an MDX query

SQL is designed to retrieve data in two dimensions: a column dimension and a row dimension. OLAP cubes, however, have multiple dimensions (which poses a bit of a problem for standard SQL). At the intersection of the dimensions in a cube, there are one or more data elements or measures. MDX returns a subset of the OLAP cube. MDX uses tuples to identify cells in a cube. A *tuple* is one member, either explicitly or implicitly referenced, from each hierarchy in the cube. If a member from a given hierarchy is not explicitly referenced in the tuple, the default member from that hierarchy is implicitly included in the tuple. Tuples identify cells of interest in a cube. Tuples can specify sections of the cube (called slices). A tuple appears in braces, and levels of a dimension appear in brackets, so that an example of a tuple is:

{Time.[2nd half], Product.[Product Category]}

A collection of tuples is a called a *set*. Because multiple dimensions can be used in MDX, each dimension is referred to as an axis. The terms "column" and "row" in MDX can be used as aliases for the first two axis dimensions in an MDX query. You can use a SELECT statement to select the dimensions and measures to be returned. You can also specify what tuple will appear in columns and what tuple will appear in rows.

MDX syntax is very robust, and it can be complex. MDX was designed to provide a simple, effective way of querying multidimensional data. There are functions like TopCount() that will retrieve the top x members of a cube satisfying the requirements of a query. An example of the MDX query required to retrieve the top 10 stores in sales for 2004 from the Reseller Sales cube is:

```
SELECT
{[Measures].[Sales Amount]} on columns,
{TopCount([Reseller].[Reseller Name].members,10,
          [Measures].[Sales Amount])} on rows
FROM [Reseller Sales]
WHERE ([Order Date].[Qtr 1 2004])
```

You will notice that the cube itself is referred to in the FROM clause. The WHERE clause can be used to further filter the tuples and sets specified in the specifications found in the SELECT clause.

Defining calculations with MDX

A *calculation* is an MDX expression or script, used to define a measure, member, set, or other object associated with a cube. Calculations allow you to add objects, such as measures, to a cube that are derived from other measures in the cube. For example, you can define the expression for Gross Profit to be Sales less Operating Cost. Calculations allow you to extend the capabilities of a cube, adding flexibility and analysis power.

Defining KPIs with MDX

Within Analysis Services, you can define business metrics, called *key performance indicators* (KPIs), that consist of relevant attributes to form industry goals and benchmarks. The performance of your business can be measured by how well the business is doing on its KPIs. A KPI collection includes a measure, a goal, display properties, and variances. Companies use KPIs to track performance and improve decision-making.

KPIs are defined within the Business Intelligence Development Studio for Analysis Services projects using the KPI window, as shown in Figure 17-3. You need to right-click on a cube in the Solution Explorer and select the option to View Designer. It requires a knowledge of MDX to define how these KPIs are calculated. You need to define the value of the KPI, the goal for the value to set the target for the KPI, the status of the KPI, which is an MDX expression to calculate status as a normalized value in the range −1 (very bad) to +1 (very good), and the trend to evaluate if the value of the KPI is better or worse than its goal.

KPIs can be browsed within the Business Intelligence Development Studio. You can click the Browse button within the KPI window to show the KPI values for the cube. This allows you to view the values of the KPIs as well as where you are compared with the target values and how it is trending relative to the goal. You can also filter on any number of dimensions to see the KPI values for that part of the cube. This is highlighted in Figure 17-4.

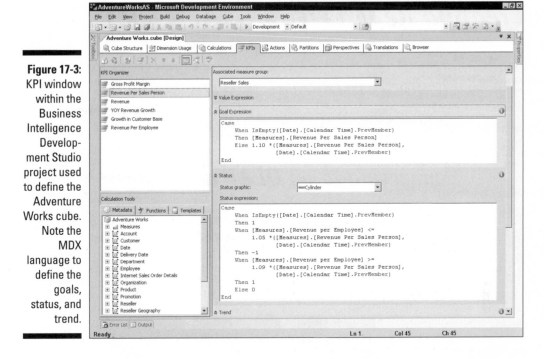

Figure 17-3:
KPI window within the Business Intelligence Development Studio project used to define the Adventure Works cube. Note the MDX language to define the goals, status, and trend.

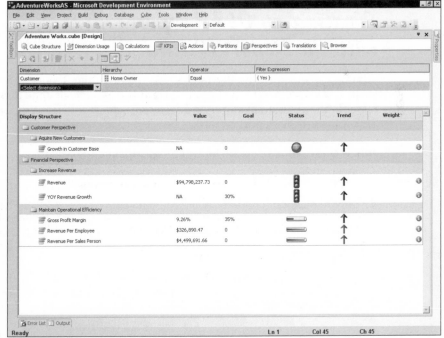

Figure 17-4:
Browsing the KPIs within the Business Intelligence Development Studio project used to define the Adventure Works cube. This shows the KPI values for homeowners.

Creating Reports with OLAP Cubes

In the previous section, I describe what you get with Microsoft Analysis Services. You can build OLAP cubes, define KPIs, and calculate members. This offers additional features from reporting from relational data sources. In this section, you will see what is involved with creating reports from OLAP data sources. You can expect performance to be much quicker with OLAP databases, especially if there are large volumes of data involved.

Connecting to an OLAP data source

The first step in creating any report is establishing a connection with the server and connecting to the data source. To connect to an SQL Server 2000 Analysis Services server, you must set the data source type to OLE DB Provider for OLAP Services 9.0 or select data source type as Microsoft SQL Server Analysis Services. The following example shows a connection string for the sample Analysis Server database Adventure Works DW running on your database server:

```
provider=MSOLAP.2;data source=<report server name>;
initial catalog= Adventure Works DW
```

Creating an OLAP report with the Report Wizard

Starting in a Business Intelligence Development Studio Reporting Services project, you can initiate the Report Wizard by right-clicking the Reports folder in the Solution Explorer and selecting Add New Report from the menu. This will start the Report Wizard.

Follow these steps to create an OLAP report using the wizard:

1. **Select the shared data source AdventureWorksAS.**

   If you have not created the shared data source yet, refer to Figure 17-5 for the connection string to connect to the sample OLAP cube that ships with SQL Server 2005. Then click the Next button.

2. **Begin designing your query.**

   Here you see the wizard screen show in Figure 17-5. If know the MDX expression for what you want to see, then you can enter it directly in the textbox with the OLAP cube measures and dimensions.

Figure 17-5:
The Design
the Query
step in the
Report
Wizard.
This step is
unique to
the OLAP
data source.
You can start
the Query
Builder
from this
dialog box.
Otherwise,
click the
Query
Builder
button and
you can
begin to
interact.

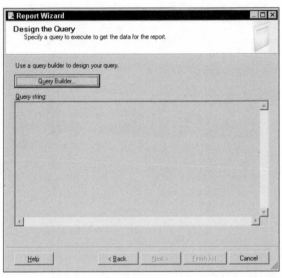

3. **Work with the Query Builder dialog box to complete your query.**

   Upon clicking the Query Builder button, you will see the Query Builder dialog box shown in Figure 17-6.

   a. You will see cube information on the left in the tree called Metadata. You can select a high-level dimension and drag this into the preview area on the right. This will show all the levels in that selected dimension as separate columns in the preview area.

   b. You can select additional columns you don't want to see and either drag them off the preview area or right-click the column heading and select Delete <column name> from the pop-up menu.

   c. You can expand the tree folder called Measures or KPIs to select individual measures to see on the report. You can also filter at the top of the page by clicking in the <Select dimension> cell.

Figure 17-6:
Query
Builder
dialog box
showing
the cube
metadata on
the left from
which you
can drag
and drop
dimensions,
measures,
and KPIs
into the
preview
area on the
right. You
can also
specify
dimension
filters at the
top right.

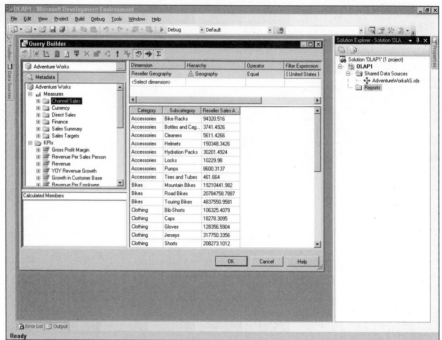

4. Create calculated members, if necessary.

You can click on the control that looks like a calculator to add calculated members to the cube. The Calculated Member Builder dialog box that appears is shown in Figure 17-7.

a. You can expand the measures and dimensions tree on the bottom right and expand the predefined functions tree to select a function you may want to use from the bottom left.

b. Double-click either of these areas to move this into the expression textbox. When you have the MDX formed, you can click the button to check the MDX syntax for completeness.

c. When you are done, enter the name of the new member and click OK. This returns you to the Query Builder dialog box.

d. You can now drag and drop the calculated member into the result set.

Figure 17-7:
Calculated
Member
Builder
dialog box
showing the
cube meta-
data and
functions
you can
select to
build an
MDX
expression
that
calculates
your new
derived
measure.

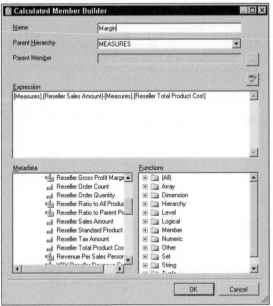

5. View the MDX that Query Builder has created by clicking the Design Mode button in the toolbar.

To view the MDX generated so far in the process, click the Design Mode button in the toolbar. This toggles you from MDX view mode to data preview mode. The MDX generated in this example is shown in Figure 17-8.

a. After you have reviewed this, you can click OK to return to the Design the Query step in the wizard. The MDX from the Query Builder is transferred into the Query String textbox where you can edit it further if desired.

b. Click the Next button to move ahead in the Report Wizard.

6. Design the table.

As with relational tables, you can design how the report table layout will look. You are prompted for Page variables (which dimension is fixed for a page), the Groups or column headings, and the Details or row headings. You can have as many variables as you need to support the report within this wizard step. This is shown in Figure 17-9.

7. Choose the table layout and the table style.

8. Click OK.

You've created your OLAP report!

Figure 17-8:
Query
Builder
showing the
MDX
generated
by the
builder
based on
your drag-
and-drop
operations
in the
design tool.

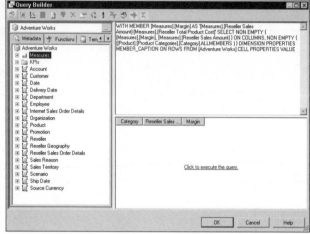

Figure 17-9:
The Design
the Table
step in the
Report
Wizard
showing the
options for
Page,
Group, and
Details from
the columns
selected in
your query.

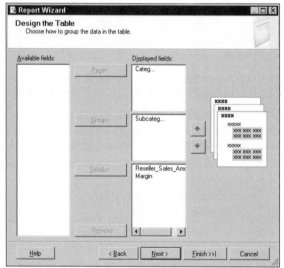

Creating an OLAP Report without the Report Wizard

The Report Wizard walks you through the steps required to create reports from OLAP databases from Microsoft Analysis Services. The options in the Report Wizard can be rather limiting. To be more unrestricted in your report development, you can bypass the Report Wizard and create a new report in a more free-form way.

In Business Intelligence Development Studio, right-click on the Reports folder in the Solution Explorer and choose Add⇨New Item. The selected report appears in the templates section of the Add New Item dialog box. This will bring you to a new Data window in the Report Designer.

Define a new dataset to be the shared data source for your OLAP data source. You can either use a shared data source as shown in the figure or define a new dataset by specifying an appropriate connection string to connect to the OLAP data source.

Click OK in the Dataset dialog box and you'll see a data designer that looks very similar to the Query Builder that you saw as part of the Report Wizard. The actual Data window is transformed into what is shown in Figure 17-10.

The beauty of working with OLAP data sources is that if you drag a dimension into your dataset, it brings along all the columns that are levels of the hierarchy of that dimension. It is a very intuitive interface to use in selecting data for query and analysis. It is also natural to design reports which have drill-down capabilities along the levels of the dimensions. This would work in both rows and columns. To see this in the sample reports shipped with SQL Server 2005, you can open the AdventureWorks Sales report which uses the Analysis Services AdventureWorksAS OLAP database as the source. See Figure 17-11.

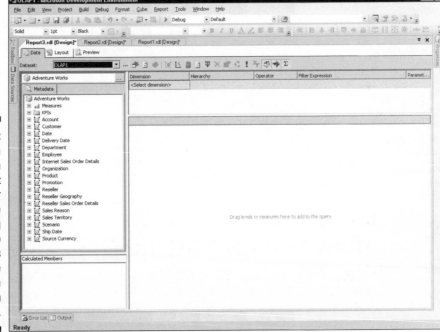

Figure 17-10: Data windows in the Report Designer encourage you to drag and drop items from the metadata tree to form your query.

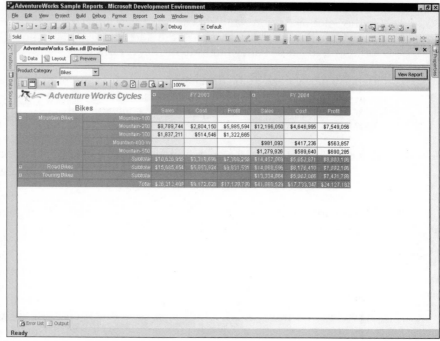

Figure 17-11:
Adventure
Works Sales
report
which
shows drill-
down along
the product
and time
dimensions
in rows and
columns,
respectively.

Chapter 18

Helping Executives See the Big Business Picture

In This Chapter

▶ Monitoring the enterprise

▶ Building the presentation

▶ Getting extra perspective

Executives are entrusted to make key decisions about their businesses. They need to monitor information, talk with experts, establish leadership in their industry, and talk with vendors, suppliers, and partners who work closely with the company to produce goods and services the company sells in the marketplace. As such, they are bombarded with information and have little time to analyze situations.

In order for their organization to move with quickness and agility in the face of competitive pressures and hidden opportunities, they need to be able to see at a high level how the company is performing in relation to its business plan and what areas need attention to correct a trend or what must be done to capitalize on short-term opportunities.

This chapter describes how you can use Reporting Services to provide executives with the information they need to make key business decisions.

Monitoring Enterprise Performance

The first challenge is how to present performance metrics to an executive in a manner that he or she can understand and interact with the information. The capabilities required to do this include the ability to see a trend over time, drill down to see more detail (by division, product, or customer), or slice the data and pivot on another dimension for analysis.

Understanding key performance indicators

In most reporting you do to support the business, there are measures or metrics, which are the numbers or dollars related to business activity. The metrics of the business are numerous and are found in every transaction of the business. However, some of the metrics of the business are key to analyzing the performance of the business. These metrics are known as *key performance indicators*. They represent key metrics of the business that can be rolled up or aggregated for the entire company. Examples of key performance metrics are as mundane as revenue and gross margin or as difficult to measure as customer defections and customer satisfaction.

Generally, the start of any analysis of company performance begins with a look at the key performance indicators, which can move up or down or remain constant. The first step in defining the true KPIs of the business is to form a direct link between corporate strategy, objectives and goals, and KPIs. You need to turn the company business strategy into a set of strategic objectives and quantifiable goals that can be translated into a set of metrics or KPIs. An analysis of KPIs and the target value of the KPI based on the company strategy tells you whether you're meeting the goals. This highlights to executives whether your organization is executing its strategies effectively.

The next step is to dig deeper into the data to discover the dimensions of the KPIs. Dimensions denote the various ways in which the KPI may be analyzed. For example, in the case of the migration rate KPI, sample dimensions (or ways to analyze the KPI) might be: geographic region, account type, time period in question, and/or customer contract type.

At this point, you may =ask "Even if I identify all the KPIs, how do I present them for the executive review?" I cover the details in the next section.

Measuring corporate performance

Researchers Kaplan and Norton introduced a new concept for how companies can measure and report performance in a way that balanced multiple perspectives, inward-facing measures like productivity, and also outward-facing measures like customer loyalty. They called this type of performance reporting a balanced scorecard for corporate performance.

The four perspectives that a balanced scorecard reports are:

- **Financial.** To succeed financially, how should we appear to our stakeholders?

- **Customer.** To achieve our vision, how should we appear to our customers?

> ✔ **Process.** To satisfy our customers and shareholders, at what business processes must we excel?
>
> ✔ **Learning and Growth.** To achieve our vision, how will we sustain our ability to change and improve?

So a balanced scorecard is a set of measures covering several perspectives where each has a target value. An example of a balanced scorecard could consist of the following measures:

> ✔ **Financial.** Percent revenue from new stores, revenue per employee, gross margin at established stores
>
> ✔ **Customer.** Average number of daily customers, number of repeat customers, average purchase in stores, average time between customer visits
>
> ✔ **Process.** Percent stores open on schedule, days to prepare stores, average lead time to delivery for fast-moving items
>
> ✔ **Learning.** Percent employees trained, percent promotions, employee retention

Typically, targets for these KPIs are established according to the business plan, and performance is evaluated against these targets. This provides a scorecard that can be used to evaluate how well the business has achieved its goals.

Offering immediate business insight

Another approach to monitoring performance is to provide an interactive summary view of the business, but not necessarily provide a scorecard perspective. In much the same way that the dashboard in your car keeps the driver constantly aware of what is happening while driving, the requirement of a digital dashboard is to keep the user aware of what is happening in the business.

The basic requirement for a dashboard is to provide business insight at a glance. That's why it can be difficult to design. It must be easy to use, personalized for each user with little customization, and interactive. The interactivity must support drilldown analysis and some ad hoc reporting capability.

Building the Presentation

I have reviewed some of the thinking about how to monitor performance. In this section, I will illustrate how you can leverage Reporting Services to provide an executive view of business performance information.

Getting a first look at indicators

The entry screen for any executive reporting solution must provide key information quickly and intuitively. The initial screen could be as simple as a set of green, yellow, or red lights on key performance indicators to indicate where executives should focus their attention.

You could create an entry screen with the following keys:

- ✔ **Colors** green, yellow, and red can indicate a plan being met, waning performance, or a crisis situation, respectively (see Figure 18-1).

- ✔ **Arrows** pointing up, down, or sideways can indicate how a number is trending and how performance changes over months or quarters.

Ensuring intuitive navigation

Intuitive navigation is essential for executives who don't have time to learn too many technical tools. Important options should be intuitive or require little training.

Figure 18-1:
Current values of key performance indicators along with the target value, trend, and status.

You can simplify a user's navigation through mountains of information by presenting a consolidated view of performance indicators (refer to Figure 18-1) and by allowing drill-down and trending options through simple mouse clicks.

Hyperlinks can instantly give users a more detailed view of information. You may even add some type of navigation to show at what consolidation level the information is presented for. The top company view may reveal one thing, but drilling down to other subsidiaries or cost centers may reveal another picture of what's happening in a business. See Figure 18-2, which shows a truer, more detailed report of performance.

Shifting to a customer view

On the dashboard start page in Figure 18-2, what would be the most natural way to investigate a customer view? One way is the find the closest fit in your list of KPIs and hyperlink the KPI name to a screen showing, say the top ten customers for the part of the organization selected for view. This customer view can be applied to the KPI Gross Profit Margin Goal. The result of taking the hyperlink from the KPI description is shown in Figure 18-3.

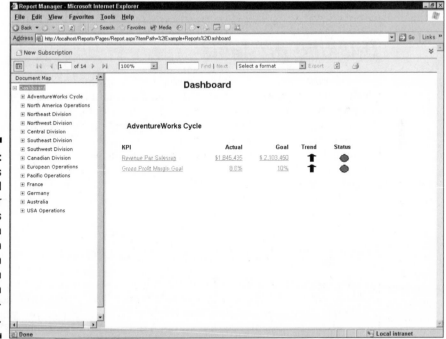

Figure 18-2:
Report cells hyperlinked to other views and an organization drill-down navigation option with the document map.

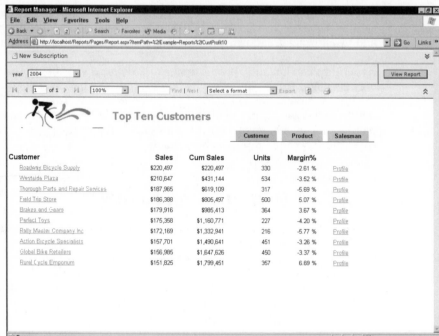

Figure 18-3:
Customer
view of the
information
from the
top-level
dashboard,
showing the
top ten
customer
sales,
cumulative
sales, unit
sales, and
margin.

Tracking products

From the customer view, you can navigate to a product or salesman view by clicking the navigation buttons at the top margin, or selecting an individual customer to see more detail. If you click the Product button, you will see the top ten products for the part of the organization selected from the initial view. Note that we are taking the approach of progressively filtering the information with each navigation decision. Hyperlinks will take you to a more detailed view of a specific product or customer or salesman, whereas the navigation buttons take you to different views at the same level of the organizational drill down selected from the dashboard start page in Figure 18-2.

Using profiles to highlight detail

Another aspect of the product and customer view reports in Figure 18-3 and 18-4 is that there is hyperlink to a profile report. The product and customer profile reports can be anything that the business thinks is important. In my business, the profile information shows a time series of sales from the last three years of history as well as a distribution of sales across product categories (for customers) and across geographic region (for products). This is shown in Figure 18-4 and 18-5 for customers and products, respectively.

The customer profile shows that Advanced Bike Components has had historically strong but seasonal sales peaking in September with the bulk coming from Bikes, and Components a distant second.

The product profile shows that Front Derailleur sales peaks in September and the bulk of the sales comes from North America. It is possible to consider allowing users to click on the sales region to drill down on the chart to show lower levels of regional sales detail within North America. The accompanying chart on the left showing the trend of sales would then show the trend for North America only at this new lower level of detail.

Searching for low margin culprits

You'll undoubtedly need to drill down on specific products and customers to see the detail activity for customer product sales by product category.

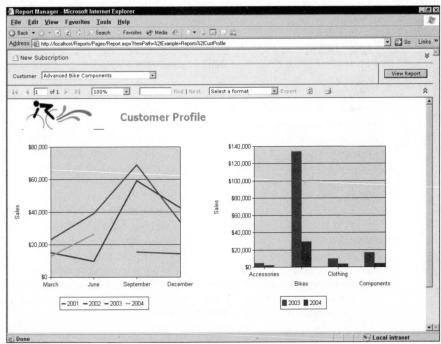

Figure 18-4:
The customer profile report for a specific customer.

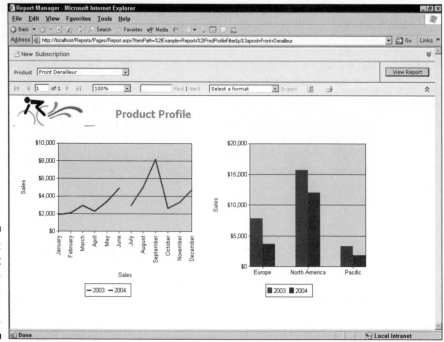

Figure 18-5:
The product
profile
report for a
specific
product.

Figure 18-6 shows the result of starting at the top ten customers analysis (shown in Figure 18-3) and drilling down on a specific customer.

This product category level report actually highlights the ability to hide lower levels of detail within a report and prompt the user to click and expand to the next level of detail. For example, to see the product sales detail levels under the Components product category and the derailleurs product subcategory level, you would click the expander button to the left of the product subcategory report line. The result of this drilldown is shown in Figure 18-6.

As you can see in Figure 18-6, the detail products are hyperlinked. This hyperlink could take the user to a view like the product profile (shown in Figure 18-5) for that product or any other view that may highlight another factor related to product sales for the selected period.

How might you return to the top dashboard to explore other reasons for performing below target? One way to do this is to add a home icon at a standard location on the report and enable each report to return to the start page of the dashboard by clicking this link.

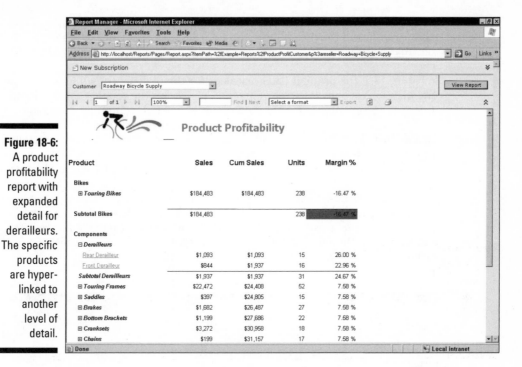

Figure 18-6:
A product
profitability
report with
expanded
detail for
derailleurs.
The specific
products
are hyper-
linked to
another
level of
detail.

Accessories to the Executive Analysis

So far in this chapter, I've talked about simple ways to mirror business
performance using Microsoft Reporting Services. You can use other tools
to accessorize information for an executive's view. The following sections
highlight opportunities where Microsoft Reporting Services can provide
some additional perspective.

Using charts for trend analysis

The use of graphics in a high-level presentation has been popularized in
PowerPoint presentations through the last decade. You can see many
aspects of a situation more easily from a graph compared to a tabular
display of data. A picture is worth a thousand words after all. The kinds
of charts that resonate with executive users involve some bar chart or

pie chart (see Figure 18-7) with interactivity built in so that clicking on a bar or a slice of the pie enables you to drill down to further levels of information.

In Figure 18-7, the product category sales for the division (or some part of the organization) is shown for a given year. This shows the relative sales volume. It does not show previous year data or any detail below product category.

Making this chart interactive and enabling the user to drill down on a particular product category of slice of the pie enables further exploration of the information. One possible view of the detail level is to display a sales trend history.

You can also use the back buttons on the Internet Explorer toolbar to navigate to a higher level of detail and take another drill-down path if necessary. You literally have hundreds of options for exploration with just a few reports and some well thought out navigation strategy that ensures an intuitive exploration through your key business information.

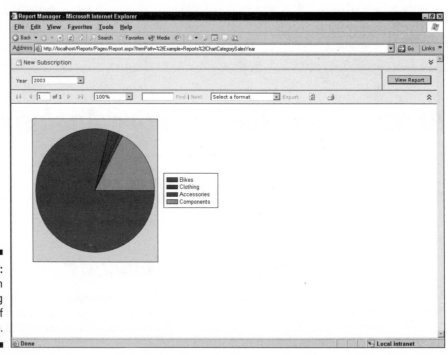

Figure 18-7:
Drill down
by clicking
a slice of
the pie.

Getting down to the details

Occasionally, you deal with executives who love to get into the details. Perhaps this is your sales executive who needs to know what types of products and services are contained within a given order — for whatever reason.

The typical scenario for analysis is that territory performance is analyzed by looking at a report like that shown in Figure 18-8. This begs the question of what is a given salesperson's selling history?

You should then be able to click on a salesperson and drill down to see a salesman summary analysis, as shown in Figures 18-9 and 18-10.

The bottom half of the report shows specific operational detail, like order history for the month.

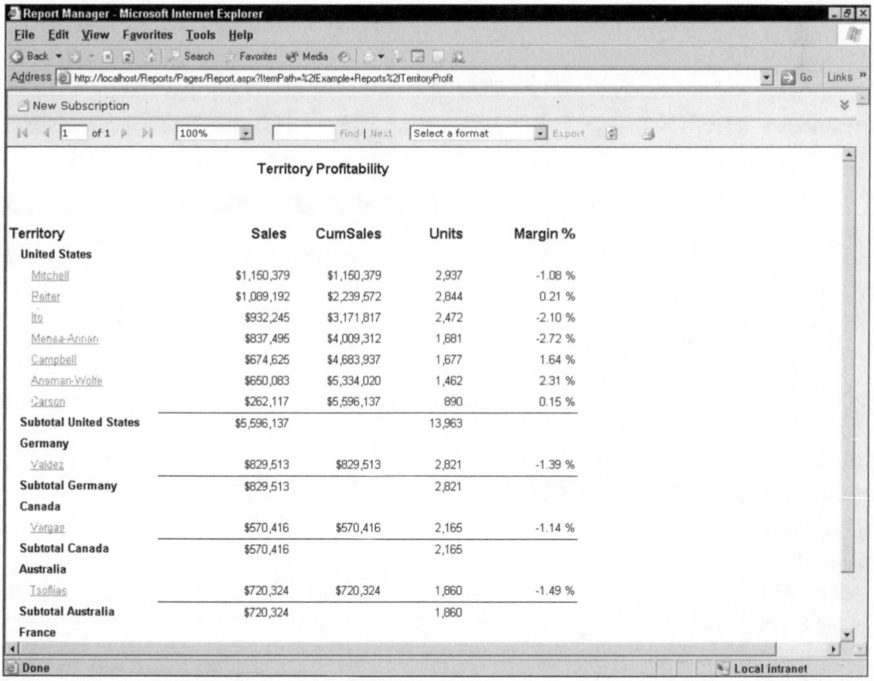

Figure 18-8:
Territory analysis showing all salespeople by territory and showing the revenue, volume, and margin on their quarterly sales.

Territory Profitability

Territory	Sales	CumSales	Units	Margin %
United States				
Mitchell	$1,150,379	$1,150,379	2,937	-1.08 %
Rafter	$1,089,192	$2,239,572	2,844	0.21 %
Ito	$932,245	$3,171,817	2,472	-2.10 %
Mensa-Annan	$837,495	$4,009,312	1,681	-2.72 %
Campbell	$674,625	$4,683,937	1,677	1.64 %
Ansman-Wolfe	$650,083	$5,334,020	1,462	2.31 %
Carson	$262,117	$5,596,137	890	0.15 %
Subtotal United States	$5,596,137		13,963	
Germany				
Valdez	$829,513	$829,513	2,821	-1.39 %
Subtotal Germany	$829,513		2,821	
Canada				
Vargas	$570,416	$570,416	2,165	-1.14 %
Subtotal Canada	$570,416		2,165	
Australia				
Tsoflias	$720,324	$720,324	1,860	-1.49 %
Subtotal Australia	$720,324		1,860	
France				

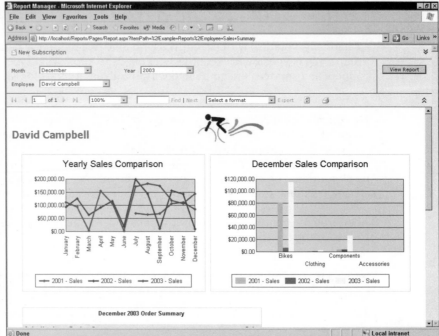

Figure 18-9:
Top half of
the Sales
Summary
report
showing
sales history
over the last
three years
as well as
the most
recent
month's
activity.

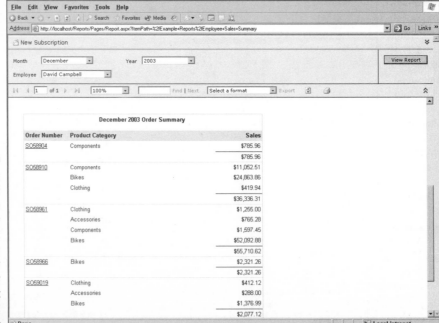

Figure 18-10:
Bottom half
of the Sales
Summary
report,
showing
order
summary for
the latest
month.

Each order summary can then be clicked to drill down to a representation of the complete sales order to examine all details of the sale (see Figure 18-11). This takes it down to the specific order of a specific product to a specific customer on a specific date. This is the lowest granularity you can expect to provide to any operational user let alone an executive user.

Integrating ad hoc analysis

Of course, we can't forget that there is a Report Builder (see Chapter 8) that will allow ad hoc reporting capabilities. You need to determine whether the Report Builder is an appropriate tool to introduce to executive users. It may be a great tool for some, but very confusing to others. The Report Builder may be a good way to allow executives to work with the information, but the tool assumes a knowledge of the information structures to create an ad hoc report from scratch.

Perhaps the best you can hope for in terms of providing ad hoc analysis capabilities to your tech-oriented executives is to provide some starter reports that are already populated with key information columns. They can open one of these reports and customize it as required, assuming they have been provided the proper training by someone like you!

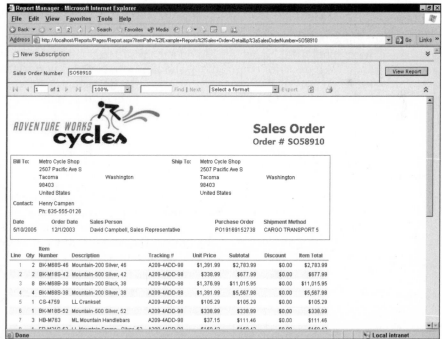

Figure 18-11: Sales order report showing all detail on a specified sales order.

Sharing the wealth of information

Of course, there is always the situation where an executive sees a report and says "Aha" and wants to share this with all his top managers! Now how should this sharing be done? What aspects of Microsoft Reporting Services or other Microsoft products can be exploited to provide this capability?

One way to encourage this sharing is to train your executive users to export information to a common format that can be e-mailed to others easily as an attachment. Appropriate formats to consider include PDFs or Excel spreadsheets or even Web Archives.

You need to be careful because multiple steps are required to pull off this maneuver! The user needs to export the report to a directory, then drag the report from the Windows directory into an e-mail message that needs to be addressed.

Another approach to this is that because you are coaching the executive through some of these areas yourself, suggest that key "Aha" reports be sent around to his team through a subscription. These subscriptions can be schedules to occur automatically with any given frequency. They can be sent through e-mail or be available in a certain Report Manager folder.

Another thought is that a collaboration portal be leveraged to enable executives and lieutenants to collaborate on a team site. Microsoft Sharepoint provides a collaboration portal experience. This is an additional Microsoft product, but Microsoft has developed "Web parts" that can snap in to the Sharepoint Portal framework. So on a team site page, there can be discussion thread Web parts for commentary about how to improve performance alongside key reporting Web parts that show all the Reporting Services reports that are available to the team. This type of integration can be very effective in assisting communication in a more virtual setting.

Reviewing reports offline

Another consideration when designing reports for executive use is that the reports may need to be viewed when a computer is offline, meaning there is no Internet connection available. This can be achieved by exporting reports to PDF or some other format. When reports are designed, the report developer should consider the formatting and specifications necessary for the exported report to be legible.

Publishing special supporting analyses

Occasionally, the executive sees a report and asks an off-the-wall question that nobody could possibly anticipate. This generally sends people scrambling trying to collect information and put it together in a report.

If a proper business intelligence environment has been developed, these questions usually can be answered (at least partially) by developing another report from this data store. This new report, written in Reporting Services, can then be published into the Special Analyses folder (or somewhere that makes sense) so that anyone with access can explore the new results. If this results in a tremendous decision bringing the company to the pinnacle of success, you can rest assured that you have provided huge value to the business from the well designed BI environment and the reporting tools available to you. Then you can ask for the raise that you deserve!

Another place to put special analyses is the folder where the dashboard reports are located. You can name them something special or put in comments indicating the type of request the report is designed to handle. If the special analysis then becomes a standard analysis (as many good ones do eventually become), you can then create new links from the dashboard reports to incorporate these new views. In this way new navigation paths grow over time within the context of a good dashboard solution.

Part VI

Migrating from Other Reporting Tools

The 5th Wave   By Rich Tennant

"MY GIRLFRIEND RAN A SPREADSHEET OF MY LIFE, AND GENERATED THIS CHART. MY BEST HOPE IS THAT SHE'LL CHANGE HER MAJOR FROM 'COMPUTER SCIENCES' TO 'REHABILITATIVE SERVICES.'"

In this part . . .

*J*ust how does *Microsoft Reporting Services 2005* stack up against other reporting tools on the market? I explore a few of the popular reporting tools as objectively as possible in this part to provide a comparison analysis. You will understand some of the similarities and differences between *Microsoft Reporting Services 2005* and these other popular reporting tools.

Okay, you have used other reporting tools before but are now convinced that *Microsoft Reporting Services 2005* is the best way to create and distribute your reports. It is time to find out how to covert some of these old reports into Reporting Services 2005 reports.

Chapter 19

Comparing Reporting Services to Other Popular Reporting Tools

. . . .

. . . .

*I*n this book, I focus mainly on the power and capabilities of Microsoft Reporting Services. But Microsoft Reporting Services isn't the only available product; other tools have been available longer than Reporting Services. This chapter provides an overview of the capabilities of some of the key reporting and analysis tools available and some comparisons of them.

Introducing Other Reporting Platforms

Among the top reporting and analysis tools on the market today is Business Objects. Business Objects integrates Crystal Reports and Business Objects reports into a new Business Objects platform. Also, COGNOS introduced a new Web-based reporting tool called ReportNet, which is the company's first new product for its new BI platform architecture. Another leading report writing tool is Microsoft Access. In the following sections, I describe in detail what each of these tools can do.

Microsoft Access reporting

Microsoft Access is part of the Microsoft Office platform. It offers reporting capabilities that have been proven over many years. Microsoft has continued to add new features and efficiencies over the years, including built-in wizards to help new users design reports quickly, and a fairly intuitive query designer that enables you to join and query tables without knowing SQL. However, Access reports are desktop reports, unless you use an approach to export a report to a snapshot and publish to the Web. Reports are authored on a desktop-based application interface, which is not supported on the Web.

Business Objects

After the acquisition of Crystal Reports in 2004, Business Objects became the largest vendor of reporting and analysis tools. Business Objects has existed for nearly 15 years and is working toward integrating Crystal Reports and Business Objects into an integrated platform. Its product development plans call for the development of Business Objects XI (XI short for Extreme Insight). Both Business Objects and Crystal standalone versions support OLAP data stores for reporting. All products can accommodate maps in reports, provide conditional formatting control of all objects and report sections, provide report designers the flexibility to resize objects onscreen, and enable you to work offline and create reports in design or preview mode. Business Objects offers a way to author reports on a Web client. Business Objects is well suited to the business user who needs to do ad hoc reporting. Anyone can create reports easily because Business Objects offers an easy-to-use metadata layer from which you can drag and drop objects with business-friendly descriptions into a report.

COGNOS ReportNet

ReportNet is a new reporting tool by COGNOS built on a Web-native architecture. ReportNet provides ad hoc, managed, and production reporting. It supports dynamic, cascading prompts, a Web-based report designer, powerful ad hoc functionality including strong drill-through, and report hyperlinking from report to report.

The data access component of ReportNet is the COGNOS connect manager, which is a Web-centric data access control. Report development environments called *studios* are geared to specific types of users. Query Studio is a flexible report designer that allows switching from tab to crosstab, creating calculations and building reports quickly with an intuitive interface. Query Studio is geared to the business user who needs to develop reports quickly for presentation. Analysis Studio is a report designer for the business analyst and facilitates doing crosstab reports quickly. Report Studio provides more reporting capabilities and is more suitable for a technically proficient report developer. In all of these studios, you can create and use templates that help you create reports. A rich set of tools (similar to the Reporting Services toolbox) enables you to create sophisticated reports with nested controls. Report Studio also contains provisions for delivering reports. You may export reports and burst them to e-mail addresses for business users. You can also develop dashboards containing navigation links to other reports with deeper levels of detail.

Reporting Services

Reporting Services is a great product for the professional report developer because of the Report Designer, and for the business user because of the Report Builder. Its Report Manager gives you a means of organizing reports easily in secure report folders as well as an administrative interface to create subscriptions, history, and other advanced features. Report Manager can connect to Analysis Services and utilize this interface to create a drag-and-drop report-authoring capability. All the tools I mention are greatly similar, and I investigate them further in the sections that follow.

Comparing Data Retrieval Features

Reporting Services is the topic of Chapter 1. In this section, I compare Reporting Services to the other reporting tools.

Retrieving data from a database

Reporting Services enables you to create shared datasets and easily prepare datasets for reporting and analysis. Each reporting tool shares this capability. Each tool has its own unique approach. Access and ReportNet do not provide access to OLAP data sources. For relational sources, there are many similar capabilities between these tools. Both can work with SQL Server databases.

ReportNet can connect to most relational database formats, but not any OLAP data sources at this time. ReportNet can connect to SAP Business Warehouse (BW) which is a hybrid data source that functions similar to an OLAP cube. To do this, the tool uses MDX (see Chapter 17 for more information on MDX) rather than SQL queries to go after BW data. ReportNet can provide a single metadata model containing both SAP BW and non-BW sources. This means that your users can have reports with data from all corporate data sources — with shared filters and prompts throughout your SAP BW implementation or while you are consolidating non-SAP data into your SAP BW solution.

Business Objects has connectivity to a wide range of different data sources — any vendor flavor (Oracle, DB2, and SQL Server), and many of the popular OLAP data sources (Hyperion Essbase and Microsoft Analysis Services). Crystal Reports supports connectivity to as many data sources.

Comparing Report Development

Each of the tools provides an interface to develop interesting reports. Some tools provide many options for developing reports geared to the type of user. A report development environment for the business analyst needs to be different than one for the professional report developer. The following sections compare the different report development environments provided by the tools.

Using a report wizard

In Chapter 4, I describe the Reporting Services Wizard for creating new reports. Microsoft Access has a wizard that has a similar look and feel. Crystal Reports provides a comparable wizard. Business Objects offers no wizard but enables efficient report creation via a drag-and-drop paradigm for creating reports. ReportNet does provide a wizardlike style of creating reports, although it is not referred to as a wizard per se. The wizard style of help is really unique with Microsoft Reporting Services. This can be a helpful tool for quickly creating reports or for learning how to design reports for new business and IT professionals.

Business Objects XI provides you with the ability to build a semantic layer or business model (similar to the report model in Chapter 8) called a *universe*. The universe consists of all the data elements of the database that are accessible expressed in business terms and not technical terms. Each data element has a short business description to define for the business user. The user can select from these elements and drag them onto the designer panel to construct a new report. This is the intuitive way of creating reports that approximates the functionality of a wizard.

Styling with report types

You saw in Chapter 5 that Reporting Services provides standard report items in a toolbox. Third-party developers also may create new controls and allow you to extend the toolbox to do new things with reports. The tools available in the toolbox include textboxes, tables, a matrix, rectangles, lists, subreports, lines, images, and charts.

Microsoft Access provides some basic report-building tools in its design interface. In some ways, you have more tool options because Access enables you to add check boxes, radio buttons, option grouping, buttons, drop-down lists, list boxes, lines, and images. You have options to build tabular or free-form reports as well as charts.

Business Objects XI offers similar tools from which you can build reports. The toolbox in the Web-based, report-development interface provides controls for a grid, chart, text, subreports, lines, and images. You can drag and drop these onto the report design interface.

ReportNet offers similar tools in the toolbox, including crosstabs, lists, and charts, as well as images, live embedded applications, dynamic HTML items, and logos that can all be linked with one another to provide greater context.

Accessorizing reports

Reporting Services provides for accessories like sorting, grouping, filtering, formatting, and using expressions. All of these tools provide good and intuitive capabilities.

Crystal Reports offers less of a free-form report creation experience since it provides the grid for you to add query fields and formula fields directly. Business Objects allows a free-form development interface that requires an administrator to set up a semantic layer, called a *universe*, which maps the data schema to business friendly objects. Dynamic prompts and cascading lists are now available in Crystal Reports and Business Objects, allowing prompt values to be populated from values in a database. Prompts can be arranged in a cascade, where one value in a prompt constrains values in subsequent picklists.

ReportNet provides a separation of report layout and query layers similar to the report design interface with Reporting Services. This allows you to select report columns from a list and place them into a Web-based grid for reporting. Prompt types can be applied to the data. These prompts allow users to modify report criteria such as date and time, and can take the form of a cascading list, a picklist, or radio buttons. ReportNet's multilingual capability means that reports can be authored once and localized automatically. In Query Studio, you can change a tabular report to a crosstab report directly. COGNOS Framework Manager delivers an enterprise data model that encapsulates all business rules, data descriptions, data relationships, and other administration tasks. It insulates the report author from the technical challenges of the underlying data. With Framework Manager, you can separate the database representation of the data from the business perspective, define single conformed definitions of metrics, and reuse the same definition in multiple business views.

Microsoft Access provides a report design interface with a toolbar of controls. This is similar to what Reporting Services offers. You can create many report styles as well as charts using the wizard or the designer interface. Reports can be designed that prompt the user for parameter values which is implemented as a popup dialog prompt for the required values.

All of these tools are capable of providing nice graphical reporting. Crosstab analysis can be done in all tools, but using different techniques. The list control in Reporting Services provides a more free-form technique to assemble repeating sections than the other reporting tools, which conform to a banded report styling

Reporting with parameters and formatting options

Reporting Services provides support for parameter-based reports, allows dynamic visibility of detail rows of a report, provides many formatting alternatives to choose from, and allows reporting from multiple datasets within a single report. You also can write expressions and use these to display information or handle processing within a report.

Business Objects can also support these capabilities. However, it can handle the drill-down reporting as requests to the database and will refresh a report to bring back more detail from the database. Crystal Reports is more comparable to Reporting Services in that there may be some drill-down in any report based on hiding detail rows and allowing users to expand these areas to reveal the detail.

ReportNet allows the development of parameter-based reports. ReportNet ships with a full set of sophisticated prompt types that can be applied to the data. These prompts allow users to modify report criteria such as date and time, and can take the form of a cascading list, a picklist, radio buttons, and more.

ReportNet provides Condition Explorer, which enables authors to easily hide or show information in a report based on specific conditions. This works much like the Reporting Services Expression Builder. Advanced report design includes multiple linked or independent queries per report, separation of presentation and query layers, and logical layout page control and conditional formatting. It also provides for multi-query compound reports and the ability to embed dynamic objects. The conditional report layout adapts dynamically to the data content and end-user requirements.

Report Builder for ad hoc reporting by business users

Also, BO XI exposes some of the common end-user needs for customizing reports. By right-clicking, you can insert a new column of information. BO XI allows you to go back to the universe or metadata for the report to add a key metric or formula to the report. You can also interactively turn a tabular report into a graphical display. Universes act as a semantic layer between the user and a database. Business Views are objects that help report designers and end users access the information they require. You can take advantage of Business Views only in Crystal Reports, whereas you can access universes in Crystal Reports and the Web-based Business Objects Web Intelligence.

ReportNet provides the capability to generate reports using a drag-and-drop interface from a set of data elements available in the Query explorer. After your administrator has created the analysis layer, you can use constructs, such as nested queries, as you would from Reporting Services.

Microsoft Access enables ad hoc report development through its report designer interface. You can create crosstabs and basic column style reporting quite easily. It is a great desktop query tool for basic reporting requirements.

On this topic, Business Objects provides much more capability to do ad hoc reporting. Most of the capabilities that you would find only when you are designing and building new reports with the other tools, you can do in the analysis interface within Business Objects. You always have access to the semantic layer (the universe) from which the report was created. You only need to drag in another data element to add it to the grid, or pull a column out of the grid to create a nested report on that variable. You can transpose rows and columns and do crosstab analysis on the fly. You can also change a tabular report into a graph with the click of a toolbar button. All of these changes can be done without leaving the viewing environment. For ease-of-use in ad hoc reporting. Business Objects has a clear advantage over the other tools.

Comparing Publish, Subscribe, and Access

After you create your report, you need to be able to get it to your anxiously awaiting business users who are starved for information. Each of these tools has somewhat different capabilities in supporting reporting on demand, scheduled reporting, and automatic distribution of this information. The following sections provide detailed analyses of these capabilities among available tools.

Publishing your reports

For Business Objects, the Live Office add-in enables users to integrate business intelligence data within Microsoft Office and easily create or modify reports to individual requirements. In addition, Business Objects Enterprise

XI Premium also includes auditing capabilities that enable IT to more easily administer individual user accounts and reports and give more insight into the actions users take and which reports they access.

You can use Live Office to embed your business intelligence data into Word documents, Excel spreadsheets, and PowerPoint presentations. Then you can share the resulting Office documents securely by using Business Objects.

Publishing capabilities formerly were provided by a separate ad-on called Broadcast agent, where reports could be scheduled and sent as e-mail attachments for report distribution. Now this functionality is embedded in BO Enterprise. Scheduling a report provides the ability to schedule documents on behalf of others. This secure mechanism allows a single report to serve the needs of multiple users by delivering only the specific subsets of information to each user according to their security profile. Business Objects supports the report history option to save a snapshot of the data at a specific point in time.

ReportNet provides robust scheduling and bursting capabilities. Data is read once and then deployed in multiple formats to a massive number of users. Reporting that's this easy to use and administer can truly be extended across the global enterprise. ReportNet reports can be rendered as HTML or PDF, or e-mailed to individual e-mail accounts. ReportNet doesn't give you the ability to produce report history, a snapshot of a report at a specific point in time.

Microsoft Access does have the capability to publish reports to the Web. This is a push capability where a Web page renders the report information from the access query. Microsoft Access doesn't support any concept like report history.

Accessing reports on demand

For optimized self-retrieval through portal access, COGNOS ReportNet uses the cache control facilities provided by the HTTP protocol. Although pages in COGNOS ReportNet are dynamically generated to provide rich content, it can intelligently decide whether a page needs to be regenerated or simply refreshed if already viewed. This capability is similar to Microsoft Reporting Services.

Business Objects also caches the reports so that if the report has been delivered through the browser based on a request by another user, it is available to any subsequent business users from the cache.

Microsoft Access doesn't handle the caching in the same way as the other tools. The report requests are always executed on demand.

Delivering reports

Business Objects users can create schedules on virtually any timetable, including daily or weekly dates and times, as well as any business calendars. Users can share documents via e-mail or send them to a system inbox, printer, or file — in several different formats — allowing further interaction.

COGNOS ReportNet can send content to eliminate the need for portal access or it can send e-mail links to eliminate the need for portal navigation. The ability to push information out to users rather than forcing them to pull content provides flexibility for the entire report user community. Scheduling tools allow these reports to be pushed automatically.

As I mention previously, Microsoft Access can publish reports to the Web. This is a push capability where a Web page renders the report information from the access query. This could possibly be scheduled to work as a macro based on an event from the Windows scheduler. However, there is no function to allow distributing Access reports via e-mail according to a schedule.

Comparing Management and Administration of Reports

Organizing your reports in a folder hierarchy and providing for high security in the access of reports are design goals for all reporting tools. Many of the vendors have focused on providing an intuitive folder-based system for organizing content, and this has become the standard. All of the vendors have in recent years expanded their platforms to provide for security management capabilities to finely control the access of users to individual reports or access to functions surrounding the management of reports, such as the ability to schedule or access underlying data.

Managing your reports

BO XI has the ability to better manage the data side of the infrastructure. Central Management Console can help integrate the security with an existing infrastructure security. You can inherit the security model from any of the popular security environments. An audit dashboard shows the users per hour, the load on the system, and the run times for specific queries monitored throughout the day. In the Rights Management module, you can set user-specific privileges to allow editing and viewing report objects. You can manage all the services of the BO infrastructure and configure which servers are allocated to running various services of Business Objects. This capability enables you to scale to a 16-server cluster without having to shut down any server or node on the system. BO XI also recently achieved the Microsoft Datacenter Certification.

Folders and categories work together to provide strong navigation capabilities. Folders are locations to store documents. Complementary to folders, categories are used for classifying documents in Business Objects Enterprise. By creating a combination of folders and categories and setting appropriate rights for them, you can organize documents according to multiple criteria and improve both security and navigation. You can upload new BO reports or any Microsoft Office document into the new report folders.

ReportNet also supports the use of public folders to organize reports. It is comparable to what Reporting Services or Business Objects has to offer in terms of folder management and organization.

Securing information

Business Objects can leverage the Office/Windows security environment so that secure information is secured with Windows rights and privileges. Also, Central Management Console is a centralized management tool that can be used to administer security. BO also provides single sign-on with Active Directory authentication. You can also define reporting and tool function privileges within the Central Management Console to finely control access to all features and functions within the BO enterprise platform.

COGNOS ReportNet is security agnostic — it works with virtually every security model. Where required, an API lets you accommodate custom authentication models. ReportNet also leverages security models of any existing COGNOS products through the COGNOS Series 7 authentication provider. ReportNet does not replicate existing enterprise models to enable application security. You can secure all report objects in COGNOS ReportNet, setting permission rights for use by the appropriate users or groups. Report objects include folders, subfolders, individual reports, data connections, and ReportNet capabilities (such as authoring).

Microsoft Access does allow some security to be built into the model. However, it does not support a robust security model and it is not integrated with any Windows security strategy. You can define user privileges of open, read, modify, and administer for each object in the database. You can set passwords and encrypt the database.

Comparing Advanced Reporting Capabilities

Here's a brief comparison of how the various reporting tools handle advanced reporting tasks.

Making reports interactive

Business Objects XI enables users (via its WebIntelligence platform) to click on an object and drill down without having to change to a different product. The document map control was originated with Crystal Reports and is now a component or report part option for any standard report within Business Objects XI. You can navigate from report to report through the Infoview portal, a component of the BO XI platform. Business Objects can provide for intuitive drill-down by the business user, or change from a quarterly trend to a monthly trend with a little setup.

ReportNet has a capability of setting up a dashboard containing drill paths to navigate to lower levels of detail.

Microsoft Access does not support hyperlinking to other reports and passing parameters as the context to the receiving report.

Reporting from OLAP sources

OLAP database sources will be introduced in this release so that customers can utilize their data stored in OLAP servers and easily standardize Business Objects XI for all of their BI requirements. Initially this capability will be available for the SAP BW, Hyperion Essbase, and Microsoft Analysis Services OLAP databases. This is referred to as OLAP intelligence in the Business Objects XI platform. In this way, Business Objects provides similar access to OLAP as Reporting Services. Neither COGNOS ReportNet nor Microsoft Access supports reporting from an OLAP data source.

Reporting for executive use

Dashboards can capture the context for a particular job. The information is actually pulled into the dashboard and is ensured to be relevant for that specific user. Click on a graphical display control (like a gauge or some similar control) on a dashboard that shows progress on a particular goal, and drill to a more detailed report to understand why.

Scorecard brings together goals, targets, and the current metrics into a view to show whether a business is performing according to the business plan. You can sort based on priority, color, or perspectives (customer, product, learning, operations). You can also drill down on the status to see a trend of how a business has performed historically compared to goals, period by period.

Business Objects believes that going into the Reporting tool should be a seamless experience. If you're accustomed to working in the Microsoft Office environment, the reporting experience should be seamless with Office. As a result, it has focused on integrating its reporting capabilities with Microsoft Office, since this is the leading spreadsheet, word processing, and personal database environment.

The presentation to the executive committee has to reflect the correct numbers at the time when the presentation is made, by making the data available in a report that is embedded and live within a PowerPoint presentation. Being able to refresh the numbers in a report on demand, you can utilize one PowerPoint slide deck to show the monthly financials that are consistent from month to month. This saves on presentation development time and provides a consistent framework for an executive review of business performance. In this way, Office products can become the front-end interface to business intelligence.

Dashboards can be developed using Business Objects technology (note that this involves buying a lot more software). You can add discussions to any document in the system either by selecting it from the document list or while the user is viewing the document. Threaded discussions can be used for collaboration to understand the details related to the top-level view of the information

A BI encyclopedia is available to show the business meaning of the report. The encyclopedia describes the purpose of the report and the type of information. It can also describe a guided analysis scenario where it can walk the user through the steps in the drill-down and trending investigation. Another facility is the context, which shows the more technical aspects of the report, such as the data source and the formula definitions on the report.

Comparing Price

COGNOS, Business Objects, and Microsoft SQL Server Reporting Services provide a powerful reporting and analysis platform suitable for enterprise reporting. One of the first questions people ask of these tools is how much they cost.

COGNOS and Business Objects have been battling for the desktop BI market-place over the last ten years. Each is priced comparably and is similar in the functionality and scalability of the platforms. Recent integration work has enabled these tools to more easily be scaled to the entire enterprise over the Web. However, these tools come with a price tag.

Since Microsoft Reporting Services is an extension of SQL Server and is built in to the price of the server product, there are obvious advantages of considering this platform's capabilities. If your company has standardized on Microsoft SQL Server or has many server deployments of the database, you can leverage this investment and provide sophisticated reporting on this platform with no additional cost. This is a significant price advantage.

Tool Comparison Takeaways

If you read the previous sections, you will see parity among the various reporting tools in many of the reporting categories. The fact that Microsoft Reporting Services comes with the SQL Server database makes it a powerful consideration for the reporting tool of choice with SQL Server, provided your requirements for analytical slice/dice/drill/pivot/filter are appropriate.

Whereas Microsoft Access is part of the Microsoft Office family and supports desktop reporting, it is a desktop-oriented product. It is a reporting tool and a database management system, but cannot scale to the number of users or speed of processing as SQL Server. Reporting Services is the next step for Access users who need to move to a more powerful platform.

COGNOS ReportNet has many similarities to Microsoft Reporting Services. However, its drill-down capabilities are not as strong as what is provided in Reporting Services. Furthermore, it does not have the report subscriptions capability that Reporting Services has to push reports to subscribing users as a Web link or an e-mail attachment on a scheduled basis.

Business Objects XI does have this report subscription capability, however. It has comparable report designer capabilities as Microsoft Reporting Services. Where BO XI excels (pardon the pun) is in interactive viewing of the report. You can drag in another data element to add it to the grid, or pull a column out of the grid to create a nested report on that variable. You can transpose rows and columns and do crosstab analysis on the fly. You can also change a tabular report into a graph with the click of a toolbar button. All of these changes can be done without ever leaving the viewing environment. This online analytical capability, plus its ability to support offline viewing of information within a report, provides a comparative advantage if these capabilities are needed. Even for SQL Server database environments, this may justify the additional expense for another reporting tool.

The future development plans for SQL Server Reporting Services will no doubt target this gap in interactive analytical capabilities where BO XI establishes its superiority. Report Builder is in its first version. Given time and additional development from third- party vendors developing new controls for it, the Microsoft Reporting Services platform will no doubt soon evolve into a more robust interactive analysis tool. But if your organization is using SQL Server currently, the price is right for starting to use Microsoft Reporting Services as your enterprise reporting platform.

Chapter 20

Converting Reports from Access

· ·

· ·

*Y*ou may be contemplating taking reports created in Access and converting them to Reporting Services reports, thinking they'd look better on an intranet compared to a desktop view.

How do you get started? One way is to start from scratch and develop the new reports using your basic understanding of the Access report or implement based on the requirements specs used in developing the Access reports.

Another alternative is to see how much of the Access report can be brought in using the Import Reports function of Reporting Services. Then you can work on this starter report to fix problems or enhance it based on the functionality available by using the new tool to compete the implementation. In this chapter, I cover all you need to know to proceed.

Importing the Access Report

You can use Report Designer to import reports from a Microsoft Access database (.mdb) or project (.adp) file. Report Designer converts each report within the database or project file to RDL and saves it within the designated report project. The data source for the Access reports must be available when the reports are imported.

You must install Access 2002 or a later version on the same computer that Report Designer is installed on in order to use the import feature.

To start using this import feature, follow these steps using the Business Intelligence Development Studio:

1. **In the Solution Explorer, right-click the Reports folder.**

   A pop-up menu appears.

2. **Select the Import Reports menu item from the pop-up menu.**

   You see tools you can import from.

3. **Select the Microsoft Access menu item.**

When you use the import feature, all reports in the database or project file are imported. If your Access file contains many reports, you may want to create a separate report project into which you can import the reports, and then open the individual RDL files in your main report project. You may have to edit the reports after they are imported into Report Designer.

Understanding how Access reports differ from Reporting Services

After you import an Access report into your project, you will find that some features convert well and other aspects are just not supported. For example, the page layout in Microsoft Access is different than in Reporting Services. Access arranges items on the page using *bands* or sections that span the width of the report. The bands can include report header, report footer, page header, page footer, groups, and detail. Reporting Services provides a more flexible layout. Data regions provide grouping and detail, and you can place multiple data regions anywhere in the body of the report. Side-by-side placement is also supported. It also includes banded page header and footer sections, similar to that in Access.

When a report is imported from Access into Reporting Services, the page header and footer from the Access report are converted into a Reporting Services report page header and footer. Groups and detail are converted into a list data region. The report header and footer are placed into the body of the report, rather than in a separate band. This may result in item placement that is slightly different than what is in the Access report.

In some Access reports, report items that appear to be adjacent to each other may actually overlap. When the report is imported using Report Designer, this overlap is not corrected and may lead to unexpected results when the report is run.

Supporting cast for Reporting Services

The following important report objects from Access are supported in Reporting Services:

- **Grouping.** Access defines a group level using a combination of three properties: the group expression, the GroupOn property, and the GroupInterval property. A group that does not have a group header or footer is merged with the group contained within it. If the group does not contain another group, sorting is applied to the detail section and the group is dropped.

- **Expressions.** Access uses expressions to specify values that appear in text boxes. Access uses Visual Basic as its expression language in addition to some aggregate functions. Reporting Services converts these expressions.

- **Functions.** A Reporting Services report definition uses Visual Basic .NET as its native expression language, while Access 2002 uses Visual Basic for Applications (VBA).

- **Array Functions.** Reporting Services supports the array functions such as LBound or UBound.

- **Parameters.** During the import process, Reporting Services scans each expression within a report for variables that do not correspond to field names or controls. These variables are added to report parameters. Furthermore, the data type for stored procedure parameters is always imported as a string. After the report is imported, you must manually change the parameter to use the correct data type.

If you import a report containing a query with query parameters, the query won't convert when you import. To import the query, temporarily replace the query parameters in the Access report with hard-coded values, and then replace them with query parameters after the report is imported.

Making sure everything converts

Some parts of Access lose a little something in the conversion between Access reports and Reporting Service reports. For example, all bitmaps that are embedded within a report are converted to BMP format when the report is imported, regardless of their initial format. So if your report includes JPG and GIF files, the resulting resources imported with the report are BMP files. The bitmaps are stored as embedded images in the report.

You should be aware that conditional formatting in Access is not converted. Also, the description field in report properties in Access is not converted.

Also, keep in mind that there are several Access objects that are not supported by Reporting Services. Examples of the report controls that Reporting Services does not support include the following controls:

```
BoundObjectFrame
CheckBox
ComboBox
CommandButton
CustomControl
ObjectFrame
OptionButton
TabControl
ToggleButton
```

Tightening up reports after conversion

After you convert a report from Access, preview it. You may see error messages in the Error List window.

You may find that the basic layout doesn't convert correctly and needs some adjustments after the import process. Consider the following example where you import XMarket.mdb from an Access database. The Sales Summary report in the Access database is shown in Figure 20-1.

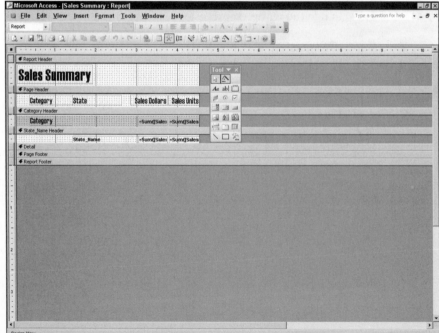

Figure 20-1: Access Report Designer showing the layout within Microsoft Access.

You see some interesting conversion artifacts in Reporting Services. The first is the columns have gone to the report header section but the report title is in the report body. The converted report initially looks like the report shown in Figure 20-2.

You can clean up an errant report in many ways. Suppose that you want the report title and header to appear at the top of each page. Then you would drag the report title text box up above the column names in the header section, as shown in Figure 20-3. Also note in the figure that the properties on the report header indicate that nothing is printed on the first page or the last page.

If you change the `PrintOn FirstPage` and `PrintOnLastPage` attribute properties to true for both, you will find that the result looks similar to the Access report from which it came (see Figure 20-4).

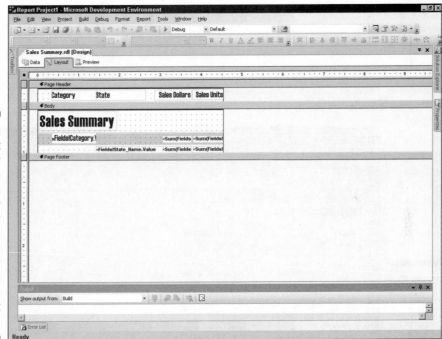

Figure 20-2:
Report Designer layout of the Sales Summary report after it has been converted and imported into the Report Designer.

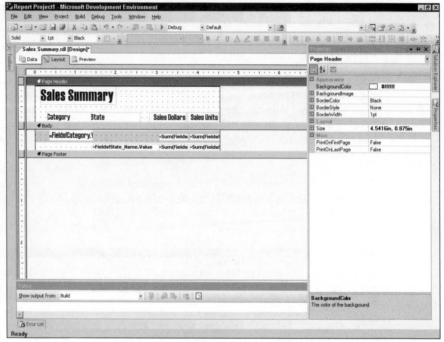

Figure 20-3:
Report
Designer
layout of the
modified
Sales
Summary
layout, also
showing the
report
header
properties.

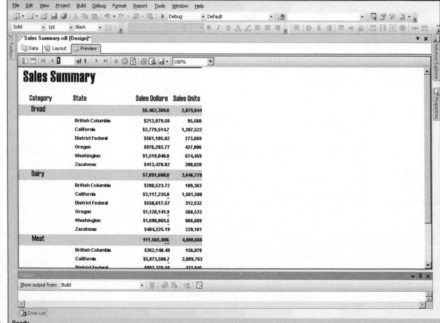

Figure 20-4:
Report
Designer
layout of the
modified
Sales
Summary
layout, also
showing the
report
header
properties.

Upsizing an Access Database and Reports

Over time, most database applications grow, become more complex, and need to support more users. At some point in the life of your Access database application, consider upsizing to SQL Server to optimize database and application performance, scalability, availability, security, reliability, and recoverability.

High performance and scalability

In many situations, SQL Server offers better performance than an Access database. SQL Server also provides support for very large, terabyte-sized databases, which is much larger than the current limit for an Access database of 2GB. Finally, SQL Server works very efficiently on Microsoft Windows 2000 or later by processing queries in parallel (using multiple native threads within a single process to handle user requests) and minimizing additional memory requirements when more users are added.

Increased availability

SQL Server allows you to do a dynamic backup, either incremental or complete, of the database while it's in use. Consequently, you do not have to force users to exit the database to back up data. This means your database can be running up to 24 hours a day, seven days a week.

Improved security

Using a trusted connection, SQL Server can integrate with the Windows 2000 or later system security to provide a single access to the network and the database, employing the best of both security systems. This makes it much easier to administer complex security schemes. An SQL Server database on a server also employs innovative security features, which helps prevent unauthorized users from getting to the database file directly, but rather they must access the server first.

Immediate recoverability

In case of system failure (such as an operating system crash or power outage), SQL Server has an automatic recovery mechanism that recovers a database to the last state of consistency in a matter of minutes, with no database administrator intervention. Critical applications can be up and running again right away.

Server-based processing

Microsoft designed SQL Server from the beginning as a client/server database, where data and indexes reside on a single server computer that is often accessed over the network by many client computers. SQL Server reduces network traffic by processing database queries on the server before sending results to the client. Thus, your client/server application can do processing where it's done best, on the server.

Your application can also use user-defined functions, stored procedures, and triggers to centralize and share application logic, business rules and policies, complex queries, and data validation and referential integrity code on the server, rather than on the client.

Upsizing your Access database

The best way to upsize an Access database is by running the wizard in Access. Not only does running the wizard save you time, the process is done right the first time. After you upsize your database to a more powerful database platform, using Reporting Services will be that much easier to implement for the reports formerly implemented in your Access database.

To begin the Upsizing Wizard, find it in the Tools menu within Access (see Figure 20-5) and follow its prompts.

The initial screen of the Upsizing Wizard will give you a choice between using an existing database or creating a new database. I would suggest starting with creating a new database.

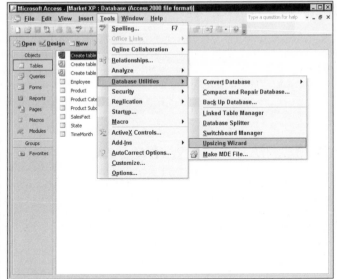

Figure 20-5:
Find the
Upsizing
Wizard in
the
Database
Utilities
menu.

The remaining prompts enable you to get an SQL Server 2005 database all set up and and ready to go for reporting. Then you can either create reports from scratch in Reporting Services, or follow the conversion routine described earlier in this chapter to get a running start at the report layouts for a one-for-one conversion.

Part VII
The Part of Tens

In this part . . .

The Part of Tens distills the information found in various sections throughout the book into lists of ten telling tidbits to enhance your reports. From cool tricks and helpful resources on the Web to more aspects of the BI platform from Microsoft and a list of third party tools that can complement your repertoire, these items can extend you into the ranks of a professional report developer.

Chapter 21

Ten Cool Tricks with Reporting Services

. . . .

. . . .

*Y*ou can do a bunch of things in Reporting Services that may involve some custom expressions or customization involving a little extra coding to your reports. This section introduces you to some interesting (and cool) tricks you can use to make your reports either stand out or fit into the existing standards you may be required to fulfill.

Greenbar Paper Formatting

If you work at a company that still runs mainframe computers, you may have seen the old "greenbar" paper stock. This is the wide paper that mainframe computers use to print out their results. The paper is lined alternatively with green and white stripes to assist in reading across the columns of a report.

In Reporting Services, to simulate the stripe effect when printing, you need to do conditional formatting on the contents of table cells. To change the `BackgroundColor` to be an expression that alternates between green and white, use this expression for the `BackgroundColor` property for all cells in the report line:

```
=iif(RowNumber(Nothing) Mod 2,"Green","White")
```

Controlling Page Breaks

If you want to better control page breaks within a report, you can do so with expressions on groups in a matrix or table. If you know that you would like to do a page break on a specific row count, you can specify that in the group expression. That way, you can introduce a hidden page break grouping. Just right-click a row on the table grid and select Edit Group from the pop-up menu. In the Expression Edit dialog box that appears, enter the following expression to insert a page break after 20 report lines:

```
=Ceiling(RowNumber(Nothing)/20)
```

Running Totals

In some reporting situations, you may want to express the cumulative total for a report column as it changes row by row. In order to do this, you need to enter an expression for the value in the table cell. Let's assume you want to specify a running total for a field called `SalesAmt`. The following aggregate function will provide you with running totals:

```
=RunningValue(Fields!SalesAmt.Value, Sum, Nothing)
```

Simulating End-User Sorting

If you want to use a parameter to provide a dynamic sorting capability, you need to create two report parameters called `Sortby` and `Direction`. The values of the `Sortby` report parameter should be set to the names of the fields by which you need to have the users sort. The values of the `Direction` parameter should be set to values `Ascending`, `Descending`, and `None`. Then enter the above information into the Report Parameters dialog box that appears.

After you create the two parameters for your report, you need to add two expressions to the table control in your report. To do this, follow these steps:

1. **Click the top-left part of the table to select it.**

   Right-click the table object to display a pop-up menu of options.

2. **Select Properties.**

   The Table Properties dialog box appears.

3. **Select the Sorting tab and enter the following expression for an ascending sort:**

```
=iif(Parameters!Direction.Value= "Ascending",
          Fields(Parameters!SortBy.Value).Value,0)
```

4. **Add the following expression for a descending sort:**

```
=iif(Parameters!Direction.Value= "Descending",
          Fields(Parameters!SortBy.Value).Value,0)
```

When you preview the report, you will see two parameters at the top of the report. Enter a value of the column in the Sortby parameter.

Simulating the All Parameter Value

Situations exist when you want to see on a parameterized report a parameter choice indicating that all values are selected. To do this, when you define the report parameter in the Report Parameter dialog box, define a valid values list of the parameter including the value All. This means that you will see the All value in the list of values for the parameter.

In the first case, consider when the parameter in question is a text field like Department. In your dataset expression in the Query Designer, you need to specify in the query the following expression:

```
WHERE department like @department
```

In this case, the All parameter should be mapped to the value of %, which is a wildcard. When the All value is specified, then the like search criteria becomes:

```
WHERE department like %
```

This expression returns rows containing anything in the Department field.

In the next case, consider when your query criteria is an integer. Assume that the report parameter is `Year`. Suppose that your dataset expression in the Query Designer, you specify a criteria like:

```
">= @MinYear"
```

and

```
"<= @MaxYear"
```

Define a query parameter expression for `MaxYear` as:

```
=iif(Parameters!Year.Value=0,10000,Parameters!Year.Value)
```

Define a query parameter expression for `MinYear` as:

```
=iif(Parameters!Year.Value=0,0,Parameters!Year.Value)
```

In this case, the `All` parameter should be mapped to the value of `0`. When `All` is selected for the parameter value, then the `like` search criteria expressions become:

```
">= 0" and "<= 10000"
```

This will return rows containing any value (other than NULL) in the year field.

Using the wildcard method above can be a security risk and could be vulnerable to SQL injection attacks. An alternative way of accomplishing this is to define the following parameter query for the parameter `@Year`:

```
SELECT 'All'
UNION ALL
SELECT Year FROM DateDim
```

Then your dataset query expression would be:

```
SELECT YearName, Col2, Col3
FROM FactTable
WHERE 1 = CASE
WHEN @Year = 'All' THEN 1
WHEN @Year = YearName THEN 1
ELSE 0
END
```

Using this dynamic filter is a very powerful form of using parameters.

Dynamically Creating a Report Query

You actually write code to dynamically create a report with parameters. The way you do this is to go to the Data tab in the Report Designer for the report and select the Generic Query Designer. Then enter a code reference like:

```
=Code.GetQuery(Parameters)
```

Then click on the Report Properties menu item on the Report main menu to open the Report Properties dialog box. On the Code tab, define a function like:

```
Public Function GetQuery(repParameters As Parameters)
        As String

   End Function
```

The logic in this function can build a query dynamically with string functions. Note that you can refer to parameters in this function with an expression like:

```
repParameters!paramname.Value
```

Changing the Report Manager Folder Icon to a Corporate Logo

You may want to customize the icon at the top left of the Report Manager home page and put your corporate logo in its place. If you browse the source of the Report Manager, home page you will see that the file reference for the folder icon is:

```
/Reports/images/48folderopen.jpg
```

Searching around in the program manager, you can locate this file in the directory:

```
C:\Program Files\Microsoft SQL Server\MSSQL.3\Reporting
        Services\ReportManager\images
```

If you open this file, you'll find that it's a 48 x 48 .jpg image. Therefore, if you can make a similar resolution .jpg of your corporate logo and save this new logo file as 48folderopen.jpg, the next time you refresh your Report Manager, you will see your corporate logo in the top-left corner of the Web page.

Suppressing Objects or Formulas in an Excel Rendering of a Report

When you don't want to see a document map or formula in an Excel rendering of your report, you can control the properties of the rendering by using the devise information settings when specifying the report using the URL access method. For example, to suppress a document map from a report in Excel, use the URL link as follows:

```
http://servername/reportserver?/SampleReports/Sales Order
        Detail&rs:Command=Render&rc:Format=HTML4.0
        &rcOmitDocumentMap=True
```

When you want only the data values and no formulas generated in Excel for the entire report, you can use the Device Information Setting of OmitFormulas to suppress formula generation as in the following expression:

```
http://servername/reportserver?/SampleReports/Employee
        Sales Summary&EmployeeID=38&rs:Command=
        Render&rs:Format=EXCEL&rc:OmitFormulas=true
```

Securing Reports with a UserID Parameter

Suppose that you want to integrate a report containing HR information in your application and it requires a value for Employee ID to specify the employee who is viewing the page. Let's assume that the data in the HR database is keyed by the EmployeeID field. One solution to this requirement is to have your application determine the value of EmployeeID for the current user, and you could pass EmployeeID as a report parameter that'll drive its queries. This seemingly natural solution is less than optimal because your users could change the parameter and pass in another EmployeeID, which leads to unwanted information disclosure.

You can try to hide the parameter so that it doesn't show up in the Report Viewer toolbar, or not show the toolbar at all. This may seem like a solution, however, parameter values will still show up in the URLs generated in the report. User entered report parameters offer opportunities to hack data from a report for savvy users. Even if you use a custom encryption, those encryptions seldom are strong enough to withstand a serious hacker. Because of this, a general rule to follow is: Never use report parameters to implement security.

Instead of using parameters, base your security decisions on the User!UserID parameter. UserID is populated as the result of the Windows authentication mechanism, so it is inherently more reliable than parameters. Use the expression:

```
User!UserID
```

Use the value of this global parameter (hidden from the user) to pass to the query in order to filter the information specific for that user.

Measuring and Improving Report Performance

In Chapter 14, I discuss techniques and provide suggestions for optimizing report performance. You should keep a few issues in mind while you are looking for ways to improve report performance on your system:

- ✔ The bulk of report execution time is spent executing queries and retrieving results. If you're using SQL Server, tools such as Query Analyzer and Profiler can help you optimize your queries. Database Tuning Advisor can suggest better indexes for your database.

- ✔ The Report Server ExecutionLog table contains data on report performance. If you want a quick look at how long it took to execute certain reports, and where the bulk of the time was spent, TimeDataRetrieval contains the number of milliseconds spent getting data from the report's data source(s). Use the following syntax in Query Analyzer: ReportServer Select * from ExecutionLog with (nolock) order by TimeStart DESC. Make sure to include nolock. The ExecutionLog table is used by the RS runtime and locking it can severely degrade your server's performance.

- ✔ If you don't need data in your report, don't retrieve it. Leveraging database operations such as filtering, grouping, and aggregates can reduce the amount of data that is processed in the report, improving performance.

- ✔ Keep your reports modest in size and complexity. Do users really want to look at a 1,000-page report?

- ✔ If performance is extremely bad even for single users, check the Application Restarts counter in the ASP.NET category. Some antivirus software is known to "touch" configuration files. For more information, search http://support.microsoft.com/ for articles relating to "antivirus and ASP.NET."

- ✔ If performance is slow on the first Web service access after there have not been any accesses for a certain time period, disable the idle timeout on the Performance tab in the Application Pool in IIS Manager.

✔ Execute reports from cached/snapshot data as opposed to live data whenever possible.

✔ Limit non-essential background processing to off-peak hours in order to avoid contention with online users.

✔ If you load your report server up with 4GB memory, remember to set the /3GB switch in `C:\boot.ini` so application processes can make use of it.

✔ If a single server can't handle the workload, consider locating the Reporting Services catalog on a remote SQL Server instance as your first step toward increasing system capacity.

✔ If one report server configured with a remote catalog still doesn't adequately support your workload, consider increasing the available resources on the system hosting your report server (scale-up), or setting up a clustered Web farm of report servers (scale-out).

Chapter 22

Ten Ways to Hook Into the Microsoft BI Platform

SQL Server 2005 offers some tremendous capabilitities in terms of fulfilling a robust set of data warehousing and business intelligence needs within one database platform. SQL Server Reporting Services is just one of the many capabilities that SQL Server offers to streamline business intelligence design and development.

This chapter talks about the top key SQL Server 2005 BI platform capabilities that, together with Reporting Services, make SQL Server 2005 an exciting platform for business intelligence.

Analysis Services

With SQL Server 2005, Analysis Services moves into the realm of real-time analytics. From scalability enhancements to deep integration with Microsoft Office, SQL Server 2005 helps extend business intelligence to every level of your business. Analysis Services offer ways to outline drill-down levels within your information and allow users to work with information in cubes where multiple dimensions of the data can be manipulated to see trends and deail in the underlying detail data.

Integration Services

DTS (Data Transformation Services) was the integration tool of SQL Server 2000. It consists of a set of graphical tools and programmable objects that you can use to extract, transform, and load (ETL) data from disparate sources and move it to single or multiple destinations. SQL Server 2005 introduces a complete redesign of DTS that is called Integration Services. Integration Services is loaded with new functionality to better control transformation logic. It automates many previously difficult tasks like handling slowly changing dimension transforms. It greatly adds to developer productivity and database scalability to provide a truly comprehensive platform for doing the basics of data integration: Extract, transform, and load operations.

Data Mining

Four new data mining algorithms are part of SQL Server 2005 Analytical Services. These algorithms assist developers in constructing complex analytical models and integrating them into business operations. Data mining is helpful in predicting what customers are most likely to buy, what products tend to be purchased together, and what the demand for a product is likely to be next month, and for segmenting customers in logical groups that represent various degrees of loyalty. The algorithms include decision trees, sequence clustering, time series, and neural nets. There are also new wizards and improved tools that will make data mining easier for businesses of any size.

Reporting Services

SQL Server 2005 Reporting Services is a service-based platform for creating, delivering, and managing traditional and interactive reports. Reports created with Reporting Services can be used for enterprise reporting on the Web, reporting to customers and partners through a secure Internet connection. Running a report is easy and intuitive for the typical business user so that self-service reporting can be achieved with little training. Ad hoc reports can be created using the Report Builder. Finally, developers can create complex and interactive reports easily to enhance the business user experience.

Clustering Support

SQL Server 2005 provides for improved availability with support for failover clustering, enhanced multi-instance support, and support for backing up and restoring database information. SQL Server running on Windows 2003 Server can support eight clustered servers all sharing in the performance of database tasks required of it. Users will have access to a database during a restore operation, within certain limits. This helps get you up and running faster after problems.

Key Performance Indicators

The key relevant measures of the business are what are known as key performance indicators or KPIs. After a company defines its key performance measures, reporting them on a daily or even real-time basis helps monitor business performance. Key performance indicators (KPIs) provide businesses with the capability to define graphic, customizable business metrics to help generate and track key corporate benchmarks.

Scalability and Performance

Features such as parallel partition processing, creation of remote relational online analytical processing (ROLAP) or hybrid online analytical processing (HOLAP) partitions, distributed partitioned cubes, persisted calculations, and proactive caching will greatly improve the scalability and performance of Analysis Services in SQL Server 2005.

One-Click Cube

When creating a cube in a data warehouse project, the Cube wizard includes an option to enable One-Click Cube detection and suggestions. This option examines the relationships in a data source view and makes suggestions for fact tables, dimension tables, and measures.

Proactive Caching

Proactive caching combines MOLAP class query performance with real-time data analysis and eliminates the need to maintain OLAP stores. The Proactive

Cache transparently synchronizes and maintains an updated copy of the data organized specifically for high-speed querying and for isolating end-users from overloading the relational databases. The structure of the cache is automatically derived from the Universal Data Model (UDM) structure and can be finely tuned to balance performance with latency of data.

Integration with Microsoft Office

Reports created by Reporting Services and executed by the Report Server can run in the context of Microsoft SharePoint Portal Server and Microsoft Office System applications such as Microsoft Word and Microsoft Excel. You can use SharePoint features to subscribe to reports, create new versions of reports, and distribute reports. You can also open reports in Word or Excel to view HTML versions of the reports.

Chapter 23

Ten Places to Find Reporting Services Support

*Y*ou can go to literally hundreds of places on the Internet to get more information or support when using Microsoft Reporting Services. These Web sites may change as the product matures, and Microsoft reserves the right to change their Web site at will. However, in my travels I have found solace in a few Internet knowledge stores that you may benefit from as well.

Microsoft SQL Server

Of course, one good place to look for information and links to what's new is to look at the vendors' Web sites. This is intuitive, but you may not know exactly where to navigate because the home page changes daily and new products are services are being offered. Well, just bookmark the Web site www.microsoft.com/sql and you will be able to find the links for SQL Server. Reporting Services will not be many clicks away and you can see other business intelligence tools from this page.

Reporting Services Web Site

The main page within the SQL Server domain for Reporting Services is found at:

```
www.microsoft.com/sql/reporting
```

Here, you can see product overviews and demos, download new service packs and report packs, and take a skills assessment exam. More links are added periodically to move you to new content.

Sample Databases for Reporting

You may be wondering where to go on the Microsoft site to find some common sample databases to try your hand at reporting in unique and different environments. Some of the popular sample databases include AdventureWorks. The AdventureWorks2000 database is installed by the Reporting Services setup if you select the Documentation and Samples option in the installation. This option installs the complete documentation set for Reporting Services, code samples, report samples, and the AdventureWorks2000 database.

In order to find the sample databases for Northwind or pubs, you must use the following link:

```
www.microsoft.com/downloads/details.aspx?FamilyID=
06616212-0356-46a0-8da2-eebc53a68034&DisplayLang=en
```

Report Packs

Microsoft has sponsored the development of sample report sets based on popular databases that are being used by mid-market businesses today. So example databases of content related to key functional applications have been constructed to provide a reference base for some interesting Reporting Services databases.

Microsoft Report Packs are available to show how Reporting Services reports would work for popular applications. Microsoft provides Report Packs for IIS Logs, Microsoft Business Solutions (MBS), Financial Reporting, Microsoft CRM, and Exchange, as well as sample OLAP reports. These can be downloaded at the following site with all related information on Reporting Services downloads:

```
www.microsoft.com/sql/reporting/downloads/default.asp
```

Reporting Services Newsgroup

If you have a question about a Reporting Services feature or want to share your experience of working with Reporting Services, you can navigate to the newsgroup to share with other developers like yourself.

The Reporting Services newsgroup has ranked frequently as one of the top five most active newsgroups for all of SQL Server. Here are some ways to get to the newsgroup:

- ✔ If you have Outlook Express, the following link should open Outlook Express and connect to the Web site for the public reporting services newsgroup:

    `news:microsoft.public.sqlserver.reportingsvcs`

- ✔ Go to the MSDN (Microsoft Development Network) site, which is a Web version of the previous site:

    `http://msdn.microsoft.com/newsgroups/default.aspx?dg=`
    `microsoft.public.sqlserver.reportingsvcs`

Chat or Webcast

As Reporting Services was completed, Microsoft provided a tremendous number of Webcasts that were archived for viewing on demand. A great number of interesting Webcasts exist for Reporting Services. By the time you read this, there will no doubt be many more Webcasts. You may even be able to take part in regular chats to discover more advanced applications with Reporting Services.

The site for the Webcasts, where you may find a great archive for viewing on demand is:

`www.microsoft.com/usa/webcasts/default.asp`

The site for seeing when chats are scheduled is:

`www.microsoft.com/communities/chats/default.mspx`

OLAP Reporting

This may be an advanced topic, but when you work with Microsoft Analysis Services, you need to understand how Reporting Services functions in this scenario. Understanding what MDX is all about can be understood by viewing a very good primer on MDX at:

```
http://msdn.microsoft.com/library/default.asp?url=/library/
en-us/olapdmad/agmdxbasics_4erb.asp
```

A nice set of links to topics related to MDX, ADO-MD, and XMLA is available at:

```
http://msdn.microsoft.com/SQL/sqlmultidata/default.aspx
```

SQL Server Magazine

This magazine is a popular one among enthusiasts of the various components of SQL Server. On the magazine Web site, you'll find links for educational or instructional opportunities so that you can find out more or test your current knowledge. You can also find information about organizations that focus on SQL Server (like PASS – Professional Association of SQL Server) where you can collaborate with others who are working with the tool. The magazine site is at:

```
www.windowsitpro.com/SQLServer/
```

SQL Server Development Center

MSDN provides an SQL Server Development Center for Reporting Services. This site is intended to provide more information and insight for how Reporting Services can help with your reporting needs. You can find this at:

```
http://msdn.microsoft.com/SQL/sqlwarehouse/Reporting
Services/default.aspx
```

General BI Links

If you're interested in Reporting Services as it relates to other BI topics, a good general business intelligence (BI) site provides a wealth of links in related topics to reporting and analysis. This site can be found at:

```
www.businessintelligenceiq.com/overview.asp
```

Chapter 24

Ten Third Party Tools to Use with Reporting Services

Microsoft provides an open environment for other software vendors to develop add-ons and extensions to Microsoft Reporting Services. This kind of grass-roots support channel with its software vendor partners gives you more alternatives for how best to leverage Microsoft SQL Server Reporting Services. Consider these ten third-party tools that work well with Reporting Services for special needs you have in your business.

Attunity

www.attunity.com

Attunity provides turnkey adapters for accessing mainframe, enterprise data sources, and legacy applications. Attunity's Adapter Suite is designed for seamless, federated, and bidirectional integration, and includes adapters such as CICS, IMS, VSAM, COBOL, RPG, DB2, Enscribe, RMS, Oracle, and many others. Founded in 1987 and a Microsoft Partner, Attunity and its worldwide operations support more than 1,000 direct end users.

Attunity's support of the Microsoft SQL Server Reporting Services offers customers real-time access to corporate and enterprise data. With Attunity Connect, you have the flexibility to analyze and generate reports with the right data at the right time.

Cizer Software

www.cizer.com

Cizer.Net Reporting for Reporting Services is the Web-based Business Intelligence suite from Cizer Software. It provides full report authoring in the browser, and does not require Visual Studio or any .Net client or download of any kind, including ActiveX controls or Java applets. The built-in Portal features configurable links to Cizer Quick Query ad hoc reports for Business Users, mid-level Cizer Report Builder reports with global libraries, charts, and parameters for intermediate authors, as well as the ability to run advanced Visual Studio reports from the Cizer Portal. Originally launched with Reporting Services in 2004, Cizer.Net Reporting has become a standard component of SQL Server BI implementations, and in December 2004 became the first Reporting Services application to pass the Microsoft Gold-level ISV BI Test.

Dundas Software

www.dundas.com

Dundas Software, founded in 1992, specializes in data visualization solutions for the Microsoft .NET Framework. Data visualization is the graphical presentation of information, with the goal of providing the viewer with a qualitative understanding of the information contents. Portions of Dundas Chart for .NET technology are currently being utilized within Microsoft SQL Server 2000 Reporting Services to display a variety of advanced charts. With the next release of Reporting Services, users will have the ability to create charts using Dundas Chart for Reporting Services, a charting add-on, which will take advantage of the extensive features found in the Enterprise Edition of Dundas Chart for .NET. This additional charting functionality will offer developers more sophisticated charts, new chart types, and many advanced customization options beyond what is standard.

Fenestrae

www.fenestrae.com

Fenestrae extends Microsoft SQL Server Reporting Services beyond the desktop to make business information more widely available within the company and business partner networks. Fenestrae Communication Server makes Business Intelligence available anywhere, anytime, and on any device. With Fenestrae and SQL Reporting Services, you can ensure real-time, automatic delivery of business information to remote locations, including reports as faxed documents or KPIs as mobile SMS and MMS messages when on the move.

GFI

www.gfi.com

GFI FAXmaker for Exchange/SMTP is a leading network fax server. It integrates with Exchange Server and popular SMTP servers, enabling you to send and receive faxes and SMS/text messages directly from your e-mail client. By using the e-mail server and Active Directory, GFI FAXmaker provides reliable fax administration through your existing infrastructure. GFI FAXmaker fully supports the use of Microsoft SQL Server Reporting Services. It can log all incoming and outgoing faxes to Microsoft SQL Server and enables users to easily create custom reports such as billing/fax usage, fax notifications, and more.

OutlookSoft

www.outlooksoft.com

OutlookSoft CPM is a fully integrated Microsoft-based Corporate Performance Management application. Microsoft Reporting Services extends the reach of OutlookSoft's CPM to a whole new level of detail. Customers can access data from relational tables as well as Analysis Services through the application interface. Reporting Services will be integrated into OutlookSoft solutions to provide greater reporting flexibility to meet business challenges in areas such as Sarbanes Oxley, Line item detail analysis, and Security and audit reporting. OutlookSoft CPM provides access to Reporting Services through a secured browser interface and through a patented Web-based Microsoft Excel interface.

Panorama Software

www.panorama.com

Panorama Software offers a powerful and intuitive front end to SQL Server Analysis Services. Panorama extends the Microsoft Platform through integrated business intelligence and corporate performance management solutions. With Panorama, decision makers at all levels and functions can easily analyze data, quickly create and distribute reports, and proactively measure performance. Companies gain a greater understanding of their business and make better decisions. These informed decisions improve profitability, increase revenues, reduce costs and time to market, and mitigate competitive risks.

Panorama is a leading innovator of business intelligence solutions and supports customers worldwide in industries such as financial services, manufacturing, healthcare, retail, telecommunications, and life sciences.

ProClarity

www.proclarity.com

Microsoft SQL Server Reporting Services integrates seamlessly with the ProClarity product family, providing customers with a comprehensive and cost-effective reporting and analysis solution that's very easy to implement. The ProClarity Analytics Server allows organizations to publish collections of views onto a middle-tier server for centralized access to analytical information. With Reporting Services, customers can launch relational reports from the ProClarity environment, making both relational and OLAP (online analytical processing) reports within a common context available to the broadest range of decision makers throughout the enterprise.

Proposion

www.proposion.com

Proposion Report Adapter connects Microsoft Reporting Services to Lotus Notes/Domino environments. This product extends Reporting Services in three ways: (1) Notes/Domino Data Extension: A fast, robust, and feature-rich data driver that turns your Notes and Domino databases into first-class data sources in Reporting Services. This connector supports images, attachments, rich text, unread marks, parent/response relationships, full-text search, formulas, and much more. (2) Notes Mail Delivery Extension: Allows any scheduled reports in Reporting Services to be routed to subscribers via native Notes mail. (3) Notes Database Delivery Extension: Allows any scheduled reports in Reporting Services to be deposited into Notes/Domino databases (great for building report archiving/workflow/distribution applications).

OfficeWriter

www.officewriter.softartisans.com

SoftArtisans OfficeWriter enables the design, publishing, and delivery of reports directly from Microsoft Excel and Word using SQL Server Reporting Services or ASP.NET. End users design and publish their Reporting Services reports without ever leaving Microsoft Office — avoiding design tools, like VS.NET, that are unfamiliar to most business users.

OfficeWriter creates Reporting Services reports (RDL files), but unlike Reporting Services' Excel output, all Excel features such as pivot tables, VBA, macros, advanced formulas, and charts are preserved by OfficeWriter. Without OfficeWriter, Reporting Services cannot deliver reports in Microsoft Word format. OfficeWriter-rendered documents preserve all the Word features contained in the user's existing Word template. All this is accomplished without the need for Microsoft Office on the server.

Index

• T •

SINESS, CAREERS & PERSONAL FINANCE

Grant Writing
FOR
DUMMIES
0-7645-5307-0

Home Buying
FOR
DUMMIES
0-7645-5331-3 *†

ME & BUSINESS COMPUTER BASICS

Windows XP
FOR
DUMMIES
0-7645-4074-2

Excel 2003
ALL-IN-ONE DESK REFERENCE
FOR
DUMMIES
0-7645-3758-X

OD, HOME, GARDEN, HOBBIES, MUSIC & PETS

Feng Shui
FOR
DUMMIES
0-7645-5295-3

Poker
FOR
DUMMIES
0-7645-5232-5

TERNET & DIGITAL MEDIA

Digital Photography
FOR
DUMMIES
0-7645-1664-7

Starting an eBay Business
FOR
DUMMIES
0-7645-6924-4

Also available:

- Accounting For Dummies †
  0-7645-5314-3
- Business Plans Kit For Dummies †
  0-7645-5365-8
- Cover Letters For Dummies
  0-7645-5224-4
- Frugal Living For Dummies
  0-7645-5403-4
- Leadership For Dummies
  0-7645-5176-0
- Managing For Dummies
  0-7645-1771-6

- Marketing For Dummies
  0-7645-5600-2
- Personal Finance For Dummies *
  0-7645-2590-5
- Project Management For Dummies
  0-7645-5283-X
- Resumes For Dummies †
  0-7645-5471-9
- Selling For Dummies
  0-7645-5363-1
- Small Business Kit For Dummies *†
  0-7645-5093-4

Also available:

- ACT! 6 For Dummies
  0-7645-2645-6
- iLife '04 All-in-One Desk Reference
  For Dummies
  0-7645-7347-0
- iPAQ For Dummies
  0-7645-6769-1
- Mac OS X Panther Timesaving
  Techniques For Dummies
  0-7645-5812-9
- Macs For Dummies
  0-7645-5656-8

- Microsoft Money 2004 For Dummies
  0-7645-4195-1
- Office 2003 All-in-One Desk Reference
  For Dummies
  0-7645-3883-7
- Outlook 2003 For Dummies
  0-7645-3759-8
- PCs For Dummies
  0-7645-4074-2
- TiVo For Dummies
  0-7645-6923-6
- Upgrading and Fixing PCs For Dummies
  0-7645-1665-5
- Windows XP Timesaving Techniques
  For Dummies
  0-7645-3748-2

Also available:

- Bass Guitar For Dummies
  0-7645-2487-9
- Diabetes Cookbook For Dummies
  0-7645-5230-9
- Gardening For Dummies *
  0-7645-5130-2
- Guitar For Dummies
  0-7645-5106-X
- Holiday Decorating For Dummies
  0-7645-2570-0
- Home Improvement All-in-One
  For Dummies
  0-7645-5680-0

- Knitting For Dummies
  0-7645-5395-X
- Piano For Dummies
  0-7645-5105-1
- Puppies For Dummies
  0-7645-5255-4
- Scrapbooking For Dummies
  0-7645-7208-3
- Senior Dogs For Dummies
  0-7645-5818-8
- Singing For Dummies
  0-7645-2475-5
- 30-Minute Meals For Dummies
  0-7645-2589-1

Also available:

- 2005 Online Shopping Directory
  For Dummies
  0-7645-7495-7
- CD & DVD Recording For Dummies
  0-7645-5956-7
- eBay For Dummies
  0-7645-5654-1
- Fighting Spam For Dummies
  0-7645-5965-6
- Genealogy Online For Dummies
  0-7645-5964-8
- Google For Dummies
  0-7645-4420-9

- Home Recording For Musicians
  For Dummies
  0-7645-1634-5
- The Internet For Dummies
  0-7645-4173-0
- iPod & iTunes For Dummies
  0-7645-7772-7
- Preventing Identity Theft For Dummies
  0-7645-7336-5
- Pro Tools All-in-One Desk Reference
  For Dummies
  0-7645-5714-9
- Roxio Easy Media Creator For Dummies
  0-7645-7131-1

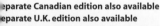

eparate Canadian edition also available
eparate U.K. edition also available

ilable wherever books are sold. For more information or to order direct: U.S. customers visit www.dummies.com or call 1-877-762-2974.
customers visit www.wileyeurope.com or call 0800 243407. Canadian customers visit www.wiley.ca or call 1-800-567-4797.

SPORTS, FITNESS, PARENTING, RELIGION & SPIRITUALITY

0-7645-5146-9

0-7645-5418-2

Also available:

- Adoption For Dummies
  0-7645-5488-3
- Basketball For Dummies
  0-7645-5248-1
- The Bible For Dummies
  0-7645-5296-1
- Buddhism For Dummies
  0-7645-5359-3
- Catholicism For Dummies
  0-7645-5391-7
- Hockey For Dummies
  0-7645-5228-7

- Judaism For Dummies
  0-7645-5299-6
- Martial Arts For Dummies
  0-7645-5358-5
- Pilates For Dummies
  0-7645-5397-6
- Religion For Dummies
  0-7645-5264-3
- Teaching Kids to Read For Dummies
  0-7645-4043-2
- Weight Training For Dummies
  0-7645-5168-X
- Yoga For Dummies
  0-7645-5117-5

TRAVEL

0-7645-5438-7

0-7645-5453-0

Also available:

- Alaska For Dummies
  0-7645-1761-9
- Arizona For Dummies
  0-7645-6938-4
- Cancún and the Yucatán For Dummies
  0-7645-2437-2
- Cruise Vacations For Dummies
  0-7645-6941-4
- Europe For Dummies
  0-7645-5456-5
- Ireland For Dummies
  0-7645-5455-7

- Las Vegas For Dummies
  0-7645-5448-4
- London For Dummies
  0-7645-4277-X
- New York City For Dummies
  0-7645-6945-7
- Paris For Dummies
  0-7645-5494-8
- RV Vacations For Dummies
  0-7645-5443-3
- Walt Disney World & Orlando For Dummies
  0-7645-6943-0

GRAPHICS, DESIGN & WEB DEVELOPMENT

0-7645-4345-8

0-7645-5589-8

Also available:

- Adobe Acrobat 6 PDF For Dummies
  0-7645-3760-1
- Building a Web Site For Dummies
  0-7645-7144-3
- Dreamweaver MX 2004 For Dummies
  0-7645-4342-3
- FrontPage 2003 For Dummies
  0-7645-3882-9
- HTML 4 For Dummies
  0-7645-1995-6
- Illustrator CS For Dummies
  0-7645-4084-X

- Macromedia Flash MX 2004 For Dummies
  0-7645-4358-X
- Photoshop 7 All-in-One Desk Reference For Dummies
  0-7645-1667-1
- Photoshop CS Timesaving Techniques For Dummies
  0-7645-6782-9
- PHP 5 For Dummies
  0-7645-4166-8
- PowerPoint 2003 For Dummies
  0-7645-3908-6
- QuarkXPress 6 For Dummies
  0-7645-2593-X

NETWORKING, SECURITY, PROGRAMMING & DATABASES

0-7645-6852-3

0-7645-5784-X

Also available:

- A+ Certification For Dummies
  0-7645-4187-0
- Access 2003 All-in-One Desk Reference For Dummies
  0-7645-3988-4
- Beginning Programming For Dummies
  0-7645-4997-9
- C For Dummies
  0-7645-7068-4
- Firewalls For Dummies
  0-7645-4048-3
- Home Networking For Dummies
  0-7645-42796

- Network Security For Dummies
  0-7645-1679-5
- Networking For Dummies
  0-7645-1677-9
- TCP/IP For Dummies
  0-7645-1760-0
- VBA For Dummies
  0-7645-3989-2
- Wireless All In-One Desk Reference For Dummies
  0-7645-7496-5
- Wireless Home Networking For Dummies
  0-7645-3910-8